Doubters and Dissenters

Doubters

AND

Dissenters

CATACLYSMIC THOUGHT
IN AMERICA, 1885-1918

Frederic Cople Jaher

THE FREE PRESS OF GLENCOE
Collier-Macmillan Limited, London

For Sue

ACKNOWLEDGMENTS

MUCH OF THE CREDIT for any book accrues from debts owed others, and I would like to express my gratitude to those who have helped me. Mrs. Abigail Homans permitted me access to the Adams Papers at the Massachusetts Historical Society and Houghton Library. Mr. Henry Cabot Lodge allowed me to use the Lodge Papers at the Massachusetts Historical Society. Professor Mark DeWolfe Howe let me examine the Oliver Wendell Holmes–Brooks Adams correspondence, and Professor Theodore S. Nydahl provided material from parts of Ignatius Donnelly's diary. The following publishing companies and Mr. Irving Shepard were generous in granting me permission to quote from printed matter: Mr. Shepard for Jack London, *The Iron Heel;* Houghton Mifflin for Worthington Chauncy Ford, editor, *The Letters of Henry Adams;* Harvard University Press for Ignatius Donnelly, *Caesar's Column;* and E. P. Dutton for John L. Heaton, *Cobb Of "The World."* I am also indebted to the staffs of the Houghton and Widener Libraries at Harvard University and to the Massachusetts Historical Society for the many ways in which they facilitated my research.

I would also like to thank my teachers at Harvard University, colleagues at City College, friends, and my father. Professor Michael Kraus suggested interesting research possibilities. Professors Sidney Ditzion and Frank Freidel and Marvin Gettleman, Michael Parenti, Richard Weiss, and Sidney M. Jaher read the manuscript and offered much valuable criticism. It is a pleasure to acknowledge the stimulating discussions in Professor Louis Hartz's seminar and his incisive reading of the manuscript. Martin Kessler was the ideal editor whose suggestions helped to turn a dissertation into a book. Professor Oscar Handlin's contributions are beyond my ability to describe but not to appreciate. Without his patience and inspiration as a teacher and thesis adviser, this book would not have been written. To my wife, Susan Jaher, even a dedication is an inadequate expression of gratitude for her editing, criticism, and encouragement.

F. C. J.

Contents

PART ONE

THE
CATACLYSMIC
VISION

I

The Problem

HISTORICAL CATEGORIES are manifold in purpose and approach. They may trace social change or probe the style of life at a given time; they may be constructed out of objectively verifiable principles or subjective impressions. America from 1885 to 1918 has been interpreted from many such perspectives but never through a study of cataclysmic thought.

Undoubtedly, the United States was on the rise in this period, but society is so delicately balanced that it cannot change without disturbing its equilibrium; for the whole to progress, some parts must retrogress. To study the era only from the top, therefore, to contemplate it only as a prelude to America's eminence is to miss a great deal. This type of analysis not only omits what was left behind but also distorts the very process of national emergence. Development is partly shaped by resistant elements that cling desperately to a vanishing order. Although the future may be eagerly anticipated by those who swim with the tide, for those who want to hold fast against the currents of change, innovation seems cataclysmic.

Since historical categories are structured by the phenomena they explain, the cataclysmic perspective is shaped by the forces that were transforming the nation. Although cities were growing, immigrants arriving, corporations forming, unions agitating, and artisans already giving way to factories before the Civil War, not until the 1880's did these forces come to dominate American life. To many who thrived on memories of a rural, agricultural, native-born, and small-propertied community, these elements embodied the threat of modern times—they were the manifestations of the cataclysmic trend of industrial capitalism.

Pessimism is a state of mind, and there is therefore a lag between the emergence of apparent cataclysmic components and their impingement upon a people's consciousness. Urbanization, industrialism, immigration, and labor organization were threatening old America during the 1870's, but not until the middle of the next decade did they assume a catastrophic role. Perhaps the euphoria of victory in the Civil War and the relatively small immigrant influx before the 1880's delayed this realization. More likely, however, the absence of a dramatic incident was the major cause. It often takes an electrifying event like the Haymarket Affair to bring fears to the surface and intensify them to the point of cataclysmic consciousness. The active presence of urbanized foreign anarchists amid a great strike attracted fearful attention to these characteristics of the new era—the apparent evidences of impending disaster.

Established élites were particularly horrified by late nineteenth-century developments. Every new strike, boatload of immigrants, or socialist cell further alarmed the bluebloods, the farmers, and others who dreamed of return to days gone by. As conditions worsened in the depression of the 1890's, rifts occurred even among the native born. Liberals and conservatives split over issues of agrarianism and monopoly. Regardless of which side individuals took, however, they were all motivated by similar anxieties. Frustrated and confused by turbulent forces, these Americans were adrift in the wave of the future.

Prosperity and adjustment to change ushered in a calmer mood after 1897. Social flux results in adaptation as well as in alienation; it helps to integrate, as well as to disintegrate, society. Many people took a second look at the city and the workers and saw some hope. The middle-class perspective became less clouded as it was discovered that foreigners, city dwellers, and unions had not in fact destroyed civilization.

Progressivism was the product of this optimistic realism, yet despite the movement's self-confidence, it could not completely eradicate despondency. This failure may be partly attributed to its environmental tenets—or its basic view of the relationship between social conditions and social control. As long as reformers think they can influence society, optimism prevails. Unfortunately, the Progressives were not certain that they had mastered all aspects of the cataclysmic syndrome. For example, the great corporations' resistance to reforms engendered further gloom about the future. The reformers themselves failed to recognize that nationality is environmental rather than genetic and, as a result, also failed to deal with the immigration problem. Newcomers continued to be regarded as a dire threat at a time when workers, socialists, and city dwellers were already becoming respectable.

America's emergence as a world power after 1898 also prevented the dissolution of cataclysmic thought. A new national role meant further disturbances and concomitant pessimism. Instead of destruction brought about by class conflict, many now saw disaster in the form of a world war. Prospects of foreign combat and the domestic limitations of Progressivism did not, of course, stifle all hope in these years. Anti-imperialists were not as somber as the Populists, nor did big business seem quite the bugaboo that anarchy had been.

World War I properly terminates this study because, in retrospect, it is clearly the only real global disaster during the period. The contemporary refusal to treat it as such raises the question of whether failure to react to catastrophe is not as neurotic as fear of a debacle that will never come. By purifying and unifying, war revived the nation. The sacrifices of 1917-1918 temporarily purged many Americans of a sense of guilt that had been building up through years of social injustice and money-making. Cynicism returned in 1919 when it was discovered that the war had not really changed human nature, but during the war itself, the frustrating contradictions of ordinary existence and the loneliness of futility were submerged in allegiance to the great cause.

Variables of time, intensity, and causation in cataclysmic thinking should be carefully distinguished. Occasional pessimists must be separated from those obsessed with doom, and forebodings induced by outside stimuli like strikes must be differentiated from fears arising out of paranoid personality. Such distinctions are crucial because cataclysmic thought can represent clear judgment or insanity depending upon the context. Furthermore, the degree and type of divergence from reality often can indicate as much about that reality as about the individual. There are, in fact, three possible types of catastrophic prediction: perceptive analysis of a decaying society or a dangerous impasse, the final step in a paranoid departure from reality, or—perhaps most interesting—a combination of both.

Homer Lea, Ignatius Donnelly, Mary Lease, Brooks and Henry Adams, and Jack London fall into that middle ground between hallucination and reality. Their thinking offers a vital vantage point from which to study their age. If these cataclysmists predicted doom for a society surging forward, it was partly because they belonged to groups that had lost their moorings in the groundswell of industrialism. Donnelly and Mrs. Lease were agrarians at a time when the farmer's position seemed to have sunk beyond redemption; the Adamses were Brahmins displaced from pre-eminence by an ascendant middle class; London was an alienated artist whose mother had skidded out of upper middle-class respectability; and Homer Lea was a militarist who despised the pacifism of big business. These figures, except for Lea, came from groups disaffected by America's industrial growth. Cataclysmic pronouncements were frequent among farmers and aristocrats—yet though the groups to which they belonged revealed symptoms of somberness, these individuals were downright melancholic. Something in their backgrounds made them more gloomy than their associates. In Mary Lease's case, it was the obstacle of a man's world and a burden of poverty extreme even for a farmer; success cut short by early defeat embittered Donnelly; the Adams brothers suffered deeper disappointment than other patricians because their family's prominence had raised higher expectations; Homer Lea was a cripple; and Jack London had suffered a ghastly childhood as the illegitimate son of an indifferent mother.

Despite their common melancholic mood, differences in age, background, education, and interests produced dissimilarities among the cataclysmists. London and Lease exhibited paranoid tendencies stemming from adverse family experiences, while the Adams brothers and Ignatius Donnelly grew morose because of worldly defeats. London, more fundamentally alienated than the others, reacted in the most extreme manner by taking his life. There were variations in tone as well as in degree and type of despondency. London and Donnelly, who had vivid imaginations, wrote catastrophic tales; others, more scholarly than fanciful, wrote ominous treatises. The fiction writers focused on problems of class conflict, while Brooks Adams, Homer Lea, and Mary Lease emphasized invasion and foreign war. Those who led urban existences—the Adamses, Lea, and London—reluctantly bowed to the new era. Donnelly and Mrs. Lease, rooted to the soil, were more uncompromising. The better educated Lea and the Adams brothers conceived of cataclysm in terms of abstract economic or scientific forces. Donnelly and London, on the other hand, were fascinated with the drama of disastrous events. They invented such characters as Prince Cabano in *Caesar's Column* and Ernest Everhard in *The Iron Heel* to personify cataclysmic forces. Descriptions of destruction and bloodshed, rather than analyses of causes, fascinated the novelists.

Differences existed within as well as among cataclysmists. Expectations of disaster shifted with alterations in personality and society. Brooks Adams, for example, was much more hopeful in

1902 with a patrician in the White House than after the election of
1912. Individuals also varied their emphases. After 1898, the
Adamses came to fear foreign defeat as much as they had always
feared the commercial élite. Conversely, with the decline of socialism
after 1904, Jack London became more worried about a capitalist
dictatorship than he had been about the Yellow Peril.

In the final dénouements as imagined by these individuals, contemporary conditions interacted with inner contradictions: For
Henry Adams, the Virgin battled against the dynamo; for his
younger brother, aristocratic contempt conflicted with a desire to
play the game. Donnelly envied the successful while sharing the
pathos of the defeated, and London would never decide between
Marx and Nietzsche. The cataclysmic conception of force ranged
from Henry Adams's aesthetic Virgin to Jack London's primitive
blond beast, but no matter what the level of the writer's intelligence
or sophistication, power always involved catastrophe.

Essentially, however, the similarities among these thinkers out-
weigh their differences. They are more fundamental, the distinguish-
ing aspects of cataclysmic thought. Mrs. Lease, Donnelly, the
Adamses, London, and Lea shared the feeling of being cheated and
swept aside by progress and they were therefore on the defensive
against modern times. Immigration, cities, industrialism, and empire
epitomized the new order and therefore seemed to be sources of
catastrophe. These elements were both blamed for contemporary
misery and feared as the instruments by which it would end. The
cataclysmists forecasted a bleak future in which sudden destruction
or slow strangulation lay in wait for a rotten civilization.

Common conceptions of the process of catastrophe, as well as
common foes, united cataclysmists: Conspiracy, inevitability, and
force were to precipitate catastrophe. The inconsistent belief that
willful conspiracies have predetermined consequences is revealing of
the paranoid obsessions of the Cassandras. Scheming Jews or unscrupulous financiers were seizing control of society, while the
noble yeoman with his simple strength, the aristocrat with fine
sensibilities and chivalric courage, the artist with his rare sensitivity were no match for slick urban and foreign conspirators.
Shifting the blame for social reverses, however, only partly assuaged
the shame of defeat and the guilt of impotence. The cataclysmists
were driven still further to predict that futility must frustrate the
victors as it had the vanquished—the conspiracy that had enabled the
new master class to triumph, must in the end impel its destruction.
The downfall of society had begun with guile but would end in
violence. Clashing forces meant drama, conflict, and finally doom.

The cataclysmists always foresaw a climax of foreign war or revolution because they projected their inner conflicts onto society. Disaster came when opposing forces—the poor and the rich, the farmer and the banker, the Slav and the Saxon—clashed. Those who felt coerced and cheated would then be revenged on a society that suppressed morality and sustained meanness. Cataclysm was to be the reward of outraged virtue.

So far, predictions of doom have been viewed as arising from certain experiences and expectancies in one period of American history. A study of such forebodings, however, can be broadened into an analysis of social change in general. This extension of the cataclysmic perspective goes beyond mere description of a phenomenon of the age to become an analytical principle that imposes intellectual order upon the whole era and provides insights into the processes of social change. Such an extension involves using the concept of catastrophe, not only to account for a given event, but also more generally as a category abstracted from history.

Criteria for general interpretations are obtained from historical models, which are hypotheses derived from the observation of history and applied to interpreting the past. Specific and concrete events are the data of history, but they are not self-explanatory. Only when they can be related in rational patterns do they take on full meaning. The perception of patterns among events, however, lies in the realm of ideas rather than the realm of recordable fact. Inevitably there will be a gap between these two realms. Generalization involves distortion. Nevertheless, only through such models can relationships among particular events be established and a meaningful order imposed on what would otherwise seem a chaos of isolated phenomena.

The cataclysmists are treated as a group here for the purpose of making significant observations about society in flux. The individuals involved in this abstraction actually belonged to different classes, shared no personal relationships and had little intellectual influence on each other. They came from groups that, while alienated, were not themselves cataclysmic. Unique personality traits and emotional commitment to an ordered system made cataclysmists go further than their associates. They were more concerned with society's basic problems, more conscious of their own estrangement, and thus more apt to carry it to the logical extreme of catastrophic prediction.

In the search for conceptual categories, it must not be forgotten that neither the contemporary situation nor the cataclysmists' responses were constant. Successes as well as failures came their way, and they did not always look despairingly upon the future. Although these qualifications are limiting factors, the only means to discover common characteristics among cataclysmists and their responses to diverse trends of their times is to pluck these individuals from their separate existences and place them in a theoretical model.

A study of American Cassandras yields insights into social change by demonstrating the interaction between personality and situation. Nostalgia, one phase of this interaction, provides a perspective from which to study negative responses to social transformation. Central to the cataclysmists' disaffection was their attachment to a "golden age"—by placing paradise in the past, they demonstrated alienation from the present. Fond remembrance is a classic response to unwelcome departures from tradition, but it would be too hasty to say that all the figures reacted uniformly in this manner. Although Donnelly, for example, dreamed of antebellum agrarianism and the Adamses sentimentalized about the aristocratic eighteenth century, London was not preoccupied with the past. His attitude toward history appeared to stem from his socialistic concern with the present and future, but the European Marxists from whom he drew much of his thought *were* interested in the past and shared the cataclysmists' views of the passing era as a prelude to society's destruction. The proletarian uprising, however, was not a disaster, but a blessed event that would end class exploitation and prepare humanity for further progress. Socialist Jack London, therefore, had no sentimental attachment to previous eras that had enslaved the group with whom he identified.

A comparison between cataclysmists and European socialists reveals other relevant strands in historical interpretation. The Cassandras, again excepting London, agreed with European Marxists that history was building up to an imminent debacle. The cataclysmists, however, claimed that the holocaust would result from rejecting tradition, while many foreign socialists saw the crisis as a termination of adherence to old ways, the ushering in of the era of promise. London differed from both groups in conceiving of catastrophe outside any stages in history. He saw the uprising, therefore, as irrelevant to civilization's transformation; it repeatedly occurred in an eternal present where there was no past to destroy and hence no future to create.

For the cataclysmists in general, glorification of previous periods compensated for failure in their own time. London, unlike the others, was a success by the Algeristic standards of his generation and had no need to cling to the past. But Brooks and Henry Adams,

Donnelly, and Mary Lease rose as defenders of Protestant, rural, or aristocratic America against contemporary subversion. They labeled modern forces un-American, and their allegiance to history was at once a claim for legitimacy and a source of alienation.

Another dimension of change appears in their dialectical analysis of contemporary developments. The master class, they felt, was causing its own downfall by expansion and oppression, which multiplied its enemies and embittered groups whose support was vital to its existence. A uniquely American aspect of the cataclysmic dialectic was its derivation from Darwin rather than from Marx. Evolutionary terminology seemed much more relevant to a nation where class structure did not stifle competition.

Although professing Darwinism, the cataclysmists found this optimistic creed ill-suited to doctrines of impending doom and therefore modified its principles in accord with their mood. Evolution portended disaster for those who felt themselves ill adapted to the struggle for existence; survival of the fittest was a dismal phrase when it meant society's ability to outlive the demise of one's own group. Doubts about these basic principles led to distortions of other evolutionary concepts. Brooks and Henry Adams, for example, made an excessively somber formulation of Darwinian doctrines, asserting that the old would always give way to the new. Ignatius Donnelly claimed that the ascendancy of the most efficient type would destroy civilization by preventing a return to the simpler state of preindustrial agrarianism. Jack London shared Donnelly's belief that adaptation to a miserable environment ensured destruction. Most social Darwinists believed that change was not only good but also natural and inevitable. The cataclysmists, however, felt that victory in the struggle for existence depended upon art and will rather than nature and fate. In the competitive jungle of human life, triumph crowned the efforts of those who carefully planned and ruthlessly implemented their programs. Power was captured by conspiracy, yet victory was never permanent. New groups, who adopted the rulers' successful traits and better assimilated themselves to the present, would rise to challenge the élite. The constant vigilance and violent repression necessary to maintain leadership would intensify friction and alienate increasingly large portions of the community. Finally, victory often sated the appetite to conquer thus blunting the fine competitive edge. Eventually, cataclysmists foresaw, success would stifle the victors by dissipating their energy and support. Then the oppressed would swoop down like hungry vultures to strip the carcass of a dying civilization.

If nostalgia gave the cataclysmists a sense of the past, dialectical reasoning made them conscious of destiny. They assumed that the evolutionary struggle for existence was a dialectical conflict in which the very policies of the dominant class engendered opposition. Conspiracies created counterconspiracies that made violent retribution inevitable. While other philosophers used the dialectical principle to describe the world's progress toward utopia, these pessimists made it a harbinger of doom. This attitude was partly due to their somber formulations of the struggle for survival, but other pessimistic philosophies contributed to the funereal interpretation of the dialectic. Even distortions of Darwin inadequately expressed the Adamses' despair, and they reached out for still more melancholy creeds. Brooks's pessimism drove him to try to synthesize contradictory notions of evolution and a cyclical theory of history. The struggle for existence, according to the younger brother, was a process of development alternating with decay rather than a progress to higher forms of life. Henry's despondency demanded a more complete break with evolution, and he eventually adapted the Second Law of Thermodynamics to the depressing notion that civilization was in gradual decline as it lost irreplaceable energy. Even for socialist Jack London, the dialectic worked itself out in defeat. Capitalistic exploitation generated an uprising, but the revolution ended with the plutocrat's iron heel crushing a prone proletariat. Only Donnelly, who viewed community conflict as a crisis of the will that could be stopped by re-establishing virtue, offered relief from an involuntary and irrevocable holocaust of clashing forces.

Negative responses to social change reflect anxiety over departures from the past. Cataclysmists remembered an intimate community life now rapidly disappearing before the encroachment of modern mass society. The prophets of disaster agreed that industrialism defied old values and disrupted trusted traditions, but specific criticisms varied with personal origins and interests. The Adamses and Homer Lea attacked their age more for sacrificing martial and cultural ideals than for denying the poor. Donnelly, on the other hand, objected to both maldistribution and materialism. London argued against maldistribution but not materialism. Views about economic inequality also shaped attitudes toward allocation of power. Brooks and Henry Adams despised a society that disestablished rank, vulgarized taste, and substituted commonness for excellence and irresponsibility for restraint. Donnelly and London, on the other hand, emphasized completely different tendencies in modern times. Contemporary capitalism, they charged, divided society into the rulers and the oppressed, resulting in a plutocracy that divided men and maintained power by mass manipulation. Not only did the cataclysmists disagree on what was at stake, they also differed over who was involved in the struggle. Donnelly and the Adamses drew the line of battle between business and older groups like the farmers and the Brahmins. Conversely, London saw entrepreneurs fighting proletarians for the spoils of industrialism.

Cataclysmists, excepting the archindividualist London, were committed to preserving the pre-eminence of their own groups. Alienation made them fear that the autonomy of others would lead to the overlordship of usurpers. They articulated élitism based on birth, race, vocation, or will. Different standards prevented them from joining forces, but all their criteria had one common factor— embittered isolation. The Adamses yearned for another aristocratic age; Donnelly sought an agrarian utopia; London worshipped Nietzsche's superman; Lea and Mrs. Lease were racial supremacists. Elitist distinctions reflected a contempt for the masses, ranging from the indifference of the Adams brothers to the mob scenes in *Caesar's Column* and *The Iron Heel*. London and Donnelly portrayed the people as alternately apathetic and wildly active, as brutal and capricious. Even evil élites were sketched with more sympathy. Writers who impugned the people while praising their rulers indicated that authority rather than autonomy was their goal. The prophets of disaster really wanted to dominate, and they therefore spurned a valuable ally in the pluralistic religious or immigrant communities. To these groups, who were also offended by the anonymity of mass society, the cataclysmists were indifferent or hostile.

Estrangement links the specific response of cataclysmism to general social change. Indeed, forecast of disaster is but the most intense and extreme form of resistance to new developments. General disaffection occurs when beliefs and expectations based on a vanishing order disintegrate, when old hopes and values become irrelevant to the new system and prevent adaptation to innovation. The need to be assimilated, however, cannot completely uproot traditions that represent customary patterns of social orientation, for they arise from the fundamental human quest for permanence. There is, consequently, an inevitable conflict between clinging to the past and adjusting to the present. Men are torn between dual roles when they live in clashing time spans.

This dualism raises ambivalent feelings about a tenderly remembered past in which there is no fulfillment and a present that, though loathsome, is yet vital for gratification. Group loyalties are undermined by such conflicting attachments. Convinced that their goals could never be achieved and conscious of being marginal, the cataclysmists felt themselves surrounded by a hostile world. They belonged to no professional or religious organizations that could mediate between the community and themselves. Untempered by other involvements, all their thoughts were focused gloomily on the vast problems of civilization—and without the intercession of more intimate and specialized associations, society seemed distant and indifferent. Faith became fatalism, and existence seemed devoid of hope. These critics were completely cut off from a past that had failed them and a present that denied them.

For the cataclysmists, hatred of society became an obsession. Vengeance, always the weapon of the defeated, would taste sweetest and would come most quickly in the irrational simplicity of sudden catastrophe. One blow would end confusion and frustration by bringing a meaningless world to a meaningful close. Debacle would mean only a partial victory though, for the writers' own groups would also be involved in the final dissolution. Fulfillment would still be denied. Despite their wish to destroy civilization, the cataclysmists' opposition was limited rather than total. The weak often identify with power. They reject, but at the same time they envy, those whom society honors. Donnelly, the Adamses, and London respected businessmen while repudiating them. The author of *Caesar's Column* mourned the commercial coterie's demise even as he destroyed it. Brooks Adams could never quite make up his mind whether industrialism was America's salvation or its ruin. Jack London was drawn to the cool efficiency of the master class despite his socialist leanings. If they were attracted to their enemies, these prophets also had conflicting feelings about their protagonists. Brooks Adams looked upon Theodore Roosevelt as the nation's savior yet thought the aristocracy an anachronism. London and Donnelly saw the people as a passive, ignorant mass led by a few aggressive and enlightened leaders. Populist Ignatius Donnelly was repelled, however, by the mob triumph he envisioned in *Caesar's Column,* and socialist Jack London took sadistic delight in the proletarian massacre of *The Iron Heel.*

The prediction of holocaust, however, amounted to more than twisted wish fulfillment. Those who were convinced that stability rested on traditional values and institutions were not illogical in their forebodings. If sustaining forces seemed incapable of regulating disruptive new elements, disaster would seem unavoidable. The cataclysmists' dilemma—dwelling in the present while being committed to the past—created friction between themselves and the rest of society, which in turn produced a status crisis in which the cataclysmists could not compensate for loss of traditional status by identifying with rising groups. To maintain position, the declining élites arrogated arbitration of community values, labeling competitors as usurpers. Legitimate order existed only in the old establishment, while new groups were designated false and conspiratorial. In addition to buttressing their slipping status, the cataclysmists used this process of claiming legitimacy to justify actions that were otherwise socially disapproved. They could displace their hostility onto new groups and call for violent revolution instead of political debate—all in the name of "defending" America. Consequently their demand for conversion or catastrophe seemed "virtuous" in spite of being revengeful; it sustained national values while destroying the nation.

Those on the periphery of the new order felt threatened and irrelevant. Their own community had been destroyed and none could be built in its place. Nowhere is this sense of loss more evident than in the cataclysmists' conspiracy theories. Contemporary leaders were supposed to be plotting to rob virtue of its just rewards. London and Donnelly favored secret cabals to counter this threat. These organizations represented aggressive withdrawal from industrial civilization, an attempt to regain group identification and vent dissatisfaction against an impervious mass society. Such devices, however, would destroy the order they were designed to protect: By advocating the "force" and "fraud" techniques of their adversaries, cataclysmists reflected alienation from the old as well as from new forces. Imitation was an admission that conformity was the only way to succeed. Clandestine coteries increased the anxiety and repression they were created to relieve by goading the rulers into sterner measures and intensifying tension because of the threat of betrayal. Aimed at regaining autonomy for the oppressed, they became vehicles of authoritarianism because survival depended upon discipline. Designed to resist a civilization that robbed people of their identities, they promoted the use of disguises to avoid detection, thereby furthering the loss of self in many selves.

Only universal, or at least Western, tenets of social change have been considered so far, but ideas peculiar to America were also involved in estrangement and cataclysmism. Alienation was intensified in the United States during these years because of equal opportunity. Open societies where there is great status mobility and continual readjustments are more likely to be tension-ridden over ambiguous expectancies. When social mobility is a value, the goal of personal success is emphasized, and getting ahead is taken as proof of achievement in a utopia where merit is the only standard of inclusion. Success or failure becomes the individual's own responsibility, and inferior social position engenders guilt and anxiety. The cataclysmists who felt they had not passed muster in modern times were embittered and sought to escape personal responsibility for not succeeding. The Adamses alternated confessions of failure with attacks on Algerism. They felt that social-climbing produced unfit leaders and diverted vital energy into gathering wealth. Donnelly's attitude was even more ambiguous because he had once championed equal opportunity. For the Adamses, status was connected with heredity; for Donnelly, with mobility. Each felt swindled, since society no longer conformed to his values. The brothers resented the displacement of a fixed élite; the Westerner of an open society. The Boston Brahmins sought to relieve the guilt of failure by directly attacking the success cult, but the Minnesota farmer excused his defeats by asserting that opportunity had ceased to be available. Populists like Donnelly and Mary Lease accepted equalitarianism but read in their own reverses America's rejection of an open society. Curiously, the agrarians, once defeated, moved close to the Adams position. Failure rigidified them into demanding a yeoman-dominated community in place of a diverse, free society. London, the only one of these figures who really rose from rags to riches, was most tragically involved in the struggle for success. Achievement, for him, ended in an all-consuming loneliness to be escaped only through suicide.

Attacking the success myth did little to alleviate the misery of defeat. Periodic attempts were made to reverse fortunes by returning to political orthodoxy or exploiting influential friendships, but, in general, relief was sought in future debacles or utopias where corruption would be crushed and the just, the cataclysmists' kind, would rule. The ruthlessness in these phantasies, the justification of any means to victory, indicates that the Cassandras shared values they professed to loathe. Once again, they were caught between desires and declarations. Their ambivalence toward Algerism was manifested by a wish to win but also to change the rules—they would end the contest by fixing status and establishing standards. Henry Adams withdrew into his static twelfth century; Brooks deprecated democratic individualism; Donnelly tried to structure an agricultural society; Mary Lease and Homer Lea hoped to stop international strife by establishment of racial supremacy. Even ending this competition, however, entailed playing the game first. Strife would cease only in victory, and triumph meant domination by the winners and destruction or enslavement of the losers.

These attempts to cope with the basic cultural pattern were born of the desperation of futility. When religion or class allegiance no longer defined goals, aspirations became infinite. Unlimited ambition was embodied in the pursuit of success. Achievement in a hierarchical society has a different meaning for each group and is visibly embodied in a multitude of forms and distinctions. In America, however, accomplishment was measured by the single vague standard of making money. Criteria like size of fortune, the termination point in active wealth-gathering, methods of acquisition and consumption, or origin of fortune were rarely used to differentiate groups or to give variety and precision to the definition of success. In one sense, ambiguity made sufficient wealth-gathering an unattainable end—undefined success could never be won. There was no real achievement but rather a striving for accomplishment that intensified its own quest and prevented people from ever arriving.

A lack of fixed roles and goals isolated individuals. Position was associated with individual effort rather than group identification, and Algerism generated high interpersonal competition. As a result, group ties were only temporary and superficial, while competition limited the gratification ordinarily derived from personal relationships. Bitterness was further increased because there were fewer places than contenders. Competition was therefore intensified, and the success of some necessarily entailed the failure of others. The frequency of failure made individual responsibility seem a burden to many, and they sought relief by claiming that rewards were often unfairly won and defeats not necessarily deserved. This truth was pushed to paranoia by the cataclysmists, who made conspirators out of competitors and attributed their own positions to society's persecution. Relations between individual and community were also exacerbated by recognition that accomplishments did not always depend upon merit or skill. Others' successes seemed even more unjust when they were based as much on manipulation of personality to maximize social attractiveness (sometimes in defiance of inner needs) as on demonstration of competence.

Ambition's tortuous route often caused crises of belief in individuals. Contemporary goals were universalized, although they often conflicted with traditional beliefs or personal desires, yet the drive for accomplishment was not always channeled through these contemporary values. Self-manipulation combined with constant readaptation to changing demands and ambiguous standards made self mastery and social adjustment difficult. Too often the pursuit, and even the attainment, of success meant conflict with both self and society.

Up to this point, the analysis of cataclysmic thought has been developed in terms of group and personal reactions to social change. There is, however, another dimension to the problem. The cataclysmists were also personalities responding to an adverse situation, and they manifested classic anxiety patterns: aggressive hostility that aims at destroying a menace, submission and withdrawal to propitiate threats. Cataclysmic literature provides evidence of hostile aggression, but the restriction of that aggression to imaginative works is a form of withdrawal before overpowering forces. The element of alienation in aggression is revealed when animosity is projected against all segments of society. The cataclysmists' ambivalence toward their own group, the involvement of their associates in the final dissolution, indicates that self contempt could not be completely displaced. Displacement of inner hostility even intensified anxiety because it demanded a desperate attempt to forestall defeat by destroying the foe—The gratification in striking while being stricken is that self hostility assumes the nobler guise of self defense.

Cataclysmic thinking links self-aggrandizement with self-deprecation, flight with assault, submission with aggression by making power the determining factor in social relations. Foretellers of doom divided civilization into the strong and the weak. The community was split between the impotence, deprivation, and submission of the underdog and the greed, aggression, and grandeur of the rulers. Henry Adams vilified industrialists while seeing himself as a weak old man who needed the protection of the Medieval Virgin. Brooks Adams thundered at commerce with all the bitterness of those who submit to what they hate. Sometimes dual images of deprecation and aggrandizement occurred in the writers' own group or even in one protagonist. The primary figure of *Caesar's Column,* Gabriel Weltstein, flees the plutocracy to escape death, but his friend, Maximilian Petion, leads the proletarian attack on the élite. Ernest Everhard, the superman in *The Iron Heel,* is killed, and his cause is suppressed. Dualism in their works reveals the authors' own divided personalities. Maximilian and Gabriel reflect both Donnelly's desire to seize power and his frustrating defeats. Ernest represents Jack London, blustering and bullying but ultimately bowing to the enemy. Brooks Adams is the enraged aristocrat who could never decide whether the world would end because it ignored his breed or whether Brahmins were irrelevant in the machine age.

Cataclysmists attributed their dismal situation to an adverse allocation of power. The gap between reality and their aspirations was caused by the irresistible strength of their enemies. The Cassandras' sense of feebleness made them feel manipulated, and they were fascinated by the techniques of the manipulators—hence, the preoccupation of these critics with Nietzschean or Darwinian power types and with such theories of pre-emption as the conspiracy theory of history. Their versions of the power configuration, apart from explaining why they lost, also excused the losers and even provided them with revenge. They claimed that ruthless repression made them blameless for their failures and the debacle resulting from misused power would extinguish their enemies. This view of force reduced the complex and frustrating web of social relationships to a paranoid syndrome. The perspective of power clarified the cataclysmists' position, an all-or-nothing position of mastery or catastrophe.

Defiance and doubt rose from the conviction that they were being victimized. These feelings in turn generated a sense of paranoid helplessness that made debacle seem inevitable—a vengeful vision of global disaster. These emotions mitigated failure either by the narcotic of belief in adverse fate or the catharsis of violence. But catastrophe is small reward because it ends all hope of achievement and self-mastery. Forecasts of doom are an admission that there is no possible *détente* between society and the individual. Healthy communities are able to harmonize self-realization with social progress, but only the negative accomplishment of destroying that which denied them was left to the cataclysmists. Holocaust would be a final resolution of the insurmountable contradictions of ambition and defeat, competition and community, change and permanence. The wish to destroy civilization produced the only unity possible in those torn apart by society.

2

Cataclysmic Thinking and Social Criticism

THE VALIDITY OF A THEORETICAL MODEL depends on its capacity to explain cogently the context from which it is abstracted. The analytical significance of cataclysmic thought is therefore determined by the degree to which it can be related to other social developments. Presumably, if the ideal type sheds light on other elements, a study of these elements will in turn furnish a more precise perspective on the conceptual category itself. A study of the connection between jeremiads and social criticism in general should be enlightening about both the cataclysmists and other critics.

There is actually no sharp distinction between cataclysmists and noncataclysmists. Utopian thinkers shared the fears of anti-utopians; Social Gospelers, notwithstanding their faith, had a deep sense of crisis; and naturalist writers, despite their pretense of objectivity, could not escape the pessimistic implications of their observations. Criticism, however, is not the same as cataclysmism and reformers do believe that society can be saved.

Social thought in the decades between 1880 and 1918 encompassed a variety of vocations and attitudes. Preachers and poets, pundits and politicians all evinced concern over the course of civilization. Some were reformers, others feared change, and still others professed to be objective observers who refused to distort their perceptions by taking sides. Amid such diversity, however, there were two constants: Everyone was highly critical, and everyone—except the cataclysmists—believed that society would survive.

In 1879, a book appeared whose title and theme, *Progress and Poverty*, defined social criticism for an entire era. For Henry George, its author, and many who came after him, industrialism was a force that impoverished the masses by diverting labor's product to rich parasites. Concentration of wealth, government corruption, and increased immorality, "the obstacles which finally bring progress to a halt are raised by the course of progress; . . . what has destroyed all previous civilizations has been the conditions produced by the growth of civilization itself."

The dualistic nature of progress caused George to view social change as a prelude to either development or disintegration. "The civilized world," he wrote, "is trembling on the verge of a great movement. Either it must be a leap upward, which will open the way to advances yet undreamed of, or it must be a plunge downward, which will carry us back toward barbarism." If iniquities were not quickly removed, industrialism would create "a despotism of the vilest and most degrading kind. . . . The sword will again be mightier than the pen, and . . . carnivals of destructive brute force and wild frenzy will alternate with the lethargy of a declining civilization."

He argued that adverse conditions were exacerbated by fallacious principles for dealing with them. Eighteenth-century doctrines on the immutability of human nature or rigid wage laws blocked adoption of realistic policies. In attacking both social conditions and methods of coping with them, George opened a two-front war that raged through the next few decades. Ministers, economists, and sociologists in this age fought formalism within their own professions, as well as the evils of the outside world.

George, who described the imminent collapse of society with words similar to those in *Caesar's Column* and *The Iron Heel,* was equally capable of grandiose utopian visions. If only the single tax panacea were adopted, "our civilization may soar" to "the Golden Age of which poets have sung and high-raised seers have told in metaphor!" Humanity would at last attain "the glorious vision which has always haunted man with gleams of fitful splendor . . . the culmination of Christianity—the City of God on earth, with its walls of jasper and its gates of pearl. It is the reign of the Prince of Peace." This passage highlights the difference between George and the Cassandras, between a sense of crisis and a certainty of catastrophe. Social change can mean poverty, but it also may result in the development of a perfect society. It means "that our own civilization has a broader base, is of a more advanced type, moves quicker and soars higher than any preceding civilization." Henry George rejected the pessimistic view that saw in every advance a sign of decay and that claimed man was chained to merciless fate. The single-taxer no longer feared since he had found the remedy for all social ills. *Progress and Poverty* had transformed despair into a conviction that peace and happiness would prevail. By discovering the laws of happiness Henry George revived in himself "a faith that was dead." [1]

At first glance, cataclysmic writing, which is anti-utopian, seems diametrically opposed to the utopian literature of that era. Such an appearance is deceiving, however, because both have a common assumption—that something is wrong with society. Edward Bellamy and William Dean Howells, the two most prominent utopians of the period, found much amiss in America. Bellamy's *Looking Backward* and *Equality* depict a nation rife with strikes, corruption, materialism, overcrowded cities, undesirable immigrants, and class conflict. The "industrial system of the United States was fast" replacing "social unity" with "the iron bands of despotism" backed by "a government of bayonets." The nation was headed for "irrepressible conflict . . . between the rights of man and the tyranny of capital" unless radical revisions were made.[2] Despite these forebodings, Bellamy was basically an optimist. A firm believer "in man's essential nobleness" and in the country's capacity to make a relatively peaceful transition from misery to paradise, he was confident "that the Golden Age lies before us and not behind us, and is not far away." [3]

Howells, in *A Traveller From Altruria,* also saw a strife-ridden and corrupt society facing a struggle for survival "more uncompromising than any such fight that the world has ever seen." Only a state without cities or trusts, where agriculture was the primary occupation and technology virtually discarded, could avoid the pitfalls of industrialism. Perfection consisted in returning to a simple life with so few needs "that the handiwork of the primitive toilers could easily supply our wants." [4]

The difference between utopian and anti-utopian literature is spectral rather than polar. The two genres share an apocalyptic vision of the end of corrupt society and differ more in emphasis than in ideology. If Howells and Bellamy began with a dismal view of capitalism, Ignatius Donnelly and Mary Lease ended with a picture of pastoral paradise. Utopians and anti-utopians returned a common indictment of nineteenth-century civilization. They charged it with being individualistic, materialistic, exploitative, and divisive. Both groups seized upon the same enemy, ruthless capitalism, and shared the apprehension that disaster could be forestalled only by immediate reform. Even disagreements over cures were similar in both camps. As Howells wanted to recreate the past and Bellamy to embrace the future, so a parallel divergence existed between modernists and reactionaries among cataclysmic thinkers. Donnelly, for example, bemoaned the loss of an antebellum Arcadia, while Brooks Adams and Jack London saw the roots of catastrophe in inability to adjust to contemporary conditions.

The crucial difference between utopians and cataclysmists lies in their degrees of faith in the future of mankind. Howells, Bellamy, Mrs. Lease, and the young Brooks Adams may be considered optimists because they believed in man's ability to establish a healthy society. Conversely, Homer Lea, Jack London, and Ignatius Donnelly believed that an adverse fate impelled civilization to chaos. Rather than dwelling on the promise of paradise, they were obsessed with the prospect of gory holocaust.

Horatio Alger is the real antagonist of cataclysmism. He writes of a world peopled with beneficent businessmen and abounding in opportunities for success. The established order, in which the good triumph and the evil fail, embodied moral perfection. Thrift, pluck, honesty, and ambition could overcome all obstacles. Virtue would prevail because equality and democracy governed the system. For Jack London, Brooks and Henry Adams, and Ignatius Donnelly, however, society was a conspiracy to crush the worthy. Ernest Everhard in London's *Iron Heel* and Gabriel Weltstein in Donnelly's *Caesar's Column* have all the right sentiments, yet they are defeated by a civilization that rewards goodness with failure. Jack London goes even further in *Martin Eden* to attack not only the means but also the goals of Alger's credo. Martin Eden realizes the dreams of Alger's newsboys and bootblacks only to become so disgusted with success that he commits suicide.

Mark Twain—unlike Henry George, the utopian novelists, or the Social Gospelers—manifested alienation without a sense of catastrophe. Samuel Clemens forecasted no horrible conspiracy about to trigger class war, nor did he anticipate a Darwinian struggle that would end in global conflict. The extent of his speculation was prediction of a gradual decline from republicanism to absolute monarchy. This prediction, passively rather than turbulently pessimistic, was the closest Twain came to imagining a debacle.

The humorist's passivity, his genuflection to fate, prevented his pessimism from becoming cataclysmic. In a sense, it was the very

depth of Twain's despair that precluded belief in disaster. Cataclysmists claimed that destruction would result from contention for
power, but Clemens believed that individuals were too weak to
challenge their destinies. The distrust and bitterness lurking in the
background of his earlier works grew into a contempt so complete
that it assumed humanity capable of nothing but capitulation to
the inevitable. The main themes of *The Mysterious Stranger,
Pudd'nhead Wilson, The Man Who Corrupted Hadleyburg,* and
What is Man? are man's hypocrisy, cowardice, and lack of free
will. The cataclysmists at least believed that the sources of power
existed in society, but Twain was so contemptuous of man that he
saw him as a mere plaything of the larger forces of fate.

Those obsessed with the idea of holocaust identified with displaced groups and associated catastrophe with the elimination of
their compatriots. Twain's estrangement, on the other hand, was
personal. He had never joined abortive crusades or belonged to defeated movements—his tragedy was death, illness in the family, and
financial failure. Consequently, his image of the social struggle was
that of a lonely, feeble individual bowing to his fate rather than
that of a defiant force involving society in its own destruction.

Although Twain did not foresee a climactic disaster, he had
much in common with cataclysmists. As might be expected from
a man whose contentment had suddenly vanished, he conceived of
life as a vast "swindle." "Traps" in which "Disaster" was "dis-
guised as Good Fortune" had been "set for man from the beginning
of time." [5] Disillusionment abounds in *Pudd'nhead Wilson, The
Man Who Corrupted Hadleyburg,* and *The Mysterious Stranger*—
those sad stories that reflect tragedies in his own life. The gentleman in *Pudd'nhead Wilson,* is really a slave, Hadleyburg's honor
is compromised, and existence is proved a huge hoax in *The
Mysterious Stranger.* Substance and appearance become so divorced
in *The Mysterious Stranger* that reality dissolves into a dream.
Twain agreed with the Cassandras that life was a swindle, but his
suspicions never crystallized into that vital ingredient of cataclysm, a
conspiracy theory. He believed all men were swindled equally because no one had mastery or autonomy. There could be no conspiracy of the "haves" against the "have nots" when everyone was a
"have not"—equal in misery and futility.

His sense of being cheated by life was the expression of a feeling of inner weakness combined with an oppressive sense of fate.
Omnipotent destiny made resistance futile. This negative determinism helped Twain to rationalize the setbacks of his later years.
A demonic destiny had wreaked those illnesses, deaths, and financial

reverses. Mark Twain, powerless to end his misery, raged against the human race for its inability to change its destiny. His bitterness, however, was really directed at himself; its source lay in his sense of guilt over his own role in the family misfortunes. Why had he not invested more wisely? Why had he not been at the deathbed of his daughter Susy? Why had he not been a better husband to Olivia? The shame of Hadleyburg and the nightmare of Eseldorf were as nothing compared to the remorse of Mark Twain.

In order to preserve his reputation as the nation's greatest humorist, Twain repressed his real thoughts. *The Mysterious Stranger* and *What Is Man?* were not published until after his death. The younger generation of novelists, however, did not feel called upon to play Pagliacci—they portrayed life in much darker tones. Stephen Crane, Frank Norris, and Theodore Dreiser filled pages with frustration, failure, conflict, vice, and corruption—but, except for Dreiser's later work, they offered critical observations rather than wholesale condemnations. While Twain became a pessimistic determinist out of bitter desperation and while London, Brooks Adams, and Donnelly were cataclysmic determinists, Crane, Norris, and Dreiser portrayed the struggle for existence as a fatalistic natural process that precluded guilt or catastrophe. Donnelly's Weltstein and London's Everhard are protagonists in a world tragedy, but in *The Octopus,* an epic about the struggle between the railroad and the farmers, Norris identified with Presley, the artist-observer. Dreiser too cautioned against judging irresistible destiny and, though sympathetic to the downtrodden, regarded conflicts involving the poor and the rich, the city, or business more as situations worthy of study than as portents of doom.

Urban strife and commercial struggles fascinated rather than horrified these authors. As Darwinists, they were drawn to areas of conflict because there were the centers of action, social change, and power. New social forces outraged Twain and the cataclysmists, but Dreiser and Norris paid homage to them. Norris in *The Octopus* sketches the railroad president sympathetically and accepts his excuse that the conflict with the farmers was shaped by forces beyond human control. Dreiser, who offered a glimpse of the emptiness of success in *Sister Carrie,* was also infatuated by the tycoon. Frank Cowperwood, hero of *The Titan, The Financier,* and *The Stoic* was modeled after a real business buccaneer—Charles T. Yerkes. Dreiser thought "the financial type . . . the most selfish and the most useful of all living phenomena. . . . a highly specialized machine for the accomplishment of some end which Nature has in view." With mixed feelings he described the magnate as "shark-like, avid, yet among the greatest constructive forces imaginable; absolutely opposed to democracy in practice, yet as useful an implement for its accomplishment as for autocracy." [6]

These writers depicted tragedy from the perspective of men basically at peace with society. They were never completely estranged, and they never declared war upon their era. To them misfortune was society's by-product—a natural life process. They never conceived of such occurrences as the results of conspiracies against them, and they therefore had no desire to destroy society to save themselves. Beneath the guise of objectivity, Dreiser, Norris, and Crane were actually far more committed to the system than Twain and the cataclysmists.

The Social Gospelers were more traditional in outlook but equally as critical as the naturalists. They shared with Henry George and the utopians a consciousness of the challenge of social change and made the same basic distinction between crisis and cataclysm. Civilization might be shaken by industrialism, but with God's help it would be saved. Religious reformers had reason to be alarmed in this period. Their faith was under attack from every quarter. Intellectually it was being undermined by biblical criticism and a growing belief in science. Socially it seemed to be growing more remote from and irrelevant to the industrial conflicts rending America. Immigrant sects threatened to undermine its influence and even to destroy the tradition of a Protestant America. There was danger from within the ranks of the religious, as well as from the outside. Conservative ministers continued to bless the *status quo* and assured their well fed flocks that they were the best of all people in the best of all worlds. Preachers who asserted that business success was a sign of divine approval and poverty a penalty for sin and indolence did not exactly inspire widespread religious devotion. Like other reformers, the Social Gospelers fought on two fronts—against the perils of social change and against the platitudes of their own colleagues.

Men like Washington Gladden, Lyman Abbott, Walter J. Rauschenbusch, and Josiah Strong were convinced that Christianity had to be revitalized. They forced Protestantism to face contemporary problems, asserting that poverty was not a character defect and that social criticism was not blasphemy. Despite their conviction that Jerusalem would finally be won, these crusaders occasionally doubted their ability to rouse the faithful and convert the sinners. Social strain, manifested in corporate greed, bloody strikes, materialistic creeds, and hidebound clergymen sometimes made even the faithful verge on a crisis outlook. Gladden felt "the state of industrial society" to be "a state of war." [7] Abbott thought that if America did not return to God "ruin" was inevitable.[8] Rauschenbusch imagined "some Gibbon of Mongolian race" writing a " 'Decline and Fall of the Christian Empire' " in which he would describe "the nineteenth and twentieth centuries as the golden age when outwardly life flourished as never before, but when that decay, which resulted in the gradual collapse of the twenty first and twenty second centuries, was largely far advanced." [9] Strong also shared the anxiety of his fellow ministers and, in a book significantly entitled *Our Country: Its Possible Future And Present Crisis,* warned that "we are preparing conditions which make possible a Reign of Terror that would beggar the scenes of the French Revolution." [10]

Despite such gloomy utterances, these ministers were not basically cataclysmic thinkers. Rauschenbusch and his colleagues found more reasons to hope than to despair in the modern era. They felt that business organizations were efficient, provided employment, and increased production and that labor unions protected workers and fostered brotherhood. If only wealth could be used in a spirit of Christian stewardship, "civilization would be on a higher plane than formerly" and there would come an age of "prosperity" and unprecedented "intellectual and spiritual development." [11]

Fundamentally though, it was the conviction that God would prevent catastrophe that distinguished religious reform from cataclysmism. The Deity, as the reformers pictured Him, was a God of Love who called on men to behave as brothers and to acknowledge His Fatherhood. Accordingly, the theology of the Social Gospel rejected tooth-and-claw Darwinism for "the higher stages of evolution." In those stages, Christlike altruism would bring "the completion of nature's process of evolution—the crown and glory of creation." The divinely ordained change from brutality to brotherhood meant that turbulent transformations would be merely a prelude to the "kingdom of God on earth." [12]

Harmony would prevail because "God intended that we should be the happiest of all His creation." [13] Social Gospelers believed that God was a protective rather than a punitive parent. He was everywhere interposing Himself between humanity and catastrophe and directing social forces toward beneficent ends. Every day Christ was bringing the "Kingdom of God" closer to this world. Ultimately Jesus would "lead his children" into a "perfect social order" with "blessedness and abundance of peace as long as the moon endureth." [14]

Henry Adams and Jack London ignored God, the aged Brooks Adams saw Him as an avenging angel, and Ignatius Donnelly considered Christianity inoperative in modern society. The Social Gospelers, however, were secure in their beliefs and inspired in their activities. Rauschenbusch, Strong, Abbott, and Gladden believed themselves to be walking with God on the path of right-eousness. They could already see their destination, the everlasting virtue and universal bliss of the "Kingdom." Men who were so sure of their message, their future, and their Maker could not long dwell upon world disaster.

Liberal clergymen extended their operations from church organ-izations to other movements. One of the most fruitful of these alliances was with the American Economic Association. As the Social Gospel had been formulated to counteract the Gospel of Wealth, the American Economic Association was founded to oppose the prevailing conservatism of most economists. Twenty-one religious reformers, including Washington Gladden and Lyman Abbott, enlisted to carry the good fight into economics. They became charter members of the new organization and the degree of their influence was evident when their views were voiced by one of its guiding lights—Richard T. Ely.

Ely shared the sense of crisis held by Rauschenbusch, Gladden, and Abbott. History, he felt, had reached a crossroads where "the potentialities for good or for evil are grand beyond precedent, and it rests with the living to say what the future will be." [15] The economist agreed with his theologian colleagues that social welfare was threatened by corruption, class conflict, cutthroat competition, and conservatism. He battled the ritualism of Manchester *laissez-faire* in the same manner as the ministers resisted ritualism in the churches.

Ely accepted the values, as well as the methods, of the religious reformers. He too eschewed the violent implications of Darwinism in favor of struggle on "higher planes" where men contend for honor and virtue rather than for power or wealth. In this elevated competition, "altruism . . . and the amelioration of man's social environment has been coexistent with the increasing strength and efficiency of men in modern civilized society." [16]

Progress was inevitable—and also beneficial—because of divine paternalism and human brotherhood. The devout economist echoed the Social Gospelers in worshipping a God of love "primarily con-cerned with this world" and desiring "to bring to pass here a king-dom of righteousness." [17] The faith that sustained these reformers was given its classical formulation when Ely declared that "in

Christ we have a personal Comforter who affords us consolation
in our weariness and disappointments." Despite the disturbances
resulting from progress, they had the "sure and steadfast hope"
that "nothing is in reality lost; that we are working for a cause
which will finally triumph because back of it there stands a Ruler
of human destinies." [18]

The position of Ely's doctrine of Christian charity as the touch-
stone of economic reform was challenged, not only by defenders of
the established order, but also by a young iconoclast from Minnesota.
Thorstein Veblen adopted a guise similar to that of Crane and
Dreiser, posing as the tough-minded, objective observer with little
patience for spiritual reformers and sentimental theorists who
hoped to solve social problems by proclaiming the coming of
Christ's Kingdom. Veblen's abrasive personality could not express
itself in the gentle beliefs of Christian brotherhood, and he was
too deeply estranged from his era to attribute social strain to
individual immorality.

Seldom has a man turned more bitterly on his age than did
Veblen. He spurned its heroes, attacked its values, and deprecated
its institutions. In total scope and in many details, Veblen's condemnation resembles those of the Cassandras. The similarity of
their critiques is not surprising, for Veblen and the cataclysmists
shared the frustration of stunted careers and a deep sense of
alienation from the community. The dissenting economist agreed
with the foretellers of doom who envisioned society irreconcilably
divided between an exploitative élite and producers who sustained
this master class. Although Veblen's criticism was more profound,
the object under attack—businessmen—was the same. He echoed
Donnelly and London in calling them predators who diverted community resources into conspicuous display, and he agreed with
Brooks Adams that capitalists had already been bypassed by social
development and were too atavistic to administer the modern
economic system. Veblen foresaw a bleak future of periodic wars,
frequent depressions, cutthroat competition, and class conflict if
production continued to be hamstrung by the price system and
society to be dominated by the captains of industry.

Despite this dismal view of the situation, Veblen did not
actually despair until after World War I, when he came to feel
that predatory finance would crush the productive forces. Before the
war, however, Veblen was not frightened. He never assumed that
class division would erupt in revolution, that the wars he expected
would terminate civilization, or that socialism would destroy society.
Veblen, like the naturalists, was too detached for cataclysmism. His

strong identification with his Norwegian background precluded a passionate commitment to America. He suffered the hurt pride of the outsider but never the pain of the defeated participant.

But a more positive state of mind than ethnic isolation helped to neutralize any cataclysmic propensity in his thought. Until his last years, Veblen believed that man's healthy instincts would ultimately override destructive environmental tendencies. If only the instincts of "workmanship" and the "parental bent" could be given free play, the perversions of modern times would disappear. The development of industrial capitalism, he felt, would breach the bastions of the master class. As modern machine techniques cut through anachronistic notions of individual competition and private property, people would finally see that progress involved economic cooperation and technical knowledge. Rationalizations for the price system would then be exposed and the business élite's expendability revealed. Once fully aware of the real interaction of economic forces, producers would assume leadership and usher in an era of peace and progress.

The critics of this era shared many convictions with the cataclysmists. Both groups were disaffected by their environment and aware of its perils. Except for Twain, however, the noncataclysmists were not alienated to the degree of regarding civilization as beyond redemption. They conceived of no brutalized mass that was irretrievably inhuman; they imagined no conspiratorial élite so devilish that it had to be destroyed. In some individuals pessimism was stifled by indifference, for only intense moral indignation engenders the apocalyptic frame of mind. Others, however, tapped deep reservoirs of faith to avoid "The Slough of Despond." Optimism welled up from various sources. Some were confident that they had found the solution to all social problems; others rested secure in their belief that a benevolent deity would rescue man. Whatever the causes, these critics never surrendered to a conviction of impending doom. They retained the sense of balance that prevents grotesque points of view and directs energy into suggestions for reform rather than schemes for disaster.

Cataclysmic thought from 1880 to 1918 has been delineated as an ideal type and differentiated from other forms of social criticism, but in order to be shown in its full dimensions, it must be compared with similar moods in other periods. From the time when the Puritans first struggled to obtain a foothold on this continent until the present day, radical social change has invariably engendered predictions of disaster in some quarters. Dismal prognostications have been voiced over adjustment to the wild new world, conflict over independence, the emergence of the common man, the struggle between secession and preservation of the union, the triumph of industrial capitalism, America's assumption of world power, and, finally, the challenge for global hegemony that carries with it the threat of total destruction. Puritan preachers read disaster into the backslidings of the chosen; Tories saw catastrophe in separation from England; unreconstructed Federalists shuddered at visions of the Jacksonian mob; Northerners and Southerners brooded over the crises of the 1850's; and in 1963, many Americans fearfully contemplate the prospect of defeat or atomic destruction.

Fin de siècle cataclysmists shared many fears with their predecessors and successors. Ignatius Donnelly and Mary Lease echoed the Jacksonian alarmists who forecasted disaster when independent artisans and yeomen were displaced by wealthy entrepreneurs; Brooks Adams and Homer Lea are still relevant voices to those who worry about world war; and Henry Adams, at odds with his age, represents men of past and present who have fought desperate rear guard actions against upstart élites. Notwithstanding similarities, there are, however, critical differences between cataclysmists of fifty years ago and those of other eras. This divergence is clearest in a comparison of their predictions with cataclysmic thought in the seventeenth and mid-twentieth centuries.

The alienation from society and types of power struggle that were crucial in the late nineteenth and early twentieth centuries concepts were not at all vital to Puritan notions of catastrophe. In a society that accepted the world's destruction as part of its creed, cataclysmic ideas did not necessarily arise from estrangements from the community. Seventeenth-century New Englanders had inherited the medieval eschatology that claimed the world would end in a Day of Judgment. Since everyone foresaw a time in which God would destroy the world by some sort of holocaust, it was not a mark of disaffection to anticipate such a debacle. The millennium was not to be a time of evil blight, but a day of justice when sinners would be punished and the pure rewarded. Since Puritans believed this world was a prelude to the next and since they saw themselves as God's chosen, the holocaust would mark the beginning rather than the end of existence.

A more tragic prospect than the end of the world was the end of Massachusetts Bay Colony. While the Judgment Day meant grace for true believers, the destruction of Massachusetts meant God's wrath visited upon those false in tongue and heart. God had covenanted with the Puritans to protect them as long as they observed His laws. Violation of the compact was a declaration of bad faith and would be sternly punished. Preoccupation with this threat of disaster, however, no more indicated alienation than did the conviction that God would someday terminate earthly existence. Whatever may be said about individual psyches in a society that dwelled so morbidly on sin and was so acutely conscious of divine wrath, it cannot be claimed that such foreboding was caused by rebellion against the community. While the later cataclysmists were on the fringes of society, it was the Puritan ruling élite itself that grimly warned against the consequences of immorality.

Another significant variation between these two periods of cataclysmic thinking lies in the different precipating factors that were envisioned. Cries of doom at the turn of the century were keyed to a Darwinian dirge of power conflicts. Donnelly predicted a debacle resulting from a war between producers and financiers; Jack London foresaw a battle between labor and capital; Brooks Adams, Mary Lease, and Homer Lea envisioned a struggle for survival between Anglo-Saxons and other races. The Adams brothers postulated another form of power-oriented catastrophe—by applying the laws of thermodynamics to society, they concluded that an inevitable declination of energy would ultimately lead to disintegration. In each case, power was crucial, either in domestic or foreign conflicts for supremacy or in a decline in physical energy. Power, however, was neither a vital consideration in Puritan eschatology nor in speculations about the future of Massachusetts. Puritan doctrines of cataclysm were rooted in morality. The world ended, not in battle between opposing groups, but in the meting out of justice by the Great Arbiter against whose omnipotence there could be no appeal to force. Similarly, jeremiads about the destiny of the colony were cast in terms of violating a sacred contract rather than of a desire for power. Predictions of catastrophe, therefore, were not necessarily caused by estrangement or envy, nor did they emerge from visions of group conflict. Apprehension came rather from fear that personal sins like inebriety or blasphemy would culminate in the legalistic moral transgression of breaking the covenant. The self-examination and self-criticism elicited by this attitude led to feelings of intense guilt and self-contempt similar to those that haunted later cataclysmists, but these earlier notions of doom never involved that bitterness toward the community that characterized subsequent Cassandras. Since the struggle involved spiritual aspirations to be achieved only through individual virtue, the more secular aims of wealth or political power and the tendency to identify with declining groups that characterized later pessimists were irrelevant to Puritan prognosticators.

Today's oracles of disaster contrast with *fin de siècle* cataclysmists in another manner. Unlike the Puritans, contemporary forecasters share the power-oriented, secular convictions of their immediate forebears. Catastrophe is pictured as the result of a struggle between Russia and America, as fifty years ago similar results were anticipated from a conflict between these nations. The two groups of cataclysmists also hold a common view about the emptiness of life. Earlier critics expressed those same fears of the sprawling city, the impersonal corporation, and the implications of wielding world power that have generated so much despair in their successors. There is, however, one vast difference between the two formulations of catastrophe. Earlier speculation was distorted by estrangement from the community and self-alienation. Today's theories, however, do not always originate in problems of social adjustment; they may actually offer realistic analysis of the world situation. When doom is a figment of the imagination or results from maladjustment, as was the case with the Puritans and the cataclysmists of fifty years ago, explanations for erroneous conclusions must be found—but when society is in real danger of annihilation, pessimistic judgments may be grounded in clear analysis of objective conditions.

PART TWO

THE
HISTORICAL
CONTEXT

CATEGORIES used to study the past may have faultless theoretical structures that are logically consistent, provide precise distinctions from other perspectives, and offer wide interpretive scope—yet if relevance to their ages cannot be demonstrated, as historical models they are meaningless. Study of cataclysmic thought from 1885 to 1918 must, therefore, help to clarify the historical context, if it is to be useful. Since social upheaval was basic to that era, modifications in cataclysmic forecasts should help to reveal the changing course of society. If there is a correspondence between the changes in ominous prediction and social flux, then we can conclude that expectation of doom played some role in public opinion. The significance of this role can be ascertained through the relationship between pessimistic prognostications and other social attitudes (as we have already seen), the extent of cataclysmism as a response to contemporary problems, and the influence of individuals or groups holding such convictions.

3

Turbulent Era

1885-1897

A CLOUD IN THE SKY: 1876-1885

THE 1880's opened auspiciously. The depression of the 1870's had subsided, and its violent labor conflicts and agrarian uprisings were memories. Almost everyone believed in capitalism, immigrants were welcomed, and the rumblings of agrarian discontent had been muted by the return of prosperity. Immigration, urbanization, socialism, and strikes were becoming problems, but they could still be treated with the traditional optimism that saw in all problems the promise of future greatness.

It had been but a few years since America had triumphed over the gravest threat to her existence, and she optimistically hoped that this rift would heal quickly. With Confederate brigadiers sitting in Congress and on the boards of railroads and banks, the power of America to convert everyone to her image seemed limitless. Certainly the immigrant, the worker, the city dweller, and even the anarchist could be redeemed.

Although the Railroad Strike of 1877 had raised a few doubts about immigration, the great weight of respectable opinion was still on the side of the newcomers.[1] The antebellum image of the United States as a refuge for the oppressed and of the foreigner as a vital factor in her development had not yet disappeared.

Labor conflict, which gave the Panic of 1873 a dimension of grim class conflict, caused more concern. The strike was a definite break in the postwar wall of security and gave rise to anxiety about

America's future. *The Nation,* for example, viewed "the occurrences of the last fortnight" as having done "much to shake or destroy the faith" that America had "solved the problem of enabling labor and capital to live together in political harmony, and that this was the one country in which there was no proletariat—no dangerous class . . ." [2] Some observers even went so far as to connect the strikers with socialism and imagined the Paris Commune transplanted to the United States. [3]

Many, however, held the line against panic. They viewed the Railroad Strike as a labor-management squabble rather than as a manifestation of a communist conspiracy. *Harper's Monthly* assured its readers that labor problems could be more intelligently solved here than in "any country in the world." The "fear of Communism in this country," it asserted, "is not reasonable." [4] Those observers who perceived the struggle as one between American groups committed to capitalism often sympathized with the working men. Indifference to employee welfare, charged *Scribner's Monthly Magazine,* "has had a great deal more to do in preparing for the strike than most people imagined." [5] The strike was followed by eight years of industrial peace and conservative trade unionism, and the optimists prevailed while fears were lulled.

The Depression of 1873 also contributed to the initial wave of Western discontent. Farmers flocked to the newly formed Granges and supported Anti-Monopoly or Independent Parties in Illinois, Michigan, Wisconsin, Minnesota, Iowa, Missouri, Kansas, and Nebraska. After some success on the state level, these groups combined to form the Greenback Party, which ran that grand old reformer Peter Cooper for president in 1876. But recovery curbed the political truculence of the farmer, and agrarian radicalism faded in the wake of high crop prices. "It is quite evident," *The Nation* could confidently assert in 1884, "that the silver craze which raged with such violence in the West and South a few years ago has died out." [6]

Budding socialist and anarchist organizations were also checked by the economic upsurge. By 1883, the Socialist Labor Party, which had established a promising beachhead of 12,000 votes in the Chicago elections of 1877, could muster only 1500 in that city. [7]

Industrial progress in this period—which was relatively free of unemployment, falling prices, and financial panics—dazzled contemporary observers. From 1880 to 1882, the labor force increased by 10 per cent, and throughout this decade capital investment in basic industries like steel more than doubled the previous ten-year

total. A writer in *The Atlantic Monthly,* observing this unprecedented activity, predicted that "the process of development seems
likely to continue with a geometrical ratio of increase." [8]

Prosperity rekindled self-confidence, but the fears of the Seventies lay dormant, ready to reawaken if conditions stirred them.
These conditions appeared in the middle Eighties and deflated the
short-lived optimism of the previous few years. Fears of danger,
doom, and disaster were awakened, and in some minds they coalesced into an image of catastrophe.

THE STORM: 1885-1897

LABOR AND THE LEFT

The years between the strikes of 1885 and the Spanish-American
War were filled with confusion, fear, and—for some—despair.
Labor's militant growth, a vast increase and shift in immigration,
the drift to the cities, an agricultural crisis, and the growing influence of revolutionaries in the Socialist Party tormented the nation
until the end of the nineteenth century. This era was ushered in by
two events occurring within nine months of each other, the Railroad Strike of 1885 and the Haymarket Affair.

In August, 1885, the Knights of Labor successfully struck
against the Wabash Railroad. Jay Gould, owner of the line, was
forced to reinstate union leaders, halt favoritism in promotions, and
agree to arbitrate future grievances. Labor's victory shocked the
substantial elements of the community. One of industry's great
titans had been brought to heel and forced to recognize an organization without respectability in polite circles. This triumph spurred
the growth of the Knights and other unions. People suddenly
became aware of the labor movement and clamored for news of its
organizations. The Knights received special attention, and exaggerated accounts of its power and numbers appeared in alarmed
newspapers. It was even claimed that the "men [who] compose
the executive board . . . of the Knights of Labor could array labor
against capital, putting labor on the offensive or the defensive, for
quiet and stubborn self-protection, or for angry, organized assault
as they will." [9]

Interest was turned to indignation by the Haymarket Affair and
the Eight Hour movement. Labor's struggles were now viewed
as harbingers of anarchy. Some observers claimed that the "strikers

have led up to the point where the anarchist begins his saturnalia of ruin." [10] The first links in the chain of cataclysmism were being forged.

Similar fears echoed from the pulpit. Socially conscious ministers like Washington Gladden and Lyman Abbott interpreted these conflicts as signs of social upheaval. Gladden envisioned "the chasm that separates the employer from the employed" getting "a great deal deeper and wider than it now is" and bearing "awful harvest through many generations." In "Is It Peace Or War," written right after the harrowing events of 1886, he warned that there were "ominous signs" that working men were disposed to employ their power "passionately and vindictively." [11]

Abbott was even more worried. He feared that "warlike" unions were "deepening the chasm and intensifying the hostility between the laboring class and the capitalist." In his anxiety, he even imagined dictatorial union coteries hatching their dangerous "designs . . . in secret conferences." [12] Fear of conspiracy, an unmistakable symptom of the cataclysmic mind, was already appearing in the respectable middle class.

The Haymarket Affair intensified concern over labor problems. On May 5, 1886, a bomb was thrown into the ranks of police officers attempting to break up a peaceful anarchist meeting in Chicago. Although only slight damage was done, the public mind, already agitated by labor struggles, magnified the incident out of all proportion.

As the center of socialism and the Eight Hour Movement, Chicago was a particularly sensitive spot. The city had once been the most formidable outpost of the Socialist Labor Party. The S.L.P., however, had been soundly beaten in the elections of the early Eighties, and its left wing, discouraged by the results of political action, seceded to form the Revolutionary Socialist Party—an organization based on the "propaganda of the deed." Unlike labor unions, which were usually driven to violence in defensive strikes during depressions, the socialists became revolutionaries because prosperity blocked any promise of success through politics.

An attempt to unite scattered socialist revolutionary groups got underway at Pittsburgh in November, 1883. The Pittsburgh Manifesto, a declaration of the new organization's aims, indicated the tone of the meeting. It called for an end to futile political action against the entrenched propertied class. There remained "but one recourse—FORCE!" The Anarchists aimed at "destruction of the existing class rule, by all means, i.e., by energetic relentless, revolutionary and international action." [13]

The convention was a success. A national organization, the International Working People's Association or, as it was more frequently called, the Black International, was formed. The Chicago contingent, led by Albert Parsons and George Spies, was the largest cell. By 1885 the Chicagoans had converted a large number of German laborers and made substantial gains among English-speaking workers.

The Party unabashedly proclaimed its terroristic policy. Official organs repeatedly declared that "simply by making ourselves masters of the use of dynamite . . . this method, and this alone, can relieve the world of this infernal monster called the 'right of property.' " [14] I.W.P.A. publications optimistically predicted an "already approaching revolution [which] promises to be much grander than that at the close of the last century." [15]

Chicago, however, secure in its prosperity and peace, was unimpressed by the sanguinary statements of these would-be revolutionaries. Mayor Carter Harrison feared no "organized resistance to authority" because "any considerable body of men mad enough to attempt any folly . . . would be as chaff, compared to the solid masses who love our institutions and are determined that law and order shall reign." [16] Outside observers, although less influenced by civic patriotism, also shared these sentiments. "The alleged Socialist conspiracy which has its headquarters in Chicago is probably very much magnified," reported the New York *Times*. "They excite no sympathy among the great body of people," it reasoned, because workers "had a stake in society equal to that of the capitalist." Indeed, the editorial glowingly concluded, "There is nothing to prevent them from becoming capitalists." [17]

Most Americans had enough faith in the traditions of free enterprise and equal opportunity not to become alarmed at what seemed to be an isolated foreign phenomenon. But faith in Algerism was wearing thin—to many who had suffered through the troubles of the 1870's and were in the midst of another conflict less than ten years later, it smacked of slogan rather than substance.

The bomb thrown into those blue ranks advancing to disperse the Haymarket meeting blasted the calm optimism of many Americans. Chicago newspapers were shocked by the incident. The Chicago *Inter Ocean* feared that the "anarchists" had "inaugurated in earnest . . . the reign of lawlessness which they have threatened and endeavored to incite for years." [18] Its sister journal, the Chicago *Tribune*, called on citizens "to meet it [the anarchist threat] with all the power of the law and put it down, or they must expect an era of anarchy and the loss of their property, if not their lives." [19]

The press spread the alarm throughout the country. New York papers, which had laughed at the anarchists, now declared them to be a serious threat to public welfare. The Cleveland *Plain Dealer,* greatly impressed with the anarchist danger, warned that "if civilization is not to be plunged into chaos, the supremacy of law must be vindicated and maintained at whatever cost." [20] In an editorial in March, 1887, the *Chautauquan* somberly summed up the events of the previous year. It declared that "American institutions have been tried and strained in an unaccustomed way." There had been an unprecedented development of mobs who gathered and raged "at so many points that there is some ground for apprehension and for systematic organization in defense of law and order." "If the people fail in self-government," concluded the magazine, "they will get at length a master to make them behave themselves." [21]

Many people panicked over the Haymarket riot. The anarchists, anticapitalist revolutionaries, were a threat to the political and economic beliefs of the nation. Predominantly urbanites and foreigners, they embodied all the forces that Americans had come to fear. The Haymarket Affair thus served to crystallize these anxieties into a catastrophic outlook.

After 1886, rumblings from the left subsided. The Chicago debacle destroyed the Black International, and the Revolutionary Socialists gave way to the milder political activism of the S.L.P. Labor was also more quiescent. The belligerent Knights of Labor lost much of their membership and were consistently defeated in strikes. Practical, conservative, wage-oriented trade unionism triumphed—not for many years would there again be a large-scale attempt to organize the unskilled or to whip workers into an insurgent frenzy. Relative calm, however, and the prosperity and industrial progress of the next five years did not reawaken the old optimism. The buoyancy of 1866 and 1878 did not reappear in 1887. The militant unionism and revolutionary socialism that had caused the alarm were quiet, but the cataclysmic mood did not vanish.

Events in the middle Eighties struck the first flicker of catastrophic thought, and events of the 1890's fanned this flame to a conflagration. All the forces contributing to the pessimism of the Eighties increased in magnitude in the next decade. Strikes were bigger, more frequent, and more violent; the Panic of 1893 was more ruinous; cities grew bigger, as the "wrong" kind of immigrants poured in; finally, there was turmoil in the West, which to some portended an agrarian revolution.

The Homestead Strike, a bloody conflict between The Amalgamated Association of Iron and Steel Workers and the Carnegie Corporation, ended five years of industrial peace. Labor's strongest union pitted itself against the mightiest corporation in the opening engagement of the great labor wars of the Nineties. After a pitched battle between Pinkerton men and strikers, the Association lost the strike and was driven from the mills. The Homestead strike taught labor and management two lessons: Even the most powerful unions could not cope with industrial giants; even the most conservative worker organizations could not avoid bloodshed in labor disputes.[22]

Public opinion was outraged and frightened by the conflict in Pennsylvania. Even sympathetic observers feared the Homestead spirit. "But what Homestead now is," said *The Standard,* a single-tax paper, "the whole country will be, unless this era of legislative privileges is brought to a speedy close. We cannot long go on surrounding millionaires with serfs." [23] A writer in *Cosmopolitan* drew a parallel with class conflict in Rome and advised management "to concede something in the way of law, lest it should be regulated through bloodshed or what is more horrible still, should throw into power, through sheer brute force, elements which will bring our Republic into anarchy." [24]

Antilabor critics were equally apprehensive, but they saw the danger in anarchy and lawlessness rather than in maldistribution of wealth. Chiefly they feared a "volcanic spirit of defiance of government" and warned that "contempt for all law must be met by a force superior to its own or the end is chaos." [25]

A few days after Homestead, the miners of Coeur D'Alene, Idaho, opened a new front in the industrial war. In August, there were labor disturbances in the Buffalo transit system and the iron and coal mines of Tennessee. Troops were called out in all three strikes, thus convincing the workers that business interests definitely controlled government. With the state apparently irrevocably ranged on the side of management, labor became more radical. The Western Federation of Miners and the American Railway Union, initiators of the most violent strikes for the next few years and instrumental in forming the International Workers of the World, were formed from defeated strikers in Idaho and Buffalo.

These struggles destroyed the uneasy truce of the previous five years and gave rise to expectations of great national peril. "We have arrived at a critical period of our history, where we must meet the demands of social progress, or our civilization will perish," predicted a commentator in the *Arena.* He was sure that he had his ear to the ground and could "already [hear] the mutterings of revolution." [26]

Hard on the heels of these labor troubles came the worst depression in twenty years. America floundered through four years of economic tribulation, in which one-quarter of all railroad capitalization went into receivership and consumption dropped to twenty-five per cent below what production capacity could support. The nadir of the depression, 1894, with more than one million men unemployed in 394 strikes, has justly been called the *année terrible* of American history.[27] Economic privation—highlighted by Coxey's Army, Populist agitation, and the Pullman Strike—served to make it a year of despair.

Depression disturbances were caused by psychological reactions as well as economic factors. Financial reverses were especially unsettling for a country that prided itself on growth and stressed status-mobility and success. Thwarted ambition generated much guilt and anxiety, and failure was not easily borne in a society that emphasized individual responsibility for achievement. The hostility resulting from these circumstances was directed at groups that could be classified as un-American. Blaming socialists, unions, and immigrants for adverse conditions absolved America and freed individuals from the burden of failure. Guilt was assuaged by the conviction that alien groups were blighting the nation's future and swindling the native-born of their just rewards.

During the panic of 1893, roving bands of unemployed men tramped the countryside, and bums became a menace to public safety. Under the leadership of Jacob Coxey and other reformers, these ragged regiments made their way to Washington to ask for relief. Only a small number actually reached the capital, and no violence was committed, but depression-agitated Americans viewed the movement with great alarm. Thomas Byrnes, the famous New York Police Superintendent, thought "this movement . . . the most dangerous this country had seen since the Civil War." To him it was "rebellion pure and simple and should be stamped out just as the great Rebellion was in 1861." For if it were to be "successfully carried out, then the United States will fall into a chaos in which mobs will be fighting everywhere." [28] Influential magazines shared his anxiety. According to *The Nation,* the tattered troops had brought us "dangerously near the conditions of things at the time of the French Revolution." [29]

Those with more compassion for poverty, looked on the march as an act of desperation, more as a "crusade of the unemployed" than "defiant lawlessness." But they also regarded the demonstration as a portent of revolution and sought to uproot the causes of a potential uprising rather than to eliminate only its menacing symptoms. "Multitudes of hungry men seemed the surest possible forerunner of the long prophesied revolution" and these critics saw the alternatives as alleviating reform or armed revolt.[30]

Another emergency that raised the specter of social upheaval was the Pullman Strike. The strike was marked by the precipitate use of Federal troops, which led to rioting, property destruction, and a long casualty list. Sweeping injunctions to prevent the union from boycotting Pullman cars or attempting to persuade other men to stop working—and the eagerness with which federal troops were dispatched—revealed once again the collusion between government and big business. By the end of July, the American Railway Union had disintegrated, admitting its defeat, and its members were blackballed by the railroads. But from the shattered remnants of the union, Eugene V. Debs was to build the Socialist Party. Once again, defeat by the alliance of the state and vested interests drove labor to the left.

This strike, coming after Coxey's march and climaxing two years of labor strife and depression, aroused more alarm than had the one in Homestead. General Nelson A. Miles, commander of the soldiers in Chicago, thought the country was in such danger that it had been saved "from a serious rebellion" only by the intervention of his army.[31] The strike was reported by conservative journals as an anarchist plot designed to destroy the nation. By "suppressing such a black-mailing conspiracy as the boycott of the Pullman cars by the American Railway Union," asserted the New York *Herald,* "the nation is fighting for its own existence just as truly as in suppressing the great rebellion." [32]

Typical of the Pullman Strike, as of other struggles, was the liberal-conservative split. William H. Garwardine, a pastor who had ministered to the strikers, warned that "we as a nation are dividing ourselves, like ancient Rome into two classes, the rich and the poor, the oppressor and the oppressed." Unless the government enforced justice he predicted, the nation would not "prosper . . . [nor] long perpetuate itself and its institutions." [33] Those who supported, as well as those who despised, labor thought the events of the Nineties were pushing the republic to the brink of chaos, but reformers blamed class oppression rather than radicalism and proposed to do away with poverty rather than to discipline it.

Despite all these forebodings, the dismal future never dawned. The workers and farmers did not rise, and the lives and property of the middle class were never touched. If Americans had not been misled by their own fears, they would perhaps have realized that these conflicts, though violent, would never be revolutionary. The industrial armies, the workers, and the Populists did not want to destroy the system; they simply wanted to secure a place within it or at least to change it back to what it had been in 1860. The strikes were defensive, aimed at very practical ends like preventing wage cuts. They were not the class-conscious assaults imagined by the left and feared by the *bourgeoisie*. Populism took its menacing tone, not from radical aims like nationalizing wealth, but from outraged conservatism. A stubborn clinging to the past, an attempt to regain lost virtues—these forces lay behind the agrarian crusades' embittered idealism. Too often, in their fear, people accepted the slogans of socialists, unions, and Populists as accurate descriptions of reality. They mistook programs for philosophies, and what they saw as the death throes of our civilization were really its growth pangs.

THE CITY

Teeming tenements; the babel of foreign tongues; foul smells rising from dirty streets; explosions of violence; criminals called Rothstein, Galantino, or O'Rourke; corrupt government run by immigrant bosses; secret socialist meetings conducted in German; rumors of anarchist plots—that is how the city seemed to the timorous and the disgusted, to all who had come to hate and fear the immigrant, the worker, and the leftist. The city, eternal force for change, became the locus of traditional America's enemies, the apparent source of sedition, socialism, and subversion. It was a danger to both the East and the West. Easterners hated it because it spawned corruption and revolution; Westerners because it was the home of the "money power" that conspired to bind them in chains of gold. Farmers, professionals, and businessmen united in condemning the city, for it housed the two groups that they felt threatened them most—the very rich and the very poor.

Until the Haymarket Affair, the metropolis had been tolerated as a commercial necessity, but that disaster helped to focus cataclysmic thoughts on the city. Even urban newspapers were quick to associate anarchy with an urban environment. "Masses of ignorant foreigners congregated in many cities," asserted the New York *Tribune,* "are the magazine of explosives to which these fiends continually try to apply the match." [34]

The city's sinister image was formed in the years of controversy following 1886, when it began to seem not only a place containing perilous forces but in itself an agent of disaster. There were three stages in this transition. The first came after the Haymarket riot when the city was criticized for housing revolutionaries. By 1893, *The Nation* had advanced to the point where it charged that the city not only sheltered corruption but had been itself corrupted. The magazine saw "the degradation of our city government" in the triumph of immigrant-supported political bosses.[35] Other critics went even further, branding the city as the corrupter. Subscribers to *Century Magazine* discovered that the city was a school of intrigue and corruption, and those who read the *Atlantic,* that the city was America's "deadliest menace." [36]

Hatred for the city was one of the few points of view commonly held in the East and West. Propertied easterners, even those who had moved to the city, feared the metropolis because they associated it with violence bred in poverty. Farmers hated it for opposite reasons: To them the city was the home of rich bankers who were living off the yeomen by taking land through mortgage foreclosures, genteely robbing them with high interest rates, and bankrupting them with the gold standard. As the farmer clung more desperately to his Jacksonian image in these years of his waning economic plenty and political prestige, he came to hate the city more bitterly—and he expressed his hatred through agrarian organizations and leaders.The Arkansas Wheel, a branch of the Southern Alliance, prohibited the formation of Wheels "within the limits of incorporated towns," and James B. Weaver warned that "the trend is toward the city, where the needy congregate and where crime becomes organized and where the Republic is stabbed." [37] The city was the great enemy—it was foreign and distant, it opposed small property from above and below, and it was crowded with pale, smooth-handed conspirators.

As outraged opinion against immigration, labor, and socialism was more an index into the mind of the objectors than a valid analysis of society, so too was the cry against the metropolis. Urban critics seized upon the pretext rather than the causes of municipal evils and were more interested in preaching against city vices than studying city problems. All the characteristics of the city confirmed their haunting fear of having been cut off from antebellum ties and imprisoned in the great impersonal metropolis. Anarchists condemned conventional forms of social organization, and immigrants came from a totally incomprehensible world. Increased mobility and life's quicker pace weakened tradition and snapped old ties, and the presence of foreign enclaves disturbed those who had grown up in homogeneous antebellum America. Massive buildings fast turning a sooty gray looked down impassively upon thousands of harried and hurrying people. Modern technology and business practices had destroyed the intimate contact between customer and producer. Human relationships were reckoned in terms of cost and governed by mania for profit.

Despite its role in social change, the city actually epitomized some of America's fundamental values. Men on the make, socially mobile and ready to seize opportunities, came to the metropolis. Farmers, foreigners, and the *nouveaux riches* moved to the city in order to realize the American dream of getting ahead. Many urban critics had themselves sought similar fulfillment through urban life, yet they ignored its role in reinforcing social mobility. Their refusal to see the city in this light indicated their doubts about the ideal of success. With the eclipse of their own groups, upward mobility ceased to seem a national virtue to them. Even where the specific belief in opportunity remained, the old faith had been compromised. By coming to the city these critics demonstrated their disbelief in a homogeneous, rural society that could also be mobile. Antebellum identity and virtue could be preserved in the country, but fame and fortune had to be courted in the city.

Those who attacked the city rarely articulated their own discontent, but it shaped their whole analyses. They erroneously attributed their negative views to factors like moral decay or foreign influx in the metropolis. Josiah Strong, however, was one critic who probed more deeply. Although Strong shared many of the contemporary notions about the city, he also touched on the real reason why his class was so alienated from it. "Where men are most crowded together they are farthest apart," he wrote. "In the towns men know each other and know what is expected of them," but in the city, not having the "bonds of race, land and religion," they are lonely individuals.[38] Rootlessness was the price demanded for success. Ambition sacrificed permanence for mobility. Even so, however, urbanization had its compensations. The city was checkered with disparate cultural groups that provided an intimacy and variety in resistance to the encroachment of mass society. But Strong's observations, limited by his own estrangement, could not penetrate urban pluralism. He sounded the same refrain that echoed through criticisms of the worker, the newcomer, and the left—a refrain that to some had already become a dirge.

IMMIGRATION

It was bewildering to see a peaceful and prosperous nation, apparently well on the way to solving the problems of industrialization, suddenly torn by conflict. Americans wondered what had diverted their course after 1885. It appeared to them that the explanation lay in the increase and shift in immigration, urban growth, and the rise of labor conflict and radicalism. When these elements were analyzed, the immigrant was usually isolated as the key factor. Critics reasoned that America had had labor violence, cities, and even radical movements before and had been able to handle them, but never before had there been immigration on such a scale. From 1880 to 1890, two and one-half million more human beings disembarked than in the previous decade. Moreover, a large percentage came from eastern and southern Europe. The new arrivals, especially those from east of the Elbe and south of the Alps, remained in the cities, contributing greatly to the urbanization of America. The foreign-dominated leftist centers in New York and Chicago seemed to provide the explanation for the confusing events of 1885-1886. Immigration was the source of the trouble. Accusing foreigners had the advantage of enabling Americans to shift the blame for the occurrences of these years. American institutions had failed, not because they were faulty, but because an alien element had undermined them. The typical citizen was a farmer, a God-fearing Protestant who spoke English without an accent, believed firmly in free enterprise, and descended from an impeccable set of Anglo-Saxon (or at least German) forebears. These people had achieved greatness for the nation. Now they were threatened by a new group who were urban-dwellers, spoke strange tongues, worshipped in despised faiths, and frequently questioned the truths of capitalism. Obviously, since they were the newcomers, they must be responsible for recent disasters. The beauty of this solution was that it explained not only what was occurring at the time but whatever might happen in the future. As the years went by and the United States continued to be torn by internal dissension, this formula was almost automatically applied. The characteristics of the immigrants were confused with the causes of conflict, and scapegoatism was often substituted for reform.

Xenophobia, however, clashed with the country's most revered traditions. Even before it became a nation, America was supposed to be a refuge for the oppressed—but that was the faith of a more confident era, an era in which American institutions were considered impregnable against any onslaught and her bounty infinite. It was a faith based on the vigor of youth, the security of inexperience, and the promise of the future. Out of the Eighties, however, emerged an older, if not a wiser, America. The sense of being a nation apart, an example to the world that the purity of democracy could remain uncontaminated by internal conflict, had been shaken.

Finally, disappointed expectations blighted the hopes of youth. The American no longer looked upon the foreigner as an example of the almost divine power of the New World to rescue the misfits of the Old. He now saw the immigrant as a potential assassin and social revolutionary, a competitor for jobs in the East and land in the West, and a general threat to established institutions and prosperity. A "safety-first" attitude came to replace the old feeling of proud and generous acceptance.

Anti-immigration feeling not only violated America's basic beliefs—it was directed against the very group that demonstrated these ideals. Foreigners were considered un-American even though they were living proof that the nation was still an open society. Ironically, xenophobia arose in a mobile society because newcomers became competitors in the struggle for success. Rejection of new arrivals was also a rejection of nonconformity as well as of equality of opportunity. The United States had always been characterized by self-contained communities that had prevented the spread of uniformity. Immigrants set up similar enclaves, thus helping to maintain the rich pluralism of American life. When older groups felt threatened, however, they foresook tolerance for compulsion. By barring the entry of new groups, they hoped to maintain their position even if it meant exchanging variety for a restricted homogeneity.

After the upheaval of the mid-Eighties, xenophobia spread from fringe groups to respectable elements in the community. Industrial and commercial organizations and business publications ceased to welcome foreigners. The National Board of Trade, for example, reversed its position of the Seventies and came out against "the scourings of foreign disease, pauperism and crime." [39]

When business began to turn against immigration, the Republican Party made gestures toward restriction. In addition to fearing radical threats, the Party was worried about the growing political power of the Democrats, who had been effective missionaries among the strangers. In the 1880's, New York and Boston elected their first Irish mayors—the Republicans were losing the cities to the Democrats and their immigrant allies. To counter this threat, G.O.P. conventions in Pennsylvania, Ohio, and California demanded restrictions on immigration, and Justin Morrill introduced a bill for this purpose in Congress.

The conservative press followed its economic and political mentors. A New York *Times* editorial entitled "Restricting Immigration," which appeared a few days after the Haymarket incident typified the new attitude. The *Times* argued that admitting "anything human or half human . . . has already degraded our citizenship especially in the large cities, and it is vitally necessary that we make an immediate and sharp change in our policy." Underlying the paper's disenchantment with unregulated immigration was a denial of old beliefs. "The theory that this Republic was founded chiefly to be a refuge for the oppressed of every nation works up beautifully in Fourth of July orations," but "its practical applications" were limited. Placed in the category of "foolish delusions" were notions "that the mere process of naturalization would transform the worst that Europe could send us into material fit for our electorate . . . that our undoubtedly glorious institutions would take care of themselves and that our country was big enough for everybody." [40]

New England Brahmins, still faithful to the transcendental tolerance of their fathers, had yet to mobilize their full opposition through the Immigration Restriction League, but events of the Eighties germinated this attitude. One scion of an old family, Francis Amasa Walker, had already swung over, and by the end of the next decade many of his class would follow.

The advent of nativist organizations accompanied the opinion shift among respected elements of the community. Here also the Haymarket Affair played a crucial role. Peter D. Wigginton, a railroad attorney in California, founded the American Party three weeks after the Chicago disaster; the Junior Order of United American Mechanics quadrupled its membership from 1885 to 1889; and 1887 was the most successful year for The Patriotic Order of the Sons of America. Two other extremist groups were founded at that time, the American League and the American Protective Association, which was destined to become the most prominent of these organizations. Although founded chiefly to fight Catholicism, these groups had plenty of hatred left over for immigrants. They agitated for "the exclusion of the restless revolutionary horde of foreigners . . . now seeking our shore from every part of the world," who had come "to terrorize the community and to exalt the red flag of the commune above the Stars and Stripes." [41]

Despite the subsidence of unrest after 1886, the melting-pot ideal continued to stir controversy. An article in *Century Magazine* expressed the now widespread animosity in the same cataclysmic tones used by alarmists who wrote about labor, socialism, and the cities. To continue to celebrate America "as the asylum of the poor and oppressed," the author declared, was "a logic that hurries into thoughtless enthusiasm . . . over the vast resources and glorious privileges of this country." This kind of "cap-in-air" patriotism "has given place in thoughtful minds to solicitude before the startling fact of immigration and the transformation of social and political life which threatens to follow." [42]

It was not easy for many citizens to accept nativism, however, and rationalizations had to be found to make it palatable for those who were uncomfortable about forsaking old ideals. The major excuse was that the old belief was valid for a time when the immigrants appreciated the American way of life, but now the nation would have to close its doors because recent arrivals were impervious to its ideals. This argument soothed American pride and justified a retreat from basic principles. On the one hand, such reasoning asserted that new immigrant types, not the abandonment of old ideals, forced the adoption of restriction; on the other hand, it denied that sheltering the oppressed had ever been a basic tenet of the national creed. Rather, it claimed that the United States was giving up the role of protector in order to preserve that creed. *The Nation* summed up the matter in an editorial declaring that "the growth of a new and distinct sort of immigration" was disturbing the existing order. "These facts," the editors warned, "are too patent to be missed and too significant to be disregarded." [43]

The minority who hung back from complete disavowal of former faith tried to justify their views by claiming that America's mission was not that of a refuge but of a showcase for liberty. "What is the function of this nation as related to other nations," they asked? "Chiefly that it shall offer to them the spectacle and example of a pure nation . . . an achievement of mercy and humanity far beyond any spasmodic and sentimental embrace of suffering humanity; it says to the nations, 'Go, and do thou likewise.' " [44]

The prevalent attitude, however, was unequivocal denial of the nation's responsibility to the world's oppressed. Even attempts to modify this rejection were more a sign of surrender than of continuing support for old ideals. For to people frightened by the conflicts of these years, the immigrant became the scapegoat for every grievance. Political corruption could be traced "to a desire to 'capture the foreign vote.' " Like "a white ant" the "hastily made and ignorant foreign voter may . . . be found eating away the political structure." [45] Labor conflict was "wholly due to this foreign element, which not only leads and comprises the mob, but so widens the range of the price of labor that the American laborer cannot endure the competition." [46] Vice and crime were strictly foreign products disseminated "through the land" by corrupt "invaders." [47] Degenerate actions were the result of decadent blood.

Inferior race "drags down the stronger," and American "stock" was in danger of "physical degeneration" through cross breeding.[48] The "persistent clannish spirit" frequently found among foreigners disturbed national unity.[49] Feared above all other immigrant evils was the threat of social revolution. "Anarchists, ultra-socialists, and dynamiters" had "found here . . . a safe place in which to preach their doctrines of hate, revenge, murder and plunder." With "such success" had the revolutionaries "carried on their proselytizing schemes . . . that for a time they seemed to threaten the very foundations of social order." [50]

The immigrants, indicted for every imagined conspiracy against public welfare, were regarded as agents of doom carrying destruction to their new land. A chorus of Cassandras rose to bewail the prospects of a foreign dominated America. An *Arena* article concluded with the warning that "no human institutions can endure indefinitely the strain which our present policy if persisted in, will inevitably put upon our social and political life." [51] A writer in the *Forum* feared that "a turbulent foreign proletariat . . . clamoring for panem et circenses, as in the days of ancient Rome, [was] threatening the existence of the republic." [52] *The Chautauquan* sounded the alarm throughout the countryside with an article predicting that America would be "another Europe" if the immigrants continued to disembark.[53]

Despite growing opposition, ships laden with immigrants continued to dock at New York and Boston. Millions of newcomers walked down the gangplanks into a land that was coming to abhor them. The negative attitude toward immigration that had emerged a decade earlier became prevalent in the Nineties. After 1893, most respectable groups, if not society as a whole, frowned on immigration. Domestic strife exacerbated middle-class fears about bomb-throwing immigrants. Public school battles and political defeats caused many to fear that arrivals would swell the ranks of spoilsmen and Catholics and assure their control over urban education and government. Even science contributed to the growing antipathy, as ingenious experts forecasted race suicide if the canons of evolution continued to be violated by inferior "hordes" diluting native stock.

By the mid-Nineties, the business community was committed to restriction. Commercial groups from New York, Boston, Chicago, Seattle, and St. Louis advocated literacy tests and consular inspection of immigrants.

Labor also rejected the immigrant. Since the early Eighties, unions had looked with increasing disfavor on job competition from new arrivals who worked for lower wages, broke strikes, and were difficult to organize. In 1892, the Knights proposed that foreigners without means for a year's support be excluded, and five years later the American Federation of Labor endorsed the literacy test.

New England bluebloods, the sons and grandsons of veterans of two wars for liberty, and the self-styled keepers of the American conscience, surrendered to the new prejudice. The vision of Boston in the hands of the Irish and of Massachusetts public schools becoming papist hatcheries made them adopt crabbed convictions of racism and restriction. Henry Cabot Lodge and Francis Amasa Walker led the way. In 1881, Lodge had welcomed the immigrants who were "in ever-increasing numbers, the best elements, both mentally and physically, of the laboring population of Europe." [54] Twelve years later, however, "the best elements" had become an "excessive . . . deteriorating . . . large body of very undesirable immigration, which in any event ought to be shut out, because it tends to lower the quality of our citizenship." [55] Walker had been converted earlier. In the Seventies, he too approved of the newcomers and felt there was "room and work enough for all." [56] But by the end of that decade, he predicted that alienation rather than assimilation would result from immigration. Walker's repudiation of his earlier position was a summary of the grievances against foreigners. He based his enmity upon exhaustion of free public lands, falling agricultural prices, labor problems, and the character of the newcomers—"beaten men from the beaten races, representing the worst failures in the struggle for existence." [57]

Other aristocrats, especially from the younger generation, followed Lodge and Walker. Prominent and aging bluebloods lent their names to the Immigration Restriction League, but its three founders had been graduated from Harvard in 1889. The League, founded in 1893, became a center for genteel, intellectual agitators who eschewed the noisy racism of the American Protective Association. Many members of the I.R.L. were both reformers and restrictionists, demonstrating the close connection between anti-immigration thought and sensitivity to social evils. During the dark days of the Nineties, even reformers had given up on the foreigners, arguing that the first step in solving the country's problems was to stop compounding them by allowing undesirable immigration.

Accusations against the immigrants proliferated in these dismal years. One phase of anti-immigrant thought received special emphasis, and it reflected the intensified bitterness toward recent arrivals. Critics made an unfavorable "contrast between this and earlier immigration." They found, "these hordes of an inferior type, least capable of understanding our institutions, or . . . responding to the opportunities and privileges of a free government." [58] Racism was the ultimate step in alienation from the old creed of tolerance. Heretofore the foreigner had been condemned chiefly because he would not assimilate, but now the racists charged that he could not assimilate.

Although ethnic exclusion had been part of the arsenal of anti-immigrant arguments for a decade, racial pleas came to prominence in the Nineties. Their advent was due to a variety of factors. Western Europeans were more akin to Americans, and in that decade, the balance of immigration finally shifted to an influx from eastern and southern Europe. When American citizens travelled or went to school abroad, they gravitated toward England, France, and Germany. Natives of these countries had filled the boats in the period when immigrants were warmly greeted and Americans were glad to share with them the credit for building the nation. Despite these considerations, however, the movement for restriction was based on something deeper and more significant than changes in nationality. Since new immigration coincided with social upheaval, it was natural for Americans to associate social troubles with the recent arrivals. When the comfortable conditions of peace and prosperity disappeared, old principles also vanished. Americans, losing faith in themselves, lost faith in their capacity to convert others—and even in their ability to maintain their creed against alien beliefs. Ethnic exclusion was the logical result of this attitude. America was no longer the easy going, self-confident nation that turned frustrated, angry, and oppressed foreigners into satisfied and independent citizens. She now feared the embrace of strangers as a clutch of death. "The question today," said Walker in *The Atlantic,* "is . . . of protecting the American rate of wages, the American standard of living, and the quality of American citizenship from degradation through the tumultuous access of vast throngs of ignorant and brutalized peasantry from the countries of eastern and southern Europe."

Social Darwinism made racism respectable. Science was replacing religion as the arbiter of man's values, and popularizations of evolution were the great scientific truths of the day. Yoking this theory to racism gave credence to ethnic arguments. The concept of a competitive struggle for survival fitted in very well with the strains America was undergoing. Pessimism generated by conflict made Americans fear defeat in this struggle. Unless the Anglo-Saxon could be preserved from the onslaughts of alien strains, America would be lost. Leaders of exclusion groups eagerly seized upon this new weapon. Intellectual giants of the anti-immigration campaign like Walker, Lodge, Nathaniel S. Shaler, and Edward Albion Ross rallied support with racist arguments. Typical of their outlook was the essay by Walker in which he asserted that the immigrants came from species already defeated in the struggle for existence. They could never adapt to American ways because "they have none of the ideas and aptitude which belong to those who are descended from the tribes that met under the oak trees of old Germany to make laws and choose chieftains."

In addition to providing a rationale for internal cataclysmism, racism forged a link between ideas of domestic conflict and expectations of an externally-caused catastrophe. In both cases, the Anglo-Saxons were a beleaguered people fighting desperately to preserve America, democracy, and civilization. And in both instances, racism was a useful reaction to a confusing, anxiety-ridden situation because it furnished an outlet for fear and frustration.

The furor over immigration caused the restrictionists of those years to echo earlier prophecies of doom. Walker anxiously questioned whether we have "the right to expose the republic to any increase of the danger from this source which now so manifestly threatens our peace and safety?" [59] Other critics came to similar ominous conclusions. They claimed that the immigrants menaced our liberties, "endanger[ed] our institutions," were "instrument[s] of degrading tyranny," and encouraged "despotic forms of administration." [60] Again and again, the immigrant threat was publicized, until it became an obsessive fear.

THE POPULIST UPRISING

Easterners who had looked to the frontier and the farmer for reassurance were shocked by the agrarian uprising. Even the native-born westerner, long-time symbol of republican virtue, now disturbed their peace of mind. It had been a long time, however, since agricultural realities had corresponded with the ideal of the substantial yeoman. With each passing year, farm conditions worsened. Crop prices fell, credit tightened, and the land bubble burst. Moreover, economic deprivation was made more painful by political and social frustration. Financial ruin was scarcely mitigated for the farmer when his sons deserted the soil for the city and there was no pleasure in exchanging the folk image of "noble yeoman" for that of backward "rube." Nor were memories of old times, when every significant group courted him, made sweeter for the farmer by the bitter experience of having the major parties ignore his demands and seduce his representatives.

He suffered social estrangement similar to that of the old eastern middle class, and he asked the same questions: Why did such things come to pass? How could they be fought? What were the chances of victory? One attempted resolution of the farmer's problems was through political protest. Initially, agrarian organizations were social clubs; later they became pressure groups; and finally in the crescendo of farm protest in the 1890's, they fused into one independent political party. Farmers did not turn radical overnight; they were driven to political action by the callous attitude of the major parties.

The conservative middle class was frightened, not only by the presence of a radical political force but also by the cataclysmic pronouncements of Populist leaders. Mary Lease and Ignatius Donnelly wrote books on this theme, and James B. Weaver and Tom Watson frequently predicted catastrophe. "We are nearing a serious crisis," warned Weaver in 1892. "If the present strained relations between wealth owners and wealth producers continue much longer they will ripen into frightful disaster." [61] Tom Watson reiterated Weaver's urgent cry. Referring to the agricultural plight, he wondered how human nature could "stand it" and asserted that "the sword of Damocles never hung by a slenderer thread than does the false system of today . . . revolution is as inevitable as the laws of the universe." [62]

At first the farmers' ferment was treated casually and, in some conservative quarters, even hopefully. H. R. Chamberlain, in *The Chautauquan,* looked forward to a "three cornered political battle." He was sure that "the struggle threatens no serious danger to our institutions or to our national welfare. It should be welcomed and fought out with good American common sense." [63]

Those who sympathized with the farmer felt that the nation had treated a noble group shabbily. They shared the yeoman's view that a group that embodied the nobility of American life was dying out. "It is plainly the duty of our government," such men reasoned, "to preserve the constantly-diminishing class once known and honored as country gentlemen." Farmers had been "the fathers of the Republic, and for a long time . . . our pure nobility." If these "country gentlemen" were displaced by "absentee landlords," they would become "an ignorant rural peasantry" and endanger our existence as a free nation.[64]

Compassion was grounded in strength. Even that bastion of eastern respectability, *The Nation,* perceived no danger in agrarianism in 1891. Confident of fundamental social harmony, the magazine predicted "the complete collapse of the Farmer's Alliance movement." [65]

Many, however, saw danger in the agricultural agitation. To them, it was a manifestation of the disappearance of the frontier. Free and open land to the West had been a symbol of America's promise. It had been one source of her expansive self-confidence, because it had provided a margin for experiment and was thought to be a safety valve for discontent. On the frontier, democracy had been revivified, the immigrant Americanized, and economic and social pressures relieved—so went the traditional argument. But now this residue of security was gone, and pressure was building up in the constricted West. Propounded by Frederick Jackson Turner and others, the theory of the disappearing frontier quickly became popular.

The widespread belief about the vanishing frontier reflected the pessimistic mood that held America in its grip. It was an admission that the golden age had passed, that the country was alienated from antebellum ideals and preindustrial traditions. Like so many other notions founded on these fears, however, it did not mirror reality. There was plenty of unsettled western land, and Alaska was still a virgin frontier. Later events were to prove these forebodings as false as those based on the danger of anarchists and immigrants.

The rise of agrarianism and the jeremiads of its leaders were alarm signals. After the election of 1892, *The Nation* dropped its smugness and began to view the Populists as a definite threat. It was shocked that Kansas, "always . . . considered a fair sample of an American commonwealth, in which the system of selfgovernment was working out its perfect fruit," should have "such an unexpected outbreak." The editors were puzzled about why this region, with "an excellent public school system . . . few cities, and not a large foreign element" should surrender to radicalism.[66] A few months later, the magazine returned to this distasteful revelation. Unconsciously reflecting on their own premature dismissal of Populism, the editors declared that "few observers were prepared for the outbreak of anarchistic violence which occurred and which seemed to indicate a condition of social unrest and mental unsoundness calculated to threaten seriously our system of popular government." [67] *The Nation,* however, is really not to be blamed for its lack of foresight. Who would have thought that the established order would be menaced by a native-born group which lived in the country, worshipped the right God, and owned property?

In the next few years, as conditions worsened and the farmers grew more intransigent, fear of an agrarian revolt loomed larger. By 1896, Populist agitation was no longer a single cloud on a calm horizon. Depression and its attendant labor troubles created a crisis outlook, in which the farm protest was exaggerated into catastrophic proportions. Even before the presidential campaign got underway, uneasy memories of the last national disaster were stirred. One writer in the April issue of *The North American Review,* noting the divergent economic interests and the disappearance of sectional bonds, felt that "The time may come, therefore—though heaven grant it otherwise—when the bustling, ambitious, independent West will see that its highest development depends upon the management of its own affairs." [68]

The presidential campaign of 1896, coming at the crest of a wave of anxiety, unloosed a torrent of frenzied feeling. With the Populists apparently on the verge of capturing one of the major parties and implementing their radical program, the conservative press came close to hysteria. The farmer, formerly the very incarnation of virtuous private ownership, was covered with the black flag of anarchy and his demands equated with confiscation. *The Nation* called upon business to close ranks and do battle against the "repudiators," and *Harper's Weekly,* made frantic by the threat to private property, even charged that the "anarchist-controlled" Democratic convention was "a declaration of war against civilization." [69]

As the campaign became more violent, accusations of disunion and confiscation proliferated. It was claimed that Bryan's cohorts were going to set the "West against the East, thereby threatening not only the commerce and labor of the entire Nation with destruction, but jeopardizing the National unity achieved with streams of precious blood." [70] Agrarians wanted to control the army so that they could "riot without fear of restraint" and bring about "the unleashing of the mob" on "a reckless and lawless crusade of sectional animosity and class antagonism." [71]

Many people in the East saw the election of McKinley as a last-ditch stand against disaster. The campaign brought back memories of the Civil War. As in 1860, thundered the Boston *Journal,* "so now there is only one side . . . Now, as then, he must be either for his country or against it." [72] Populist victory, solemnly editorialized the New York *Times,* would be "the darkest menace to which free government has ever yet been exposed in this country." [73]

Prominent individuals added their voices to the hue and cry. Andrew D. White, first President of Cornell and former Minister to Russia and Germany, implored the Democrats to join the Republican Party as the "one way . . . to prevent a National catastrophe." [74] Theodore Roosevelt, always ready to race off and do battle, especially against the Democrats, belligerently asserted that "when war does come I shall be found at the head of my regiment." Speaking "with the greatest soberness," he accused Populist leaders of "plotting a social revolution and the subversion of the American Republic." Roosevelt proposed to follow his sober words with equally judicious deeds by suppressing the movement "as the Commune in Paris was suppressed, by taking ten or a dozen of their leaders out, standing . . . them against a wall and shooting them dead." [75]

Perhaps the most vituperative mixture of intimidation, inaccuracy, and invective was an editorial in the Philadelphia *Press*. The intensity of this expression shows the extent to which eastern conservatives were emotionally committed in this election.

> The Jacobins are in full control at Chicago. No large political movement in America has ever before spawned such hideous and repulsive vipers. The Vallindighams of the war period were odious, but even they did not belong to this serpent brood. The Altgelds and Tillmans who have thrust aside the old leaders of the Democracy and have seized the reins of control incarnate a spirit of communism and anarchy which is new to American politics on any large scale. This riotous platform is the concrete creed of the mob. It is rank Populism intensified and edged with hate and venom. It rests upon the four-corner-stones of organized repudiation, deliberate confiscation, chartered communism, and enthroned anarchy. . . . It begins with falsehood, advances through war upon the social fabric, and ends with the unleashing of the mob.[76]

McKinley's victory seemed a great deliverance, and a collective sigh of relief could be heard among the pillars of the community. The New York *Tribune* got down on its editorial knees to "Thank God!" "Nothing else," it reverentially declared, "expresses the profound emotion, the deep and almost unutterable sense of gratitude which pervades the whole country this morning." [77] The New York *World* grandiloquently declared that "This great deliverance is not a party triumph. It is a triumph of morality and patriotism. . . . It goes beyond the seas and all over the world as a declaration that the institutions of human freedom and political equality are absolutely secure." [78] The heartfelt thanks and recurrent comparisons with the Civil War reveal the deep emotional impact of the election. The victors had not merely won a political battle—they had been saved from chaos. They counted their blessings while looking back at their singed coattails.

Even utopia seemed possible the morning after this brilliant triumph. "It is the beginnings of a new era," said the Brooklyn *Times,* "the dawn of an epoch of prosperity and greatness and to every citizen in it such as no country in the world has ever seen." [79] After the judgment day, the promised land was at hand, for the triumph of the righteous had created an era of unprecedented national bliss.

Victory dispelled gloom—the devilish plot to destroy everything that was good and true had been crushed, and the *bourgeoisie* had hurled back the forces of disintegration. But did the new feeling indicate the return of self-confidence, or did its very passion reveal a core of fear that would remain even after this particular threat was removed?

4

Partial Recovery

1897-1916

AN ERA OF PROSPERITY and national glory began in 1897. There were no longer desperate men wandering through the countryside, and workers had full dinner pails. No longer did the farmer have to use his crops for fuel or watch his land go under foreclosure. The middle class forgot that it had trembled at news of bullets at Homestead and ballots in Kansas. Small property-owners, white-collar workers, teachers, and preachers no longer quaked at reports of strikes, Populism, or municipal corruption. At the same time, socialists, union leaders, and farmers stopped uttering fiery denunciations of the established order. Prosperity and assimilation to contemporary American life tamed these agitators. In the face of these changing conditions and responses, only die-hard cataclysmists like Jack London and the Adams brothers despaired over the domestic disturbances of these years.

When such respectable media as *The Forum* and *The Nation* ceased to publish cataclysmic predictions about urban, labor, and agrarian developments, the differences between the cataclysmists and other pessimistic critics were highlighted. These differences were obscured as long as the moods of both groups overlapped, but now that prosperity had stilled middle-class forecasts of domestic uprisings, it was apparent that the cataclysmists had gone far beyond other critics in the nature and degree of their despair.

Spokesmen for outraged farmers and fearful businessmen had responded to objective conditions—and their forebodings ended as conditions improved—but the Cassandras continued to despair because their prognostications sprang from minds obsessed with destruction.

THE CESSATION OF OLD THREATS

General economic recovery rescued agriculture. Crop prices rose, credit eased, and land values boomed. Writers from magazines that had previously been alarmed over agrarian agitation now believed that "the period of settlement on which the West is entering gives promise of being one of permanent prosperity." [1]

Improvement in the financial position of the farmer undermined Populist support. In the campaigns of 1904 and 1908, the People's Party drew only a fraction of its vote in the 1890's. By 1908, when the Party entered its last election, even its chief, Tom Watson, admitted that "when the fusion movement of 1896 had run its course Populism was prostrate." [2]

As the movement grew weaker, easterners became more indulgent. After 1896, Bryan dropped agrarian reform for the issue of anti-imperialism and was no longer considered an incendiary revolutionist. The Boston *Traveller,* which had argued in 1896 that his defeat was a prerequisite for "prosperity," four years later praised "the proceedings of the National Convention" as "such . . . to thrill the heart of every loyal Democrat with pride." For the party's candidate, the paper had nothing but encomiums: "William Jennings Bryan demands loyalty. . . . He is a typical American. . . . He is the ideal candidate." [3] Conservative critics quickly forgot their terror and ushered the agrarian movement out with casual post mortems: "Its noisy leaders frightened the East, denounced the 'money power' on all occasions, wrote some foolish laws on the statute books, furnished a good deal of material for the sensation newspapers—and did little else." [4]

The once frightening Populists passed from the public consciousness, and their passing roused only derision or gentle condescension. But Populism's demise meant more to the faithful. Tom Watson, bitter in the loneliness of defeat, turned to racism, yet along with his angry tirades against Catholics and Jews, he whimpered that "the People's Party . . . was to me almost as a beloved child, for whose life and growth I had labored much, sacrificed much, and suffered much—and after all it died, leaving me grieved beyond consolation." [5]

Nor did the threat of the labor unions seem quite so formidable after the Nineties. Lessening tension in this area, however, could scarcely be attributed to a subsidence of strife. Strikes were more numerous, as bloody and on the whole more successful.

The opening gun in labor's offensive was the United Mine Workers' strike of 1897. After tying up the bituminous coal regions of West Virginia, Pennsylvania, Illinois, and Indiana, the union won a wage increase. This victory was repeated in the anthracite fields in 1900 and in the famous coal strike of 1902. Other triumphs followed, notably in the garment industry. Despite a grave defeat by United States Steel in 1901, the labor picture brightened considerably in the first decade of the new century.

These strikes were far from bloodless. Rifles and dynamite were standard equipment for miners in Colorado, Montana, and Idaho, where pitched battles between the militia and the western unions were as frequent as in the railroad and steel conflicts of the Nineties. But neither single acts of violence like Steunenberg's murder or the dynamiting of the Los Angeles *Times* Building nor the activities of the Western Federation of Miners and the International Workers of the World brought back the widespread antilabor feeling of the previous years.[6] Public opinion was cushioned against the shock of union violence by the prevalent feeling of security and prosperity. It could not be panicked into seeing cataclysms in these conflicts.

A good indication of the new attitude was the reaction to the Lawrence Massachusetts Strike of 1912. This conflict had all the characteristics that had formerly caused widespread panic. The strike broke out among unskilled foreign workers and was led by the International Workers of the World, an organization born out of the merger of socialists with America's most militant union, the Western Federation of Miners. It was an organization that promised a battle to the death with capitalism and professed willingness to use force to gain its end. When the militia was called up and a woman killed, it seemed as if another dangerous situation had been created.

Despite these developments, the public did not panic. The I.W.W. and the troubles at Lawrence were discussed dispassionately in a large section of the press. One commentator, in the *North American Review* for example, did not even mention the Wobblies or communism in his analysis of the strike. He stressed unfavorable living conditions and unassimilated foreigners as the chief dangers at Lawrence.[7] When the strike was over, the I.W.W. continued to be discussed in calm, scholarly terms—unlike the preceding generation of social scientists, many contemporary experts were unimpressed with the magnitude of labor conflicts. R. F. Hoxie, in an

article for the *Journal of Political Economy,* wrote "that this body
. . . is pathetically weak in effective membership and has failed
utterly in its efforts to attach to itself permanently a considerable
body of men representative of any section of American workers." [8]
While Hoxie questioned the strength of the union, the New York
Post doubted its belligerence. This journal, emphasizing the similarity between the I.W.W. and other unions, did not see how the
Wobblies' occasional use of force "differ[ed] from the conduct of
any other strike." [9]

Still further evidence of internal stability was the tendency of
reporters from respectable magazines to criticize management in a
manner reminiscent of the 1870's. As in those years there was
sympathy for the workers' plight. "Absentee ownership in a factory
should not exempt stock-holders from all interest in the lives of
their laborers," said one critic.[10] A writer in the conservative
Atlantic Monthly even went so far as to suggest that "the way to
make anarchism grow in this country is to refuse to allow organization and collective bargaining." [11]

Growing prolabor sentiment was also manifested in a change
in government policy. During the bituminous coal strike, the gov-
ernors of Indiana and Illinois befriended the workers. In 1898,
when trouble again broke out, Governor Tanner of Indiana sent
in the militia to protect the strikers! The federal government also
modified its outlook with Thedore Roosevelt's 1902 invitation to
the head of the United Mine Workers to visit the White House
for an unprecedented arbitration conference.

Such recognition helped to legitimize the union as labor's representative. Business, as well as government, began to accept the
unions' new role. Prominent businessmen joined with labor leaders
and representatives of the general public to found an organization
that would arbitrate industrial disputes. This group, the National
Civic League, was formed, according to the preamble of its charter,
"to show that organized labor cannot be destroyed without debase-
ment of the masses. . . . That capital can be taught the practicability
of securing industrial peace in accordance with business methods
. . . that the twin foes of industrial peace are the anti-union
employers and the Socialists." [12]

Why was this new approval forthcoming? The intensity and
violence of union activity rules out an explanation similar to that
for the softening of opinion toward the agrarian movement. Fear
of labor did not cease because workers became satisfied and their
organization fell apart. Instead, there was a realization that labor
was not revolutionary, that it was operating within American values

and institutions rather than trying to destroy them. This awareness was demonstrated by the National Civic League when it associated instability with the extremes of reactionary employers and revolutionary socialists. At long last, unions had been separated in the public mind from leftist groups and could be judged as independent organizations.

Progressive reform, a reflection of the new confident spirit, did much to create this new sympathy for labor. The Progressives were encouraged, by their belief in environmentalism, to battle social evils. Unlike its formulation in the 1880's and 1890's, the theory of environmental change was no longer a conservative concept. Most social Darwinists had formerly pointed to man's living conditions to show the futility of conscious social improvement, but in the new century the existence of an unfavorable environment became a challenge for reform. Called "instrumentalism" in philosophy and "naturalism" in literature, this doctrine became the dominant ideology. Reformers applied it in a variety of ways. Muckraking, civic reform, settlement houses, striving for improved working conditions, the social gospel, and the drive for "scientific legislation" all stemmed from the ideas that man was a product of his surroundings. In the light of environmentalism, strikes appeared neither as diabolical plots to destroy society nor as the schemes of greedy union leaders. They were the results of poor living and working conditions and represented a healthy attempt on the part of sufferers to better their lot. The way to stop industrial strife, therefore, was not to persecute the unions but to remove dangerous situations that caused labor struggles. As one observer at Lawrence put it, "The I.W.W. has an ability to organize discontent; where there is no serious discontent it cannot operate." [13]

The rapprochement between labor and society as a whole was due in no small degree to the A.F. of L. and its leader, Samuel Gompers. He fought doctrinaire leftists like Daniel DeLeon, who urged the labor movement toward revolution. By 1900, Gompers, victorious in the battle for "pure and simple" trade unionism, had succeeded in making the A.F. of L. the representative for the vast body of unionized workers—thus committing organized labor to work within capitalism for higher wages and better working conditions. These were goals with which the middle class progressives could sympathize. They were aimed not at society in general but at big business, which was also the enemy of the older *bourgeoisie* of professionals, clerks, and shopkeepers. Trade unionism, directed at improving the workers' environment, coincided with progressivism. Reformers could now cooperate with union leaders in making the amelioration of working conditions and the arbitration of strikes one of their basic projects.

Underlying all these factors were the economic recovery and political resurgence of the eastern middle class.[14] The decline of Populism and the termination of the depression had restored their self confidence. Confident in victory, they once again felt free to express sympathy for justice and reform.

When the struggle to preserve *bourgeois* lives and property ended, the struggle for political power emerged. Fear of expropriation had ranged the middle class against labor; the power conflict ranged them against monopoly. In this new alignment, labor-management relations took on a different meaning for the middle class. Theirs was no longer a fight to save property; it was a battle to prevent big business from getting out of control. Workers were now allies of the *bourgeoisie* in its attempt to maintain a balance of economic and political power, a balance dictated by the middle class and upon which its supremacy depended.

After 1890, the formation of gigantic trusts in major industries, highlighted by the decisive defeat of a strong union by U.S. Steel in 1901, helped to forge the new alliance. Labor and the middle class first acted together in the Anthracite Strike of 1902. The coal companies' refusal to negotiate a settlement advertised the arrogance of the vested interests. The union's willingness to arbitrate reinforced the new view that labor was conciliatory rather than revolutionary.

These shifting attitudes were reflected in the press. The Boston *Traveller* took the owners to task as "the most oppressive of all trusts and the bloated and arrogant monopoly who refuses to submit the present question to the most responsible labor tribunal that the world has ever seen." [15] A writer in *The Atlantic* went even further by attacking, not only the specific case, but the old relationship of capital and labor.

> It is a useful service of labor organizations to destroy not only the old conception of industrial overlordship, with its harshness, but even to destroy those of its implications which are attractive but enfeebling, and to leave in its place, free from all accessories the naked contract of purchase and sale . . . The old inequality at its best means dependence on one side and condescension on the other.[16]

Trusts became the new threat to national welfare. Big business however, did not arouse the same frenzied fear that had greeted previous perils. The corporate menace was mitigated because the titans of industry, having the biggest vested interest in private ownership, could scarcely alarm small property owners by demanding expropriation. Corporate loyalty to property could not completely calm the fears of the small owner, however—the old middle class had once called the Populists "confiscators," despite the myth of the noble yeoman as the ideal property owner. One cannot assume, therefore, a common belief in the sanctity of personal ownership as the sole basis for the public's imperturbability.

A more important factor was the financial recovery that had shifted the focus of cataclysmic fear. In a period of plenty, people no longer feared disaster from conflicts over wealth. America again seemed to be offering opportunity in such abundance that there was enough for everybody. Improved prospects stimulated a feeling of affinity for big businessmen that mitigated anxieties about monopoly encroachments. The great magnates were symbols of success —the most prosperous in an era of prosperity, the one's who had made it in a land of opportunity. These titans were Alger heroes brought to life. They had once been one of us, reasoned the small entrepreneurs. If they could rise, why can't we? Boys read Alger books in quantities unimagined when they first came out in the Eighties and Nineties, and shopkeepers dreamed of brilliant commercial careers.[17]

The American dream had failed to calm the nightmarish Nineties because aspirations to wealth seemed unrealistic in depressed times when property itself was threatened. Domestic struggles lost much of their terror, however, when the issue was one of distribution rather than destruction of property. Certainly small businessmen were more threatened by concentration than by agrarian reform and strikes. Bad times had disappeared, however, and the middle class, no longer worried about confiscation, did not fear corporations so much as they had feared anarchists, unions, and Populists. Progressives dealt with magnates on the same terms that they treated with labor. There were no more last ditch stands against disaster; no fears of oblivion following failure.

There were three attitudes toward trusts: wholesale condemnation, complete approval, and limited criticism. Limited criticism was the position most common, and it reflected the moderation of the Progressive Era. It conceded that some kind of concentration was necessary. "Our aim is not to do away with corporations," said Theodore Roosevelt. "These big aggregations are an inevitable development of modern industrialism . . . We draw the line against misconduct not against wealth."[18] The distinction between aggregations that helped or hindered society was a restatement of America's traditional commercial ethic. Businesses that did not prevent small tradesmen from getting ahead were good; those that swallowed him up were bad. Corporations were therefore to be corrected, not destroyed. They were viewed not as an inevitable threat to be ruthlessly rooted out, but rather as commercial sinners who had to be saved by Progressive consciences.

Progressives feared and criticized big business, but they also admired the power and efficiency of their foes. They were forever playing forces against each other, now using labor and now capital to maintain the balance that ensured their position of arbiter between classes. "We shall guard as zealously the rights of the strikers as those of the employer," said Theodore Roosevelt in a typical statement of this philosophy.[19] For this reason some Progressives feared any agreement between labor and capital that was not brought about through their intervention. Common policy could become conspiracy if it was not carefully watched by the middle class. Thus muckraker Ray Stannard Baker said of one agreement between these two groups, "We have been sighing for labor and capital to get together . . . Here they are together; are we any better off."[20]

One great obstacle to die-hard opposition against monopoly was that the means of prosperity clashed with the mode of reform. As Roosevelt put it, "a few men recognized that corporations and combinations had become indispensable in the business world, that it was folly to try to prohibit them, but that it was also folly to leave them alone."[21] This dilemma could be satisfactorily met neither by the despair that had convinced farmers of the evil of all big capitalists nor by the socialists' assurance of the justice and eventual triumph of their own cause. The middle class remained in an ambiguous position, a position that created confusion and frustration. Prosperity, which had diminished fears of class conflict, had also created tension for Progressives because of their ambivalence toward the forces that contributed to that prosperity. The strain of balancing two forces antagonistic to its basic values, of aspiring to a position of supremacy in the face of superior strength, sought an outlet: If anxiety were repressed in domestic matters, it would eventually emerge in foreign affairs.

Western Progressives, inheriting the ideology and the rhetoric of Populism, were more intransigent in opposing trusts. Robert M. LaFollette, George W. Norris, William E. Borah, Albert B. Cummins, Jonathan P. Dolliver, and Albert J. Beveridge led the fight to regulate railroads and even broke with the administration over the issue of that "mother of trusts," the protective tariff. The westerners castigated the monopolies in Populist rhetoric: LaFollette asserted that "the power of special interest . . . strikes down the very foundation of our institutions," and Borah envisioned a "war of extinction" between "the Republic and monopoly." [22]

Most of these men, however, did not share the bitterness of their Populist forebears. They were too willing to admit with Cummins that "corporations are necessary to the business of the country" or to see both sides of the issue, as did Borah, who thought that monopoly "has brought many comforts and many blessings, but also many evils and wrongs and gigantic problems." [23]

Their more moderate temper led these Progressives to look askance at some of the stern old agrarian panaceas. "I am not able to agree to this remedy," said Cummins of Bryan's proposal to nationalize the railroads. He fell back to the Progressive position of regulation: "I am not willing to concede the possibility of a failure of the government to bring into subjection either the railroads or any form of corporate power." [24] These leaders saw the trust issue more in terms similar to those of their eastern colleagues than in the old western spirit of uncompromising fight between producers and parasites. "It is also a question of government," said Borah speaking about concentration, "but it is more, it has at its base a question of morals." [25]

This group's commitment to the established order was revealed by its political policy. No Populist could accept Cleveland, and many were unable to support the Democratic Party when Bryan was its candidate, but Borah and Cummins supported Taft. Others like Beveridge, William Allen White, and Hiram Johnson fought for Teddy at Armageddon in an army containing a millionaire publisher, a Morgan partner, and political bosses from Ohio and Pennsylvania. Most western Progressives were more like their brethren in the East than their fathers in the West. They had come to accept what had been damned fifteen years before, their agrarian invective against business often concealed accommodation to these interests, making the ringing slogans of Populism sound hollow on their lips.

Leftist groups were also included in the amnesty granted to enemies of past years. In September, 1901, McKinley was shot by an anarchist. For the first time in fifteen years an act of violence— and a much graver act than the alleged killing of a policeman— was committed under the black flag. But times had changed; no longer was radical violence considered a prelude to social dissolution. Unlike the Haymarket Affair, which was treated as a harbinger of doom, McKinley's murder was attributed to a band of criminals who were a threat to the peace, but not to the existence, of the republic. The public thought of the anarchists as "a small band of skulking cowards" whose "deeds avail nothing." [26] The press, which had panicked in 1886, took this killing in its stride. In 1886, the Cleveland *Plain Dealer* editorialized that "if civilization is not to be plunged into chaos, the supremacy of law must be vindicated and maintained at whatever cost." Fifteen years later, the journal greeted a new anarchist conspiracy with the casual remark that "the anarchists form but an infinitesimally small element of the population." [27]

Reluctance to use repressive measures against anarchists demonstrated renewed faith in America. In the Eighties and Nineties a frightened populace called for summary tactics in removing this threat, but now, liberty seemed the antidote for poisons in the body politic. "If the thoughtless and even the malignant are allowed freedom of speech," editorialized the New York *Post*, "they are likely to work less evil, to excite less sympathy than if they are choked off." [28] Anarchy no longer haunted the public. The people discarded fears of proletarian confiscation and socialist revolution because they were secure in their property and confident of their institutions. It was this cushion of invulnerability that enabled them to continue to look for enemies on the right.

The Socialist Party reflected the temperateness of Progressivism. It emerged, in 1901, from the ashes of Debs's Social-Democrat Party and the anti-DeLeon wing of the Socialist Labor Party, as a mild pink rather than blood red version of earlier leftist groups. The party enjoyed a tremendous growth, and its leaders already glimpsed the promised land. A.M. Simons, weighty in party councils and editor of the influential *International Socialist Review*, saw "America . . . filled with signs of the growth of this new all-conquering international world power." [29]

Neither the party's growth nor the optimism of its members frightened America. The Socialists, unlike the embittered failures of the Eighties, eschewed violent revolution. Spared frustrating political defeat, every electoral success made them more respectable and guaranteed their remaining within the established order. Critics began to distinguish between these Americanized political activists and the remnants of old foreign bands who tried to destroy the social framework. After one outburst of leftist violence, observers claimed that "it is not fair . . . to accuse the Socialist and labor elements of the American metropolis." They "themselves repudiate it, and it must never be forgotten that far from conspiring to destroy government, Socialism—the precise opposite of anarchism —aims at vastly increasing the powers of government." [30]

Socialists did their best to fulfill the faith of the middle class. Party organs reassuringly declared that "there is no place in the political movement for the midnight revolution, and the cataclysmic transformation." [31] Party leaders ran for office and became so committed to the electoral system that they warned Socialist conventions to eschew revolutionary pronouncements and concentrate on formulating "a working program for the present national campaign, and working programs for the coming state and municipal elections." By 1912, these moderates controlled the National Executive Committee and had pushed through an amendment calling for expulsion of those who opposed "political action" or advocated "violence as a weapon of the working class to aid in its emancipation." When Big Bill Haywood was recalled from the Committee for violating this rule, the political activists had won complete victory.[32] They had not disappointed the hopes of *bourgeois* critics.

Observers of the movement, heartened by the Party's course, gave it strange but not inaccurate praise. One writer in the *Atlantic* commented "that the intelligent socialist" wanted none of the following: "pay mind and muscle alike;" "destroy private property;" "divide up" "or even do away with the 'survival of the fittest.' " [33] Another contributor to *The Atlantic* ventured a speculation on Socialism's triumph. His vision was a far cry from the nightmare of death and destruction so widely imagined in the years of upheaval:

> The Socialist Party . . . would simply take the plan of our Republican or our Democratic Party, as the "party in power," and would exercise its power in the customary party modes. The keen scented fortune-hunters and professional experts of politics would already have swarmed to it from the old parties; would have wormed themselves into its counsels and perfected its "organization," with a full equipment of the most approved "machines." [34]

The Socialists mellowed as the middle class grew more tolerant. When the party found increased sympathy in society, they came to accept the system and, conversely, their assimilation to society's ways increased public security and tolerance. Once again, prosperity neutralized cataclysmic fears and forces. Through economic recovery, the *bourgeoisie* gained the confidence that enabled them to accept the Socialists, and it was this acceptance that made possible the Socialists' political success, convincing them that the nation could be converted by peaceful persuasion.

Optimism also transformed the city from a symbol of disintegration to an inspiration for reform. When labor unions and the Socialists lost their ominous attributes, the image of the city brightened too. If these forces were not evil, the places where they were housed were also innocent. Environmentalists blamed urban conditions—but not urbanism—for social evils. Everyone had the capacity for good citizenship; it was merely a question of modifying situational factors so that this potential could be realized. Thus Frederic Howe claimed that "even the evils of the city are not necessarily inherent in urban life. They are due to the backwardness of political thought and social science and the failure of cooperation to keep pace with the needs of the community." [35]

The task then was to change living conditions so that the city would become a positive force. This goal was to be accomplished through "social science." The social-science cure meant the use of techniques like statistics and the commission form of government to unravel the mysteries of municipal finance and bring virtue into corrupt metropolitan politics. Typical of this approach was John J. Hamilton's criteria for judging the success of the commission type of city administration. This plan, he thought, would create order, efficiency, promptness, and lower taxes. [36] More than one enthusiastic expert was carried away by his pet technique. There was, for example, Raymond Bridgeman, who, in "Civic Righteousness Via Percentages," stated that "a new promise of success has come to the reformers of municipal government . . . through a new application of statistics, and its potency lies in the application of percentage of result to expense." [37]

In affirming the work of the metropolis, reformers demonstrated their belief that the citizen and his city had been reconciled. Critics in the Eighties and Nineties claimed that the city subverted the nation. But every victory over bosses, bad housing, or other evils made the Progressives feel that urbanites had regained republican virtue. Reformers spoke of an "independent vote," by which they meant those freed from the corrupt elements that had dominated the city. As this free individual appeared, the Progressives discovered that "municipal evil was chiefly due to poor environment." They counted on this enlightened citizen to improve his surroundings. Emancipation thus meant ultimate reintegration, "the reconciliation of the citizen and his city; the new birth of his faith in it and in himself as a factor in its public life . . ." [38]

The movement for municipal reform intensified in 1894 with

the formation of the National Municipal League. By the turn of the century, the election of reform administrations in Cleveland, Detroit, New York, and other cities had given the drive great momentum. Widespread use of reform techniques and the victories of reform candidates filled Progressives with hope. Urban purification was a "new birth," a "revival" of the citizens' "hopes for the republic as a thing that is not going to languish and die from absorption of the toxins evolved within itself, but is to go on for unreckoned ages, playing a good part in the drama of national life." [39] For some, even the claim of republican renaissance did not do justice to the rejuvenated city. Frederick C. Howe thought that "the city is the greatest agency of civilization," the midwife of progress that "forecasts a movement for the improvement of human society more hopeful than anything the world has known." [40]

THE UNREGENERATE

Pessimistic critics in the 1880's and 1890's regarded the city, leftist groups, labor, and immigration as different facets of a cataclysmic force. In the happier days of the new century, these elements were more clearly differentiated, and all but foreigners were freed from subversive taints. Workers were no longer regarded as foreign-born anarchists; the city apparently ceased to be the home of evil wealth, social revolution, and unassimilated foreigners; even socialists were distinguished from anarchists. This differentiation worked against the immigrants, however. Despite the general tolerance extended to other groups, the newcomers were left isolated to bear alone the brunt of society's antagonism. Consequently, when the other groups became respectable, socially repulsive attributes were fastened even more firmly upon immigrants. This differentiation and transference are evident in the Lawrence strike. Progressive writers blamed bad working conditions and management rather than socialists for the strike. Although they disassociated labor from the revolutionary left, they still accused the foreigners of anarchism. Workers were supported but immigrants condemned. The solution to the labor problem was better working and living conditions; the answer to the anarchist threat was "a careful consideration of our immigration laws." [41]

Xenophobia resisted the palliative that brought the city, the socialists, and the unions to acceptance. Prosperity had very little influence in making newcomers more welcome. Nor were their greater numbers and European origin an adequate explanation for anti-immigrant feelings. Populists were native-born and anarchists were not plentiful, yet this had not stopped Americans from fearing them.

What prevented environmentalism from carrying the day in immigration as it had for labor and the city? Why did the Progressives violate the logic of their own philosophy by refusing to extend the principles of environmentalism to the immigrant? [42] Part of the answer lies in the one great difference between the immigrants and the groups that reformers welcomed into the fold. The influx of so-called "alien races" reversed the tolerant tendencies of Progressivism. Race was the only insurmountable obstacle to reform; it was the obstacle that environmental improvements were unable to remedy or remove. It could not be eliminated by social science, ameliorated by settlement houses, or nullified by scientific legislation. Consequently, the immigrant was still beyond the pale, still rejected by the middle classes. Even Progressive tolerance and the logic of environmentalism could not bridge the gap.

Race might have been forgiven had not the newcomers been associated with the menace of foreign conflict. Increased confidence in the nation's ability to cope with its internal problems might have made it obvious that immigrants were accommodating to America, that the now respectable socialists, laborers, and urban dwellers were largely foreign born. But cataclysmic concern had shifted, and its new focus was America's relations with other countries. Emergence as a world power meant international difficulties and new enemies and frustrations. The anxieties generated by this role were projected on the immigrant. Once again, he suited the part perfectly. He was the alien subversive who could be linked with threats abroad. Racism, a door double barred by its defiance of environmentalism and its rationalization for international mishaps, was slammed in the faces of refugees seeking fulfillment in their new land.

AN ERA OF HOPE

On the whole, things brightened considerably as the new century dawned. Concern over immigrants and trusts did not motivate dire predictions. Old enemies either became respectable or disappeared from the public scene. Americans once again believed their country to be uniquely harmonious. *The Arena,* notable in the past for its dim view of the future, now ran articles asserting that "the crescent promise of the Twentieth Century is the harmonious and fair

partnership and cooperation of labor and capital." [43] *The Nation,*
also shaken in the storms of former years, optimistically stated that
"there is no land on earth where the transition from the so-called
lower classes to the middle and the higher is easier and more
frequent." [44]

Rejuvenated by prosperity, Americans enthusiastically contemplated domestic prospects. People felt young and free; the nation
had been reborn, and the future belonged to America. "He must
be blind," asserted Benjamin Flower, himself once afflicted with the
astigmatism of pessimism, "who fails to see the multitudinous signs
that point to the gathering together and forward movement of the
hosts of fundamental democracy." [45] "Everywhere," said Benjamin
Parke DeWitt in a contemporary study of the Progressive movement, "there are evidences that the nation has passed into a new
political era." [46] The Progressives themselves, however, best captured the spirit of the age and remembered it the longest. When
well along in years they would look back on this time of hope,
youth, and happiness:

> The spirit of this young America was generous, hospitable,
> brilliant; it was care-free and full of variety. The young people
> in whom it leaped to expression hated injustice. They had no
> question about the soundness of American democracy. They had
> supreme confidence in the mind.[47]

It was wonderful, in those years, to be young and to be a
Progressive.

5

Foreign Threats

EXPECTATIONS OF CIVIL STRIFE had scarcely diminished before attention had shifted to the dangers of foreign involvement. This change in cataclysmic orientation occurred both among the Cassandras and among critics not temperamentally obsessed with destruction. The Adamses and Mary Lease shifted focus in a manner similar to magazines like *The Arena* and *The Nation*. The continuity between cataclysmists and more conventional critics reflected, as it had in earlier preoccupations with internal dissension, the interplay of social conditions and subjective perception of these conditions. Widespread forecasts of catastrophe indicated that the objective situation raised fears of destruction. Once again, however, personality factors made the cataclysmists' fears more intense than the more tentative and desultory feelings of other observers.

THE BATTLE OVER IMPERIALISM

Gloomy predictions about international affairs stemmed from anxieties similar to those that motivated dire forecasts in the 1880's and 1890's. In both periods, America was making difficult adjustments. Previously, the nation had been accommodating itself to industrial capitalism—after the Spanish-American War, it assumed the position of a world power. This new role represented a break with the past. From colonial days until the end of the nineteenth century, the period of America's drive for expansion, its "manifest destiny," was to subdue the continent. Even aspirations emerging from the Revolutionary War were bounded by the Western Hemisphere. The United States in 1783, unlike France in 1789 or Russia in 1917, thought of itself as the refuge, rather than the knight errant, of liberty. The country would not venture forth to convert others to the eternal truths of freedom but would gather the world's oppressed and teach them what it had discovered. When the nineteenth century ended, however, the continent had been conquered, and America, with its expansionist energies unsated, sought an empire across the sea.

After 1898, America had commitments that spanned the globe. Speculation about this awesome turn of events led to two divergent notions of impending doom. Anti-imperialists feared that expansion would erode republican institutions and virtues; imperialists, on the other hand, felt that we had started too late and acquired too little. These two sets of observers were divided over the necessity for social change. The expansionists saw the disintegration of the old way of life in its apparent failure to meet the new challenge. They wondered if we were flexible and inventive enough to achieve great power status. The Anti-imperialists, on the other hand, doubted America's ability to preserve its institutions in the face of changes caused by new foreign policy. One group perceived disaster because America was not changing; the other because it was.

Anti-imperialism revealed a distaste for modern times not unlike that expressed in the pessimism of the 1880's and 1890's. Both generations of critics believed they were fighting a desperate holding action in order to preserve the old national spirit. This opposition to empire-building appeared among older men who were resisting the encroachments of the new era. Mugwumps, older Republicans, Gold Democrats, Brahmins, and Populists manned this rampart of conservatism. Moorfield Storey, Charles Eliot Norton, Thomas Wentworth Higginson, Tom Watson, and Pitchfork Ben Tillman may appear unlikely allies, but blueblood Mugwumps and the earthier Populists shared the same dream of a preindustrial America, and, now that the rifts of the Nineties had been healed, they united to defend their dream. The union of these former foes revealed the changing focus of cataclysmic thought. George S. Boutwell, one of the anti-imperialist leaders and a former Republican senator and governor of Massachusetts, blessed the new coalition by coming out "for Bryan in spite of what he may believe concerning the currency or finances of the country." Now that imperialism was "a question of life and death to the republic," who could "stop to consider whether silver should be worth more or less than it is." [1] Faced with a new catastrophe, men of Boutwell's stripe had to embrace the pariah of the plains, and so the Anti-Imperialist League supported William Jennings Bryan for the Presidency in 1900.

Many anti-imperialists feared that territorial acquisition would be a death blow to the Republic. Moorfield Storey, Brahmin by birth and Mugwump by conviction, expressed these fears when he told fellow blueblood reformer George F. Hoar that the administration's policy would "involve this country in the very gravest difficulties and [eventually] . . . result in the overthrow of self-government." [2]

John Clark Ridpath, relieving Flower as editor of *The Arena,* spoke for more radical critics when he declared that a conspiracy of wealth lay behind imperial schemes. "Since the Civil War the class of nabobs has been constantly increasing," he wrote. "They all belong to one political party—the Party of the Empire." If America continued a policy of possession, predicted Ridpath, "ere the century closes" the nation would see "the wreck of our old-time institutions." [3]

The course of empire would end in disaster because freedom and imperialism were incompatible. A favorite theme of *The Nation* was to raise the specter of Rome as a republic that had been undermined by expansion and its by-products of militarism and war. "Once Rome was forced to be a military republic," warned the editors, "one civil war followed another, until she found relief in a monarchy which gave her peace in exchange for liberty." [4] Moorfield Storey echoed these sentiments when he claimed, in a speech significantly entitled "The New Departure," that "we have abandoned the ideals and principles of liberty which we have cherished from our birth, and we have adopted the principles and practices of tyranny, which we have always condemned." [5] Liberty would die here if we killed it in other lands. "If we once concede any ground for any distinction between men in their fundamental rights," it was argued, "there is no obstacle save force to the establishment over us of the same tyrannous oppression." [6]

Despite these dismal prognostications, the agitation against empire was of short duration. Even at its height, the influence of the Anti-Imperialist League was not widespread, and its members were already past their political prime. In dissolving internal dissension, Americans had proven their ability to march in step with the times. If other phases of industrial capitalism had been mastered, why doubt the nation's capacity to conquer competitors in the contest for foreign territory and new markets? After 1902, only a few dissenters clung to the cause, and by 1905, Boston could claim the sole surviving chapter of the League.

The imperialists, on the other hand, were for the most part younger men who prided themselves on keeping abreast of the changing times. Some of them were realists in politics like Henry Cabot Lodge and Theodore Roosevelt, who had broken with their class over civil-service reform rather than give up their political careers. Joseph Pulitzer and William Randolph Hearst represented a second type attracted to this movement. Where others dreaded immigrants, laborers, and city dwellers, these journalistic entrepreneurs had made their fortunes by meeting—and even manufacturing—the needs of these groups, and now they were trying to make imperialism a mass crusade. Expansionism also attracted intellectuals like Homer Lea, Alfred T. Mahan, Brooks Adams, John Fisk, and John W. Burgess who marshalled contemporary theories in history, science, and anthropology to convince their countrymen of the necessity of conquering foreign markets and protecting the Anglo-Saxon race. Such allies from the clergy as Josiah Strong made imperialism a crusade, while politicians like Lodge and Beveridge fought the good fight in Congress.

Despite its accent on youth, vigor, and power, imperialism contained pessimistic elements. If expansionists thought that America's great potential could be realized through empire, they also believed far-flung possessions were necessary to forestall foreign threats. In fact, this rationalization for conquest became a self-fulfilling prophecy. The very territorial acquisition that was considered vital for protection against other nations intensified enmity between the United States and those nations. The expansion that was to provide security actually increased anxiety.

Another source of fear appeared in the expansionists' Darwinian conception of international relations. Disputes over colonies were viewed as struggles for existence in a world of voracious national organisms whose survival depended upon gobbling up the markets of Asia and Africa. Imperialists believed that although national power involved domestic harmony and productivity, it also required markets to sustain economic growth and prosperity. Most expansionists believed that America had solved her domestic problems, but they feared that the flow of goods would choke the United States unless it was diverted to foreign markets.

The quest for empire also heightened xenophobic and racist fears. The American dream of competitive achievement made enemies out of immigrants, who represented contenders for wealth and power. The formula for accomplishment through interpersonal strife was also applied to foreign affairs, and hostility was directed against those countries who stood in the way of the United States' international success. When clashing interests brought America into conflict with nations whose emigrants were landing on its shores, the familiar arguments for excluding foreigners were augmented with the charge that they were agents of unfriendly powers—and that free admission would put the United States at a disadvantage in global competition.

Racism, which was an even stronger strain in American xenophobia than were fears of competition or suspicions of subversion, was also intensified by imperialism. Since all human relationships were supposed to be governed by evolutionary principles, it was easy for Social Darwinists to extend racial categories into foreign conflicts. At home, the fittest species succeeded at the expense of inferior groups, and it would be so abroad. Conflicts over markets and trade routes were really struggles for existence among different nationalities. Magnified into wars for racial survival, these contests took on cataclysmic proportions. The struggle between America and other states was put on the most elemental and, at the same time, the most abstract plane. Victory depended upon more than material strength; it was basically a matter of ethnic rearmament, in which immigrant dilution would mean "race suicide." Although flushed with recent conquests, America was facing a world simmering with conflict, ready at any moment to erupt into total war. Vigilance and preparation were necessary to ensure triumph—and triumph the nation must have, for defeat meant annihilation.

The intensity of foreign conflicts from the Spanish-American to the First World War were determined by clashing imperial interests and by ethnic fears. Geopolitical grievances between England and America diminished, partly because Britain was casting about for alliances against new enemies but also because Americans suddenly saw other Anglo-Saxons as highly desirable friends. Conversely, disputes between this country and Russia and Japan became, in the loose language of early ethnologists (and every jingo considered himself an expert on race), conflicts between the Anglo-Saxon and the Slavs or the Yellow Peril.

In relations with Germany, as with England, apparent racial similarity minimized friction. Despite clashes with Germany in South America, Samoa, China, and over its flagrant support of Spain in 1898, Americans never considered the Teutonic nation as dangerous as Russia or Japan. Germany and the United States, both recently embarked on imperialist ventures, might be bitter rivals for miscellaneous territories not yet swallowed up by the other major powers; Kaiser Wilhelm, dedicated to the monarchical principle, might execrate the upstart democracy across the Atlantic, but cataclysmic thought was not focused on Germany until 1914. Only a small minority among the Cassandras and imperialist ideologues expressed alarm over Germany. Occasionally, Homer Lea or Alfred T. Mahan interrupted pursuit of their primary concerns to issue warnings about the commercial and colonial threat from Germany. But such warnings were ignored, because most people thought of the Germans as those "old immigrants," virtuous and industrious citizens who had helped to make the country great. Few could believe that a nation so closely related to the Anglo-Saxon heritage could constitute a peril. At a time when more than one historian seriously claimed that American democracy had originated in the forests of Germany, a Teutonic threat was unimaginable.

Objectively, there was no more reason to fear Russia than Germany. Certainly "Willy" was as much an autocrat as "Nicky," and if Russia was a more prominent rival in the Far East, she had not interfered so flagrantly with American interests in South America or during the Spanish-American War. But Russian-American relations were deteriorating at precisely the same time that Slavic immigrants were inundating the northeastern seaboard. The Russian threat appeared grave in the context of fears that these "inferior hordes" would destroy the American way of life. Czarist "absolutism," Russia's "insatiable ambition," and the Slavic menace to Anglo-Saxon supremacy made Russia "the natural foe of England and the United States." [7] Observers anxiously awaited "the final grapple" that would determine whether "the future of civilization" lay with "the English-speaking people of the world or the Russian Empire." [8]

After 1905, the Slavs ceased to be feared as the bane of civilization; a combination of domestic grievances and foreign fears focused attention on the "Yellow Peril" as the new menace. Japan's victory in the Russo-Japanese War allayed fears of Slavic encroachment only to raise the greater bugaboo of Mongolian domination. Not only was Japan the ascendant power in the Far East, but it seemed to be overrunning the American West Coast. The decade before 1905 was a period of heavy Japanese emigration to California. The Nipponese, accustomed to a lower standard of living and poorer working conditions, competed effectively with American labor. The unions and their Progressive allies abhorred these newcomers who destroyed hard won gains. Mongolians became the most detested of all the new types of immigrant. At least the Slavs had come from Europe and were physically similar to real Americans. Mongolians, on the other hand, came from cultures even more alien than those of Eastern Europe and were biologically distinguishable.

Evidence of the more intense anxiety raised by the "Yellow Peril" can be seen in the unique measures taken against immigration and immigrants from the Far East and in the proliferation of cataclysmic predictions about war between Japan and the United States. Armed conflict between the two nations was forecasted as early as 1907. "If the war would come tomorrow, Japan could whip us in the Pacific with ease," Captain Richmond Hobson, U.S.N., wrote ominously.[9] Important foreign-service officers like Charlemagne Tower, our Ambassador to Germany, and Charles Denby, American Consul at Shanghai, shared Hobson's apprehension. When Roosevelt sent the fleet to the Pacific in 1908, many anticipated war.

The first wave of war scares subsided when the Root-Takahira agreement reaffirmed China's territorial integrity. Fear was again revived in 1913, however, when the Hearst papers spread a rumor that a Japanese syndicate was seeking a naval base in Mexico. Anxiety increased when Japan built three battleships—our soldiers at Corregidor were alerted for a possible invasion.[10] After the balance of power in the East was destroyed by the outbreak of the World War, "the Japanese Menace" became "more sinister and more imminent . . . to our peace and security." [11] The July, 1916, issue of *The Forum* contained an article summarizing the areas of difficulty between the two nations. America's refusal to accede to all of Japan's demands at the conclusion of the Russo-Japanese war and her resistance to Japanese commercial supremacy in the Far East were considered more than adequate pretexts for a Japanese declaration of war. Its formidable navy, Far Eastern bases, spies in our Pacific possessions, and the numbers of ex-soldiers emigrating to the Pacific Coast were indications that Japan was already preparing to attack.[12] With Russia and Germany out of the Pacific, and the allies occupied elsewhere, Japan loomed as the greatest threat. When the United States entered the war, however, this peril gave way to that of the Teutonic ogre. The United States and Japan were now allies, and difficulties in the Far East were temporarily forgotten.

All aspects of the imperialist outlook were expressed by Homer Lea. He feared Germany, Russia, and Japan in the described orthodox order. His pronouncements demonstrated the connection between xenophobia, racism, and foreign affairs; voiced the usual economic and geopolitical arguments for empire; and, finally, predicted the inevitable racial showdown. This orthodoxy however, is not what made Lea one of the most interesting expositors of international perils. He was not only an observer of these matters, but, in typical cataclysmist fashion, his way of life was governed by his analysis. Eventually Lea devoted himself entirely to the fight against the foes who would destroy America.

One source of Lea's imperialism was his own wish to be a great general. Barred from other activities by a crippled body, his chief childhood pleasure had been playing soldiers. As he grew older, his youthful passion for blasting his sisters out of impregnable positions in the backyard gave way to close study of the great military captains. On entering college, Lea acquired another attachment: He made friends among Chinese students and joined the Po-Wong-Wui, a secret society dedicated to overthrowing the Manchu Dynasty. Lea's desire for martial glory now focused on making China a republic. In 1899, he embarked on a crusade against the Empress, asserting that "all great careers are carved out by a sword. Mine, too, I shall carve that way." [13]

Lea became a general in the revolutionary forces and co-operated with Western powers in the hope that they would depose the old Empress. After the Boxer rebellion, Lea, a general without an army, gave his services to Sun Yat-sen. The Empress, however, was able to repress this new uprising, and Lea fled to Japan. In 1901, Sun Yat-sen and Lea went to California to raise another army to free China. Five years later, they returned to China for another abortive liberation attempt.

Lea first predicted a Japanese attack on America in *The Valor of Ignorance,* published in 1909. The book had a limited success, selling 18,000 copies before going out of print in 1922. Abroad and in domestic military circles, however, it was considered quite important. In Japan, it went through twenty-four editions and became required reading for all officers. German and Russian military academies also assigned it, and Hitler cribbed passages from it for *Mein Kampf.* Even American military leaders were impressed with the volume. "We do not know of any work in military literature published in the United States more deserving the attention of men who study the history of the United States and the Science of War than this—*The Valor of Ignorance,*" said Lieutenant-General Adna R. Chaffee, former Army Chief of Staff.[14]

In 1911, Lea accepted the invitation of Britain's Field Marshall Lord Roberts to come to Europe to study German army maneuvers and advise him on the defense of the empire. The following year, Lea wrote a second book of warning, *The Day Of The Saxon,*

which had only a sparse sale of 7000 before going out of print in
1932. He also planned a third work, *The Swarming Of The Slav,*
but died before it was completed.

1911 was the year of crowning glory for the little warrior. He
went back to China, this time to lead a victorious campaign, which
resulted in Sun Yat-sen's election to the presidency of the new
Chinese Republic. But Lea's opportunity to enjoy his achievement
was cut short by death. Early in 1912, his five-feet, eighty-eight-
pound, hunchbacked body gave up its burden of pain and ambition.
One of the strangest careers in American history was ended.

The Valor Of Ignorance is a justification of militaristic imperialism and an analysis of the American-Japanese conflict in the
Far East. The first part of the book is devoted to an exposition of
general principles in the struggle for national supremacy, the concluding section to a case study of two countries involved in such a
struggle.

According to Lea's organic concept of the state, nations were
Darwinian organisms controlled by nature's laws of struggle and
survival. "Struggle for existence" and "survival of the fittest" were
the sanctions of political action.

War, however, was not only a biological and political necessity,
but also the inevitable concomitant of evolutionary growth in
nations and individuals. It was the noblest expression of man, "a
composite exemplification of the struggle of man upward; the
multiplication of his individual efforts into one, and the . . . turn
toward a greater and nobler end, not of himself but of his race."

Since war and expansion could produce national greatness,
forces that opposed them were the commonwealth's gravest dangers. Foremost among those perils was commercial activity for personal gain. Private wealth weakened the sinews of the nation by
feeding on national resources and encouraging the soft life. Such
selfish individualism, by placing "the interest of countless individuals . . . paramount to those of the state," caused "disintegration,
disaster and destruction."

Since institutional stability depended on "homogeneity of race,"
ethnic mixture was another cause of national downfall. The introduction of inferior hordes obliterated racial "superiority," eroded
morals, weakened patriotism, and destroyed "those primitive rights
upon which the great but fragile edifice of this Republic was built."
In short, immigration was national suicide.

The cataclysmic nature of *The Valor of Ignorance* lies not so
much in its delineation of national disintegration as in its projection
of such disintegration on America. Lea believed that the twin evils

of commercialism and mongrelization were eating away the country's vitality. Commercialism, "having seized hold of the American people, overshadows and tends to destroy not only the aspirations and world wide career open to the nation, but the republic." Ethnic deterioration was also sapping America's strength. Since the Civil War, "homogeneity of population has declined" and the "declination of primitive Americanism has gone on at even greater speed."

Disintegration through decadence would be completed by defeat in an international struggle. Competition for diminishing markets was shortly going to end in war. The necessity to expand brought the United States into conflict with other countries driven by the same inexorable need. Since European expansion had been stopped in the East and Asian expansion in the West, "West must the peoples of Europe go, and Eastward those of Asia, until . . . on American continents, these two sides, shall meet and struggle and subside." The champion of the West was America; the great threat was Japan, and the stakes were global supremacy.

In the ensuing contest, Japan would have the edge. Her armed forces were stronger, she was prepared for war, she had discovered our weaknesses in the Pacific, and, most important, her people had the martial spirit. "Unless there is an immediate military renascence in this Republic," warned Lea, "the approaching struggle will be relegated to that class of conflicts exemplified in the Chinese-Japanese War of 1894." He foresaw Japan taking the Philippines and Hawaii with little trouble and then moving on to her "main objective, the Pacific Coast." Once she possessed California, the United States would be crippled, and Japanese supremacy in the Pacific would be assured. Lea ended his work with a somber sketch of defeated America:

> The inevitable consummation that follows the investment [sic] of San Francisco becomes apparent in the utter helplessness of the Republic. In the entire nation there is not another regiment of regular troops; no generals, no corporals. Not months, but years, must elapse before armies equal to the Japanese are able to pass in parade. These must then . . . [attempt] the militarily impossible; turning the mountain-gorges into the ossuaries of their dead, and burdening desert winds with the spirits of their slain. The repulsed and distracted forces to scatter, as heretofore, dissension throughout the Union, brood rebellions, class and sectional insurrections, until the heterogeneous Republic, in its principles, shall disintegrate, and again into the palm of reestablished monarchy pay the toll of its vanity and its scorn.[15]

In 1912, the California Cassandra issued another solemn prophecy. Once again he used the prediction of world war as a clarion call for the "Saxon people" "to arouse themselves to the somber consequences of their neglect and to break away from the pleasant security of their delusions." If they did not heed his call, they would "awake at a predetermined hour to find themselves upon a savage dawn, stripped and desolate."

Lea broadened the scope of his version of doom in *The Day Of The Saxon.* In addition to the United States, the whole Anglo-Saxon race was in danger, menaced not only from Japan but from Russia and Germany as well. Russia's next move would be against India, while Germany, inspired by memories of Bismarck, would strike at the heart of the empire, England. The opposition was homogeneous and militant, virtues that the beleaguered Anglo-Saxons were rapidly losing. Unless the English-speaking peoples rejuvenated themselves, the coming war of races would result in a crushing defeat and "the dismalest of twilights shall fall . . . a twilight that knows no other day." [16]

From Homer Lea's desire for adventure and the need to seek it abroad had come his belief that America was unprepared and unable to fight. His crusade in China caused his hatred for Japan, and his frustrated desire for military glory made him suspicious of commerce. Were all his fears and suspicions, however, the results of unfulfilled ambition, and failure to achieve the accolades he desired? The outbreak of world war within a few years and the subsequent struggle between Japan and the United States showed that Lea's predicted cataclysm was not merely a catastrophe of his imagination.

WORLD WAR I

On August 1, 1914, holocaust finally occurred—World War I began. This spectacle of death and destruction was certainly cataclysmic, and some observers saw it as disastrous. For them, belligerency signified the collapse of Christianity, a resurgence of barbarism. They argued that patriotism and courage would be distorted by the war into repression and militarism. Pacifists feared that "a conflagration so vast as this cannot rage without scorching the abodes of mankind throughout the world." Shocked by violence and fearing that the holocaust would spread, they sought solace in the hope that "at a terrible cost the world has already learned a new lesson: That even in this twentieth century there is civilization only in peace; war is always barbarism." [17]

Not everyone agreed that the war was a great tragedy. Many saw it as an inspiration for individuals and nations. If disaster resulted, it would be due to America's lack of preparation rather than to the horror of world strife. This thinking was in line with the warnings of the imperialists. They had condemned defeat rather than armed conflict itself. In fact, they regarded war as inevitable and desirable—destruction awaited only the unprepared. Nor did the legacy of anti-imperialism arouse fears of catastrophe. The anti-imperialists had never feared war. Their main concern had been that victory might transform the Republic into an empire. They worried more over the possibilities of corruption and conquest than the possibility of defeat or the reality of destruction and death. Even if anti-imperialists had emphasized the connection between war and expansion, they would not necessarily have viewed the contest as cataclysmic. War had started over differences among European powers that had little to do with American involvements abroad. Furthermore, the administration had repeatedly disavowed any territorial ambitions and proclaimed this country's allegiance to the antiexpansionist ideals of national self-determination and defense of democracy.

Those who worried over America's unpreparedness criticized the nation's military defense and predicted defeat if war was declared. "As matters stand to-day," one author said, "our nation is doomed to irretrievable disaster in its next war." [18] These accounts pictured the enemy, usually Germany, invading the United States and forcing its unmobilized people to sue for peace. An indemnity would be demanded and often land would be occupied, but almost always the nation could be saved by a miraculous invention that would blow up the invading army. Such books, far from emphasizing the abomination of war, were "preparedness" propaganda designed to frighten people into supporting a large army.

What then, of the many Americans who approved of the war? Why, when fear of cataclysm had haunted America for years, did they gladly embrace a real catastrophe? The most obvious explanation—that the United States could afford to be undisturbed because she was not a belligerent—can be disposed of immediately, for our entry into the war only increased this enthusiasm.[19]

Of course, there was that most tangible of motives, material gain. Almost everybody benefited by the war. There was much sentiment among businessmen and bankers who were making profits on sales and loans to the allies. Agriculture and labor also had a vested interest in the war. Farmers and workers "never had it so good."

Prosperity, however, had not always been able to dispel gloom. The twenty years before the war had for the most part been an era of plenty, but the voices of doom had not been stilled. Nor did prosperous German-American farmers welcome belligerency. Before this country entered the conflict, some people were even ashamed of the bounty gained in the war. "We are in a perilous period of American democracy," declared a writer in *The Atlantic*. "We are threatened with what bankers and fools call prosperity; we are threatened with wealth which we have not earned and do not deserve." [20]

There was something else, some element that made many Americans seek salvation in the marching of armies and the reports of battle courage—that enabled them to find reassurance in destruction and hope in death. This element was the reawakening of national pride. Even before our entry into the war, people envied the war-inspired patriotism in Europe. A *Nation* editorial praised "the resources of patriotic heroism, the sense of the true meaning of national life, and the willingness to do and suffer everything for the sake of country." Not even a "champion of international peace can be so indifferent, as not to be profoundly touched by these moving exhibitions of the grandeur of human nature under mighty stress." [21] One enthusiast thought that "this war is creating in every European country a flood of new and finer loyalties, patriotic affects born of sacrifice and tears." He wondered whether "the sea which separates us from the war [would not] separate us from these finer things also." [22]

Such enthusiasts stressed individual fulfillment as well as national spirit. Novelist Robert W. Herrick repudiated his pacifism after he came to see that "war is a great developer as well as a destroyer of life. Nothing else, it would seem in our present stage of development presses the cup of human experience so full of realization and understanding as battle and death." [23]

Those who believed that war would reinvigorate patriotism were not disappointed in 1917. Disaffected groups rallied to the nation. New England Brahmins, long alienated from modern America, responded to the apparent return to older traditions. Aristocrats who had grown ever more conscious of their ties with England and France as they felt America diverge from her proper course, found reaffirmation in the fight on the side of the Allies. For them, "the anguish of the night . . . [was] past." [24] Even the Socialist Party embraced the cause. Such leading lights as John Spargo, Max Eastman, John Reed, Charles Edward Russell, William J. Ghent, William English Walling, and the 1916 Presidential candidate, Allen Benson, substituted patriotism for class consciousness.[25]

The new unity made Americans more confident. They became skeptical of ominous oracles. A writer in *The Century* disagreed with the faint-hearted "who have foreseen a race war in store for us," "who fear a new secession as the land fills up or if interests grow more contradictory," or "who prophesy a conflict of class amounting to a revolution." The war, he declared, "has come to everyone of us, of whatever region or whatever class. We know that we shall stand or fall together, and all the more because we have now seen the one other country of our size in the world fall before our enemy because it was divided." [26] *The Nation* shared this confidence born out of the great outburst of patriotism. It scoffed at those who had thought America impotent or divided. Even "talk of the achievement of American unity" made the magazine impatient because it implied previous dissension. Far "nearer the truth," claimed the periodical, was that the war "has revealed American unity." [27]

Unitey, however, was a symptom, not a cause. Why were all her people suddenly behind America? Unity for what aim? Patriotism from what source? There were as many answers to these questions as there were opinions about the war. Some rushed to the nation's defense because she was threatened with violent destruction. "I join no crusade," were the words of William E. Borah. "I make war alone for my countrymen and their rights, for my country and its honor." [28] Many eastern patricians saw in the war a broader purpose than self-defense. They were fighting to preserve a common culture, a common way of life shared by the United States, England, and France. Henry James applied for British citizenship because he wished "to testify at this crisis to the force of any attachment and devotion to England and to the cause for which she is fighting, . . ." [29] But the most visionary conceived of the conflict as a world-wide struggle for liberty. This vision was held by those who followed Woodrow Wilson down the historic path of American idealism.

America had been a country with a mission since the Pilgrims disembarked at Plymouth Rock. At first, that mission had been to set up a commonwealth of God's chosen, to create a nation in His image that would teach the world how to walk with God. One hundred fifty years later the specific message had changed, but America was still to be the deliverer of the world—the last refuge of liberty, the land that received the world's oppressed and recreated them in the womb of freedom. Almost another century passed before national messianism again came to the fore. Once more the United States was to be an example to the world. Other countries would be shown that freedom could stand the test of time, the strain of every-day existence. America preserved liberty in the face of the gravest of threats, civil war. By 1917, there had been fifty years since the last crusade. The nation had prospered and progressed, but Americans were not satisfied with material accomplishments alone. There had always been a strong undercurrent of idealism ready to burst forth and wash away the stains of the every-day, make-a-living world. For a brief period in 1898, it seemed as if that might happen. But imperialism contradicted the best part of the American creed—it did not have the ring of freedom, and it was quickly cast aside. Now another challenge rose. The challenge of making the world safe for democracy. American messianism had taken a new turn. No longer was this country merely the refuge of democracy; she was now its missionary. The United States was engaged in a crusade to convert the world to that holiest of all American beliefs, liberty. Swept up in this great crusade, in this new mission, citizens forgot the confusion and the fear of disaster that had been so widespread in the years of industrialization and growing imperialism. Like Anteus returning to the earth, America regained its strength by turning back to its bedrock of idealism.

No one had been more eager for peace, no one had feared war more than the President. In 1911, he told his private secretary, "I do not know, Tumulty, that I would care to be President during the next four years. . . . For the next President will have a war on his hands, and I am not sure I will make a good war President." [30] As late as January, 1917, he promised Edward M. House that "this country does not intend to become involved in this war. We are the only one of the great white nations that is free from war to-day and it would be a crime against civilization for us to go in." [31] On the very eve of his war message to Congress, Wilson sickened at the thought of taking the country into battle. He called in an old newspaper friend and spilled out his heart to him. When Frank Cobb came to the White House that night, the President looked worn from worry and lack of sleep. Speech tumbled out from the depths of his sadness. He told Cobb of the internal and international danger of involvement. War would "overturn the world we had known" as people turned irrationally bellicose. When the struggle ended, the belligerent powers would "attempt to reconstruct peacetime civilization with war standards, and at the end of the war there will be no bystanders with sufficient power to influence the terms." Domestic institutions and values would suffer as much as international relations. Single-minded pursuit of victory was bound to encourage repression and brutality. "Once lead this people into war and they will forget there ever was such a thing as tolerance. To fight you must be brutal and ruthless, and the spirit of ruthless brutality will enter into the very fibre of our national life." He doubted whether the Constitution or the Bill of Rights would survive the duration. Wilson ended his desperate soliloquy with the plea that "if there is any alternative, for God's sake, let's take it." [32] The next day he turned to Tumulty and said, "Our life, therefore, until this thing is over, and God only knows when it will be over, will be full of tragedy and heartache." Then his head sunk to the cabinet table and he sobbed unashamedly.[33] No one had felt the tragedy of the war more deeply; no one would be more caught up in the hope of victory.

Once war had been declared, Wilson cast off his somber doubts and treated it as a great crusade. This son of a Presbyterian minister used the Presidency as his pulpit and preached his militant sermons to a nation-wide congregation. He asked America to embark on a new mission of fighting to end all future conflict, to take up the sword to spread the principles of peace and democracy throughout the world. No man believed so much in this great purpose, expressed the ideal better, or was more tragically involved in its bitter aftermath than its great prophet, Woodrow Wilson.

On many occasions, Wilson gave voice to his message, but he was seldom more eloquent or more moving than on Memorial Day, 1917. The struggle he said was not merely one "in defense of American honor and American rights." It was "even greater than that." It was "the struggle of men who love liberty everywhere." In it America would attain her full dignity and "the full fruition of her great purpose." Tragic as the event was, it was also an opportunity to show by "the pouring out of our blood and treasure" the principles by which we profess to live. In "the providence of God," the time had come in which "America will once more have an opportunity to show to the world that she was born to serve mankind." [34]

Freedom and sacrifice, who could withstand their call? Certainly not Americans who for years had been haunted by the fear of losing the one for lack of the other. Would not this wave of idealism roll back the dark waters of despondency? Would not all thoughts of disaster be drowned in this crest of hope?

Enthusiasm for the war rose from radically different motives. On the one hand, the war brought great material advantages; running counter to this trend was the spirit of idealism, of sacrifice for the principle of world democracy. Was this idealism a rationalization for profits grasped with bloody hands, or was it the reaffirmation of what was noblest in the American spirit, a nobility that had been striving in vain for expression through more than fifty years of unscrupulous wealth-gathering? More than likely it was both. At least both existed, and perhaps the emphasis depended upon the individual. Yet even today, one is carried away from such rational explanations by memories of the tight-lipped figure of Wilson, in whom burned the flame of American idealism: the man who could not reach the people yet expressed their noblest sentiments; a truly tragic figure who carried America on the strength of his convictions and was deserted by her at the moment of their realization; a self-made idol who fell victim to his dream, to the American dream.

PART THREE

THE

CATACLYSMISTS

A STUDY of its historical context indicates the scope of cataclysmic thought, but only by probing the personalities of prominent cataclysmists can the intensity of this feeling be discerned. The biographical approach provides material from which to make finer distinctions between oracles of doom and other social critics, between gloomy remarks and cataclysmic convictions.

The biographical dimension is especially necessary when reality and opinion diverge, when there is a gap between expectations and events. If catastrophic forecasts prove to be false, subjective factors must have distorted perspectives. Since personal outlook is shaped by social position and determines social consciousness, character analysis permits a finer perception of the mentality that makes erroneous judgments. Cataclysmic thought is a constant interplay of inner feelings and outer forces. How they influence each other is as much a matter of individual motivation as of objective conditions.

6

Populist Portraits

WHEN AMERICA WAS YOUNG, the farmers boldly claimed national hegemony. They felt that leadership was theirs by right—by right of their labor, which brought forth the sustenance of life from the soil, and by right of the position of agriculture as the repository of republican virtue. With the coming of industrialization, however, America forsook the "noble yeoman," who responded by grimly prophecying disaster for a country that had fallen from agrarian virtue. The farmer, eclipsed politically and socially, was also harried by a twenty-five year depression. His economic plight would have seemed more endurable had it been caused by poor crops or bad soil. But the sight of splendid yields rotting because there were no consumers embittered him. To bring forth abundance by loving and skilled efforts on the land epitomized the agricultural spirit. When experts blamed agricultural productivity for the farmer's poverty, it was as if society were telling him that the reason for his existence was the condition of his failure.

Faced with such a situation, the farmer had two alternatives. He could discard the myth of the noble yeoman and attune himself to the needs of the market, or he could attack the society in which his values were irrelevant. He could either accept the business ethic and adjust to industrial America or make one last defense of a way of life that had been celebrated since Hesiod.

Such a defense rested on two assumptions. The first was that agriculture was both morally and economically necessary to national survival and that in denying the farmer the country imperiled its own existence. The other was that the farmer was emotionally, as well as intellectually, disturbed about his alienation from modern America. From beliefs in the rectitude and necessity of his way of life came the refusal to adapt to industrialism. From his deep commitment to agrarian values and genuine despair over their decline in postbellum America came his utterances of impending doom.

Out of these feelings arose a literature of protest. It reflected the loneliness of rejection and the suspicion that stemmed from seeing the fruits of one's dearest labor go unappreciated while others pre-empted the places of honor and power. This literature was not confined to isolated statements, stump speeches, occasional pamphlets, and fire-eating editorials. Two Populist leaders wrote full-fledged documents of doom. In point of time, literary importance, and the author's eminence, the first was Ignatius Donnelly's *Caesar's Column*.

IGNATIUS DONNELLY

Unlike most other Populists, Donnelly had not been born a farmer and a westerner. He was already a young man when he left Philadelphia in 1856 to seek his fortune as a land speculator and real-estate operator in Minnesota. For a while he rode the western land boom, his only care being how to "dispose" of the "great fortune" he was about to acquire.[1] Identifying his own prospects with those of the nation, he brimmed over with the spirit of "Young America." "There is scarcely an active or enterprising mind in this country but has at this time a look Westward," wrote Ignatius in 1857. "The West has been for years, still is, and for years will continue to be the realized El Dorado of the world." [2]

Individualism was the only way of life for those who dwelled in the promised land. "You should act for yourselves," said Donnelly with the certainty of a man whom fortune was about to honor for effort and resourcefulness. "Communism" would never "work in the Western prairie" because "where many are united in equality, important matters are often neglected." [3]

Ignatius went west intending to become rich—and went bankrupt instead. Nininger City, Minnesota, the germ of his dream of a great metropolis, was destroyed in the Panic of 1857, and with it went his creed of rugged individualism. This early defeat set a lifelong pattern. Great schemes ending in repeated failures eventually turned the cocksure, enthusiastic youth into a skeptic who doubted the future of the country that denied him fame and fortune.

Donnelly turned to politics after his dreams of material success were shattered. At twenty-eight, he was elected lieutenant-governor of Minnesota and went to Congress in 1862. For a time, the "Sage of Nininger" was the rising star in state politics. He was only thirty-one and, except for James Garfield, who was a few days his junior, the youngest member of the House. Once again, however, Donnelly was stopped short on the edge of success. His downfall came about when he embarrassed his party by uncovering fraud in the Indian Bureau and antagonized powerful leaders by an impetuous and undignified attack on another congressman. After his failure to be elected to a fourth term in the House, Donnelly's political career revolved more about seeking than holding office. Never again did he achieve a position as high as congressman.

Before his defeat, Donnelly sounded very much like other G.O.P. fledglings. He loudly proclaimed the nationalism, westernism, and Republican orthodoxy that were standard equipment for young politicians trying to sell themselves to party chieftains. Ignatius, however, leavened this conventional creed with sympathy for the underprivileged. Here was the one area in which he opposed the party sachems, and, in the case of the Indian frauds, it cost him his career. At first, his humanitarianism competed with opportunism, but it became the dominating impulse when his own political and economic losses finally drove him into the ranks of the reformers.

In the stirring years of the 1860's, however, Donnelly was chiefly distinguished for Spread-Eagle nationalism. His creed expressed patriotic belief in continental domination, democracy on trial before the world, America's ability to turn immigrants into productive citizens, and the indispensability of a strong central government. It was a belief that combined the soul of "Young America" with the fleshly federal dispensations of the "Pork Barrel" era.[4]

Like his nationalism, Donnelly's support for immigration was a carry-over from his Democratic days in Philadelphia. America had been good to his father, an Irish farmer who became a physician, a member of the city school board, and founder of the Philadelphia College of Medicine. Donnelly, personally familiar with this chapter of the immigrant success story, sought to make it come true for others. His maiden speech in Congress was a paean to the newcomers who contributed mightily to western prosperity.

Donnelly's sympathies were motivated by more than practical calculations. With impassioned equalitarianism he declared that "a new era in the development of the human race . . . is to be found in its breaking down of old prejudices and illiberalities; in its opening to all men of all races and colors equal opportunities of advancement." America advanced the principle of tolerance and its own greatness by fusing "the heterogeneous mass into a population intelligent, enterprising, patriotic, ready to spend their hearts' best blood in defense of the institutions transmitted to them by their emigrant fathers, and which have so incalculably blessed and benefitted them." [5]

A less noble variation of nationalism was Donnelly's use of nationalism to justify exploiting a bountiful federal government. As a westerner and a Republican, he felt that the nation could be best developed through the benevolent cooperation of government and business. From this conviction came his fight for railroads, internal improvements, and other party measures. He criticized the "poor, lame, blind, State sovereignty" as a "bastard of the old Confederacy," and echoed former generations of western representatives that "we look to the nation for protection. . . . We are willing to trust the nation." [6]

Public spirit was not the only reason why Donnelly blessed the union of federalism with vested interests. He had his eye on the main chance and was not above accepting emoluments. There was, for example, the $10,000 in stock given him by the Lake Superior and Mississippi Railroad for legislative services.[7] He served not only for cold cash—the way of political advancement also lay in aiding the corporations.

What, then, was Donnelly's primary reason for serving eager feeders at the "great barbecue?" Was he looking for personal economic gain and political triumph, was he sincerely determined to protect the West, did he really believe that prosperity would percolate down to the poor? When personal ambition and public welfare conveniently harmonized, Donnelly could rationalize support for the privileged. But there were occasions when altruists had to stand up and be counted, when Ignatius Donnelly had to make his choice and could not cloak opportunism with a few kind words to the unfortunate.

At such moments, Donnelly usually remembered that he had been a farmer as well as a plunger and a politician. He, too, had tilled the soil in Nininger City. He, too, was falling behind in the race for wealth, power, and prestige. A crusader for agrarianism, he considered "the subdivision of the land among the people" of prime importance. Land was "the original parent of all wealth; its blessing should be wide-spread and should reach as many as possible." Otherwise, "it will concentrate in a few hands, and then will follow plethora for the few and pauperism for the many, until at last we realize the pitiful lamentable conditions of Europe." [8] To ensure wide distribution Donnelly advocated the sale of Indian lands at a low and fixed price, and he sought to extend the payment time on homesteads.

When the interests of the small farmer were at stake, even the G.O.P.'s most treasured schemes were not safe from Donnelly's attacks. The Representative from Minnesota presented bills to tax government bondholders and opposed a party plan to make United States bonds and notes redeemable in gold. His speech against a gold-backed currency previewed later western radicalism. The Nininger farmer argued that the bill would drive out greenbacks, thus placing "the debtor class of this country entirely at the mercy of the creditor class and . . . result[ing] in widespread injustice and injury to the country." [9] When the yeomanry was attacked, Donnelly ceased to be a rubberstamp Republican.

Human compassion often turned Donnelly from the path of orthodoxy. Cries from the weak and the poor rarely penetrated the Republican elephant's tough hide as it fed at the trough of big business. But Donnelly's skin was thinner, and his sensitivity frequently led him to champion groups that the party ignored or exploited. This humanitarianism was reflected and reinforced by the tenderness of a loving family.[10]

His warmth was not restricted to the family, however. Donnelly loved to be with people. Such notations as "Met many friends"; "great fun and good humor"; and "Eller and I passed the time agreeably discoursing about philosophy, law and literature," abound in his diary. Even more fun than informal gatherings were the crowds that came to hear him speak. The plaudits he received at the podium or the stump occasioned the most gratifying entries. "I am glad to see that my reputation is growing as indicated by the increasing size of the audiences that greet me," he once confided. Even more gleeful was another statement: "Made a great hit. Audience did not want me to stop." A man who exists on popular praise, however, takes the risk of seeing crowds surround other platforms and of hearing someone else's applause. How did Donnelly react when the spotlight shone on others, when the cheers changed to jeers and the hurrahs sounded only in his memory?

Donnelly may have lived for the people's praise but he did not live off them. He was not a demagogue who detested men while trying to use them. Ignatius loved humanity as individuals, trusted them in the mass, and fought to give them a chance for happiness. A conviction of innate human goodness and a sense of justice inspired all his crusades. As early as 1866, while still a young politico, he declared this faith:

> I challenge the history of the past to produce a single instance where a revolution has occurred under equal laws in the attempt of any class to rise above the level of common rights to oppress any other portion of the population. The selfishness of human nature is not capable of such an effort. But I likewise challenge the historian to point to a single community where unjust laws did not sooner or later result in wars and turbulence,—both attempts springing from deep-seated sentiments of the human heart.[11]

His very first political conversion was made in the name of equity. Soon after arriving in Minnesota, Donnelly repudiated the Democrats because they denied the right of human dignity to the Negro. Later, as Lieutenant-Governor, he aided another depressed class, the farmers, by supporting debtor-agitated relief measures— a "Stay Law" extending mortgage payments, an "Interest Law" lowering interest rates, and an "Appraisement Law" to prevent creditors from getting foreclosed property at depreciated values.

As a Congressman, Donnelly continued to fight for the oppressed. His speech for immigration was the first in a series of pleas for the unfortunate. In those days, Donnelly believed that education offered the best chance for improvement. He had great faith in its ability to raise the prospects of others, for he had seen how learning lifted his own family. From a poor immigrant background, his father had become a physician, his sister a nationally known poet, and he a prominent politician. Enabling the underprivileged to improve themselves would facilitate wide acceptance of national ideals and institutions. Education would encourage social harmony.[12] Opportunity, however, was not the only consideration. His own intellectual curiosity was a deeper source of his interest in education. When the young settler first came to Nininger, he assumed responsibility for the community's cultural life. For his part in starting a newspaper and initiating other intellectual activities, he was dubbed the "Sage of Nininger" by fellow pioneers. Throughout his life, Ignatius remained an omnivorous reader and an avid researcher. He always admired learning, both in himself and in others, and his diary is full of references to the well informed, "cultured" men and women whom he met.

When the interests of persecuted minorities were at issue, Donnelly would not compromise even if it meant his career. He had already antagonized powerful Republicans by exposing chicanery in the conduct of Indian affairs when he gave further offense by expressing sympathy for the party's bitterest foe, advocating a Reconstruction policy of firmness without harshness. "Surely Mr. Speaker," he once said, "we should approach this grave and solemn question with none of the bitter sentiments of partisans." [13] In 1867, when the South was suffering a food shortage because of crop failures, he backed these words with action. The South's plight offered a chance to restore national unity and to help people in distress, two goals close to his heart. Through northern assistance, the South would be shown that "this war is at an end." Once again, brotherhood would prevail and "this Government of ours" would be based "upon the love of the people."

Ultimately Donnelly's purpose was not calculating. It was the heartfelt plea of a humanitarian who knew no friend and no enemy, no North and no South.

> It is not for us to ask by what means they have reached that condition, . . . It is sufficient for us to know that within the limits of our country, under the flag of the United States, human beings, our fellow citizens, are suffering from the pangs of starvation, are in imminent danger of that most terrible of all deaths, to silence all political hatred. In the presence of death the acrimony of politics should disappear; nothing should be heard but the voice of humanity.[14]

Donnelly's notion of justice was firm in the face of economic and racial bounds, nor was it limited to one sex. In a day when few doubted the inferiority of women, he was appalled at their subservient status. Here again family experience shaped his attitude, for his feminism was based on his love and admiration for his wife, mother, and sister. These feelings were buttressed by his life in the West, where pioneer women gravely coped with everything from childbirth to Indian raids. It was Donnelly the devoted son, brother, and husband, and Donnelly the frontier settler who saw "wicked usage" in giving "to the best and most deserving portion of the race one half the wages of men for the same kind and amount of work" and in excluding "women from trades and professions they are fitted to enter."

Indians, immigrants, farmers, Confederates, Negroes, and women—the persecuted and the denied had found a champion. Perhaps it was not so much Donnelly's values as the organizations through which he strove to implement them that changed when he became associated with unpopular causes and pariah parties. But in the 1860's, tomorrow still held promise, and it seemed as

if the United States was indeed a republic of virtue in which all
social ills would eventually be cured. "We are a free people," he
declared. America was an "eminence" from which liberty "plumes
her wings for loftier flights," a "fulcrum where from she shall
move the world." [15] To the young congressman, riding the crest of
his success, freedom meant progress, and progress would end in
perfection. "And who will dare to say," he demanded optimistically
in 1864, "that in the long fight of the centuries error is not hourly
losing blood and strength and life; . . . that truth is imperishable,
and that no human power can destroy it." [16]

Eventually, however, Donnelly went plummeting down, while
the world passed him by. After he failed to get re-elected, the edifice of his Republicanism, built to house a successful political career,
began to crumble. It did not fall at once, and there was more than
one attempt at reconstruction, but gradually—through an idea here,
a conviction there—it declined until, with another decade, Donnelly found shelter in the reform movement. The first breach
occurred in 1869, when Donnelly denounced the protective tariff.
The following year, he drifted even further from his conservative
moorings by coming out for an income tax and joining an independent agrarian party.

His reform activities intensified Donnelly's bitterness at being
rejected by the Republicans, and this rejection in turn strengthened
his maverick predispositions, driving him still further from his
earlier orthodoxy. "There is no other political party in the world
that would have permitted one of its representative men, one of its
most laborious laborers to be trampled under the feet of a stranger,"
went the first of many such allusions in his diary. "I am not
disgraced for I defended myself in a manner that the foul beast
who attacked me will never forget," he continued in a tone of self-
justification, "but the State of Minnesota and the Republican Party
stand disgraced before the world as a cowardly, cringing, time-
serving community." A few weeks later, the Republicans were
"these foul beasts who sought to kill me as skunks kill their prey—
first dishonoring and then destroying me." Donnelly's initial
reverse revealed characteristics that were to mark subsequent setbacks. Egotism prevented him from accepting defeat. His failure
was not the private disappointment of a minor officeholder—it was
a blot on the state and the party, a sign of their cravenness and corruption, a mark of Cain before the world. Nor were his opponents
mere rival candidates; they were arch conspirators who would stop
at nothing to crush him. Donnelly transformed his defeat into a
gallant crusade against evil forces, a brave struggle in which he

was finally overcome by vicious tactics and superior force. The office was theirs, but the glory was his.

Defeat sensitized as well as embittered him. "Poverty is a horrible thing," wrote Donnelly in 1870. "It is nothing but unsatisfied wants, restricted capabilities, undeveloped virtues." [17] To the ebullient congressman poverty had seemed temporary and easily cured, but the defeated man acquired a deeper awareness. He knew that he and the poor shared a common bond—failure.

Despite occasional lapses. Donnelly continued to shed old loyalties. In 1871, he cast off the railroads. "I have not . . . been benefitted a farthing by the construction of the road," he wrote Jay Cooke on July 29. Not only was he bitter about failing to cash in on Cooke's schemes, but he also felt that the Northern Pacific had been "the principal means of my defeat [for Congress] last fall." [18] As usual, personal disappointment registered itself in a change of public position. In a speech on July 4, Donnelly warned that railroads were bidding for control of the nation's "politics" and attempting to "corrupt its law." "If they can't behave themselves," he demanded that the people "put them in irons." [19]

Despite his political and economic disappointments Donnelly did once again adhere to orthodox politics in support of that champion of *bourgeois* respectability, Horace Greeley. Mugwumpery, however, was only a stopover for one who was now permanently moving out of the orbit of the major parties. In 1873, after organizing a Patrons Of Husbandry Lodge and becoming a Grange lecturer, Donnelly irrevocably committed himself to agrarian dissent. At the first convention of the Anti-Monopoly Party, in 1873, he wrote off the older organizations: "We can't look for a remedy in the Republican Party," he asserted. "Its brains and its pocketbook were in New England." As for the Democrats, Ignatius placed "its brains and its pocketbook" in the "South." [20]

Donnelly followed the course of the farmers' protest. He moved to the Greenback Party when the ebbing of the Grange tide stymied his attempts to regulate railroads. Switching to the new party involved discarding the last remnant of his Republicanism— a hard-money policy. As late as 1875, Donnelly had claimed that money "must in any event, rest upon a gold basis." [21] Two years later he recanted, claiming that gold no longer had to be "the exclusive currency of the nation." [22]

Ignatius Donnelly became a power in the new party. He was temporary chairman of the convention in 1876; two years later, he was a Greenback candidate for Congress. Donnelly lost the seat by a narrow margin in a bitterly fought campaign. Defeat was doubly painful because he was beaten by William H. Washburn, brother of Elihu Washburn, with whom Donnelly had had a scurrilous exchange on the House floor. The defeated candidate, charging that his opponent had won through bribery, took his case to the House Committee on Elections. At first, his prospects seemed favorable, but he met with reverses and by March, 1880, was "quite sick" with "nervous prostration . . . weak and depressed, with the feeling that the ground is being bought away under my feet and that I am powerless to prevent it."

The long drawn-out defeat left Donnelly despondent. His diary for 1880 is filled with self-pitying comments. "I make no headway," he wrote in May. "An adverse fate seems to drag me back." It galled him to see "men with much less real ability— riding on the top of the tidal wave of success while I am dashed around, despite heroic efforts, amid the sand and dirt of the breakers." October 27, his forty-ninth birthday, was "a sad day." He compared his career with that of his former colleague, Garfield. The divergence of their fortunes convinced him that his life had "been a failure and a mistake." So often had his hopes "come to naught" that he had ceased even "to hope."

He amplified his personal failure into national disaster. A private catastrophe meant that the United States was verging on ruin. When Donnelly took time from his self-pity to contemplate the forthcoming presidential campaign of 1880, he imagined "a battle of money against money—The capital of the East against Tilden's personal millions. We are repeating the experiences of the Roman Empire when money settled everything." [23] Donnelly's faith in America had been part of his faith in himself. For a while, it had seemed as if his faith were justified. But fate raised his expectations, only to deny their fulfillment. A similar destiny appeared to be awaiting America. She too would be cut down in her prime; she too would be denied when her hopes seemed about to be realized.

Deeply disappointed in politics, Donnelly temporarily turned to literature. He completed three books in the 1880's and had almost finished a fourth when the decade ended. These works dealt with such diverse topics as glacial drift, the disappearance of Atlantis, literary criticism, and fictional cataclysm. Behind the disparity of the subject matter, however, lay two common elements: nonconformity and catastrophe.

Atlantis: The Antediluvian World was Donnelly's first effort. Originally appearing in 1882, the volume became one of the most popular and influential Atlantis studies. Prominent believers in

Atlantis credited him with founding modern Atlantism by applying the scientific method to the problem of the lost continent. Such compliments, particularly one from William Gladstone, temporarily dispelled the gloom of 1880.

Atlantis was the product of a quest for knowledge that encompassed everything from Egyptian myths to geology. It is an interesting example of Donnelly's quick but undisciplined mind and of the pride he took in intellectual endeavor. After several years of scientific study, Donnelly set out to prove the truth of the ancient story of fabled Atlantis, an Atlantic island supposedly sunk by volcanic action. His attempts to establish the existence and destruction of the island smack of the popular science of his day. The imaginative and superficially educated Donnelly had no difficulty in combining natural phenomena with myth.

More important than the author's pseudoscientific reasoning, however, was his concept of cataclysm, and his defiance of orthodox opinion. Atlantis, the highest ancient civilization, a country that had given birth to all subsequent culture, was destroyed with one blow. Only today, after thousands of groping years, had mankind surpassed the ancient civilization. Equally significant was Donnelly's defense of a minority view in science, similar to his stances in politics. As he defied political and economic experts with agrarian arguments, so he opposed scientists by insisting on the existence of Atlantis.

Thoughts of disaster agitated Donnelly. While he was writing *Atlantis,* he quoted a proverb about the world ending in 1881. While laughing off this dire prediction, he noted that man had "a continual apprehension of the smashing-up of all things." [24]

Although he denied that there would be such an end for our civilization, catastrophe fascinated Donnelly. It became the theme of his next book, *Ragnarok: The Age of Fire and Gravel,* written in 1883. Encouraged by the response to *Atlantis,* the Sage of Nininger attempted to explain another scientific curiosity, the origin of glacial drift. *Ragnarok* is characterized by two of Donnelly's favorite preoccupations: disputing experts and discussing disaster. He tried to prove that drift was not caused by a continental glacier but by a cataclysmic comet. As in *Atlantis,* a natural debacle had destroyed "a fair and lovely world, a world far better adapted to give happiness to its inhabitants than this storm tossed planet on which we now live." A failure in his own time, he allowed nostalgia for a golden age to pervade all his books.

Donnelly described this "world-convulsing catastrophe" with the same blood-curdling language he later used in *Caesar's Column.*

Fancy "a storm of stones and gravel and calydust," he asked his readers, "leveling valleys, tearing away and grinding down hills, changing the whole aspect of the habitable globe." In the devastating storm "roars the earthquaking voice of the terrible explosions." Burning "drifts of debris," deposited by the holocaust, produce "an unearthly heat, under which rivers, ponds, lakes, springs, disappear." People, "burned, bruised, wild, crazed, stumbling, blown about like feathers in the hurricane, smitten by mighty rocks, . . . perish by the million." After the tempest, a grim period of icy blackness descended upon a world over which "the remnants of poor humanity wander . . . stumbling awe-struck but filled with an insatiable hunger . . . living upon the bark of the few trees that have escaped, or on the bodies of the animals that have perished and even upon one another."

Catastrophe having blighted the preglacial "high stage of civilization," man began the long climb back from the cannibalistic savagery "of the Drift Age." Painstakingly, civilization was rebuilt, only to be destroyed once more when Atlantis disappeared.

Donnelly remained optimistic in the face of all this destruction. "So far as we can judge," he wrote, "after every cataclysm the world has risen to higher levels of creative development." Despite former cycles of civilization and savagery, divinely ordained "evolution" would continuously create "higher levels of development." Some day man would be emancipated from the vicious cycle of history; then would "the Cainlike in the race . . . gradually pass away, and the Christlike dominate the planet."

Despite this vision of ultimate utopia, Donnelly was less hopeful than he had been in *Atlantis*. In a thought that foreshadowed *Caesar's Column,* he predicted another catastrophe "if sensual sins grow huge; if brother spoils brother; if Sodom and Gomorrah come again." Should evil triumph "who can say that God may not bring out of the depths of space a rejuvenating comet."

The nature of the cataclysm in *Ragnarok* differed from that in *Atlantis*. In the later work, Donnelly predicted a future catastrophe and gave the disaster a moral dimension. Destruction was more than a physical phenomenon—it was divine punishment for sinful living. With this idea in mind, the author concluded his book with a sermon on the avoidance of doom. "Establish spiritual relations," he preached. "Open communications with God," and He "will fend off the comets with His great right arm and the angels will exult over it in heaven." [25] But man did not turn to God. More and more he chained himself to material desires, and a despairing

Donnelly ultimately issued *Caesar's Column,* an even more urgent warning that humanity stood on the edge of chaos.

Encouraged by his initial successes, Donnelly entered the field of literary criticism. Again he took an unpopular position, trying to prove that Francis Bacon was the author of the plays attributed to William Shakespeare. Donnelly championed Bacon, who had "saved the English yeomanry from being reduced to the present condition of the Irish peasantry," against Shakespeare, who had come from peasant stock and betrayed it.[26]

The Great Cryptogram was a failure: It received bad reviews and did not sell. As a result, Donnelly was "greatly disheartened and disappointed." Depressing thoughts of political defeat and personal "ill fortune," temporarily banished by the favorable receptions of *Atlantis* and *Ragnarok,* returned to plague him. Once more, "despite profound thoughts and superhuman industry," he was fated to "make no headway towards fortune." Another wave of paranoia engulfed him. The book had been "howled down by a corrupt press." Again, he became "poor and powerless," only able to "grind my teeth and cry out to heaven." The nation that rejected him must be rotten to the core. America was a country "where the rich are growing richer and the poor poorer; where corporations and capitalists are grinding the face of labor; where the sum of human misery is increasing everyday." Haunted by fears of national disintegration and personal impotence, he wondered how "God looks on and permits it all." [27]

By 1889, Donnelly's literary career seemed entombed beside his political prospects. In 1884, he had been defeated in a congressional campaign. Two years later, he was elected to the State Assembly on the Farmers' Alliance ticket, but he had a dreary term in the legislature. In the election of 1888, Donnelly repudiated the Farmer and Labor gubernatorial nomination to campaign for the Republicans. He did not regain the G.O.P.'s favor by stumping for them, but, in this way, he lost his place in the agrarian party. The following year, Donnelly met his most galling defeat. He failed to prevent Elihu Washburn, his old enemy in the House, from becoming Minnesota's senator. In the wake of this setback, he wrote *Caesar's Column.*

Rarely has a remark so clearly summed up a motive as the declaration of Ignatius Donnelly that "the idea of such a work came to me the night after Washburn was elected to the United States Senate." [28] *Caesar's Column* was written by an author who had confessed himself a failure as writer and politician. The aging reformer had completely changed from the youth who went west to court success.

Now a man of fifty-eight, Donnelly was reliving the frustrating memory of a career halted by a series of mishaps and reverses. The bitterness of defeat, combined with his reform ideas and humanitarianism, led him into agrarianism. Through a penchant for exaggeration, his disappointments had been magnified into global disasters. His personal frustrations, alienation from the dominant forces of society, and association with a great organization of dissent and reform—the stuff out of which Donnelly made his nightmarish book—finally coalesced and turned him into an American Jeremiah.

CAESAR'S COLUMN

On the day he finished *Caesar's Column,* Donnelly declared that he "was incited to write it by two motives—first to do some good; secondly to make some money, which I greatly need." [29] Such purposes could be aptly served by writing a utopian novel. The sale of Edward Bellamy's *Looking Backward* had uncovered a great demand for marketing political ideas in the form of utopias, a demand that authors hastened to fill. Donnelly's financial aim was splendidly accomplished. The novel went through twelve editions in six months; in a little over a year, 60,000 copies had been sold. Foreign readers were interested enough to warrant editions in Sweden, Norway, and three in England. By 1906, 260,000 copies had been sold, and the total sale has been estimated at 700,000. *Caesar's Column* became, next to *Looking Backward,* the most popular of the utopian novels. [30]

The utopian framework also suited Ignatius because it was a facile vehicle for social criticism. Portraying an ideal state easily led to discussion of America's failure to achieve such perfection. Furthermore, Donnelly felt at home with such a theme because he had already made a study of Atlantis, the father of all modern utopias. Donnelly, however, wrote more than a description of paradise. Despondency and eccentricity led him to modify the medium by introducing an antiutopian theme. Although he wrote in Bellamy's genre, he depicted a civilization where evil triumphed. Not until the very end did a model society emerge.

Several publishers found *Caesar's Column* too incendiary, but it was lauded by many reformers. Cardinal Gibbons gave the book "unstinted praise"; Frances E. Willard hailed "Gabriel's triumph"; *The Arena* celebrated it as "the most remarkable and thought provoking novel that the disturbed industrial and social conditions of the present have produced"; and it had a great vogue among Bellamy nationalists and the Knights of Labor.[31] As was to be expected, however, the agrarians gave the volume its greatest acclaim. "Bellamy looks backward on what is impossible as well as improbable. *Caesar's Column* looks forward to what is not only possible, but probable," said Alliance leader Milton George.[32]

Much in *Caesar's Column,* designed to appeal to the public's taste, typifies the literature of the day. Taking his example from *Looking Backward,* Donnelly heavily flavored his work with science fiction. Like Bellamy's, his story abounds with references to electric trains, airships and air terminals, glass-covered roofs, and television. One of the popular pastimes of the age was speculating on the physical appearance of the future, and Donnelly regaled his readers with descriptions of New York City in 1988.

Another passion of the era was the sentimental love story. In standard melodramatic style, Gabriel Weltstein, Donnelly's hero, glimpses a beautiful blonde girl. From his friend, Maximilian Petion, he learns that she is unwittingly being groomed as the mistress for a corrupt millionaire. Our hero, determined to save her from a fate worse than death, steals into the plutocrat's palace to give warning. The heroine, whose soul is as bright as her hair, is shocked and indignant at hearing about her future prospects. She takes a knife from Gabriel to defend her virtue and, if necesssary (preferring death before dishonor), to turn it on herself. In a scene to which only Douglas Fairbanks could do justice, she is spirited away from the palace while the villain besieges her door. Gabriel, smitten with this chaste beauty, discovers that she returns his love. After appropriate blunderings, blushes, and declarations, they are united in holy matrimony. The melodrama is not without a touch of patriotism, for the object of Gabriel's affections is named Estella Washington and is supposed to be a direct descendant of the father of our country. Since Weltstein is a husbandman and her captor is called Prince Cabano, leader of a banking cabal that has enslaved the world, the rescue is symbolic of America's rescue by farmers from the financiers' depradations.

Petion also falls in love. His fair lady is Christina Olsen (also inevitably blessed with long golden tresses), the daughter of a poor but honest Scandinavian blacksmith. Max, a rich lawyer, must be absolved in Populist eyes. Purification is accomplished by his love for a daughter of the working class. It is typical of Donnelly's iconoclasm and intellectual pretensions that he idealized a cultured and wealthy lawyer, despite agrarian mistrust of this type. But

Donnelly could never forget that he himself had been born in Philadelphia, had become a lawyer, and had scholarly proclivities. Also typical, this time of Populist views, are the rural nuptials of both couples, for only pastoral innocence can be the scene of such pure marriages.

Popular science and romantic sentimentality were, however, only trappings for the real purpose of the book. The author had a three-fold aim. He wanted to publicize the terrible conditions of society, to point up the possibility of a holocaust if such evils remained uncorrected, and finally to offer a solution.

In accordance with Donnelly's goals, the first part of the novel is a bitter indictment of contemporary life. Twentieth-century civilization is described as the offspring of industrial capitalism. Measured by material accomplishments, it is impressive—Weltstein is at first overwhelmed by New York City's airships, glass-covered roofs, and exotic food. But all this luxury is merely a resplendent cover for a "civilization grown to be a gorgeous shell; a mere mockery, a sham outwardly beautiful and lovely, but inwardly full of dead men's bones and all uncleanliness."

This impression is confirmed when Gabriel visits what passes for a church and listens to what is supposed to be a sermon. The church is built of cold, white marble and is luxuriously furnished but without religious symbols. Its pulpit is occupied by a sensualist whose message is embellished with lewd invitations to the female members of his congregation. The minister, a materialist, asserts that, since there is no afterlife, his flock should seek worldly pleasures. He concludes by titillating the women with a lascivious pronouncement that sexual love is the only real love: "Love! Love! Entrancing, enrapturing Love! With its glowing cheeks—its burning eyes—its hot lips—its wreathing arms—its showering kisses—its palpitating bosom—its intertwining symmetry of beauty and loveliness." To the innocent Weltstein these words are blasphemy; to the more worldly Donnelly, however, they are the occasion of half-repressed envy expressed in condemnation of the successful.

Twentieth-century religion is thus viewed as apologia for the values and actions of the ruling class. A rationalization for selfishness, it is based on the prevailing Spencerian philosophy of tooth-and-claw competition. All animals, claims the minister, prey on each other in a merciless nature whose "skirts are wet with blood; her creation is based on destruction, her lives live only by murder." If this be the way of the world, man can not and should not help the unfortunate. Rather, "Let us rejoice that out of the misery of the universe we are reserved for happiness." Science no longer quests for truth; religion no longer serves the soul. They have perverted their original meanings and exist only to defend the old order in all its falseness and ruthlessness.

This sermon is an agrarian accusation against industrialism. Populists believed that the new modes of production reduced human relationships to matters of power and profit. No longer did the yeoman and the craftsman have personal contact with their colleagues and employees. The modern drive for colossal wealth through technological development forced people to think of each other in terms of adaptability and efficiency. Huge corporations widened the gap between owners and workers, robbed the skilled of personal pride in their product, and reduced labor to a unit of production to be reckoned by costs. This outlook even influenced those who fought it. Donnelly abhorred indifference to human suffering as the most vicious by-product of the machine age, but it molded his thinking nonetheless. The international organization of capitalism enabled him to conceive of disaster in global proportions; familiarity with technological impersonalism enabled him to describe, without wilting, the carnage and destruction of a world revolution.

Nowhere did denial of humanity seem more marked than in the city. To the agrarians, the city was the locus of Wall Street's schemes, the breeding ground of the infinitely corrupt and fabulously wealthy financiers. In *Caesar's Column,* the metropolis is the scene of a ghastly struggle between the haves and the have-nots, the center of wealth concentration and its progeny, class conflict and revolution. To Donnelly, propagandist of Populism, New York was a place where humanity had the weight of a feather when balanced against hard gold. The insane quest for gain had resulted in such self-estrangement that in "this city they actually facilitate suicide!" In "this vast, overcrowded city, man is a drug,— a superfluity,— and I think many men and women end their lives out of an overwhelming sense of their own insignificance;—in other words, from a mere weariness of feeling that they are nothing, they become nothing." Could the modern economic system be more completely censured than through the charge that human indifference had reached a point where ending existence had become more desirable than maintaining it?

So far in his book, Donnelly has been discussing the upper classes, the leaders of society. If their acquisitiveness has made them vicious, poverty has not exactly ennobled the masses. While visiting the slums, Gabriel sees that squalor has standardized the poor as wealth has molded the rich into selfish uniformity. What strikes him most "was their incalculable multitude and their silence." It is like "the resurrection of the dead; . . . these vast, streaming swarms were the condemned, marching noiselessly as shades to unavoidable and everlasting misery." They are "merely automata, . . . without heart or hope." Determined by "some ruthless and unrelenting destiny," they know "to-morrow could bring them nothing better than to-day—the same shameful, pitiable, contemptible, sordid struggle for mere existence."

Donnelly blamed the lot of the poor on "that 'Iron law of wages' . . . the reduction, by competition of the wages of the worker to the least sum that will maintain life." If "there is a hell in the spiritual universe," he would put in it "the souls of the men who originated, or justified, or enforced that damnable creed." Earlier, Donnelly had struck at religious and scientific rationalizations for the irresponsible quest after wealth. Now he attacked those descendants of Adam Smith who made economics a justification for the same ruthless individualism. *Laissez-faire,* to Donnelly, was based on disregard for the obligations of human brotherhood and social responsibility, and he abhorred it, whether it hid behind the sanctity of Darwin or the reputation of Smith. Neither truth nor virtue was embodied in the dismal pronouncements of Ricardo and Malthus or in the jungle-like utterances of Sumner and Spencer. Their doctrines led to the miserable existence of the work-wracked, mentally stunted, frightened, and frustrated poor. They had sentenced the masses to "toil, toil, toil, from early morn until late at night"; doomed them to an "endless, mirthless, hopeless round; until, in a few years, consumed with disease, mere rotten masses of painful wretchedness, they die, and are wheeled off to the great furnaces, and their bodies are eaten by the flames, even as their lives have been eaten up by society."

The division of society into the carefree rich and the hopeless poor had come about since the Civil War. Vote-buying, drinking, and atheism encouraged an oppressive plutocracy, which crushed the yeoman and expropriated his wealth. "At the close of the Nineteenth Century, in all the great cities of America there was a terrible outbreak of the working men," but that and similar uprisings had been crushed by the moneyed coterie. Since then, laborers "have become more and more desperate. . . . the yeomanry have lost possession of their lands; their farms have been sold under their feet, cunning laws transferred the fruit of their industry into the pockets of great combinations, . . . and the men who once tilled the fields as their owners, are driven to the city to swell the cohorts of the miserable, or remain on the land a wretched peasantry."

The antebellum yeoman, small businessman, and artisan had been destroyed by the machine age. Without the cement of these small property owners, Donnelly thought the country had split into two belligerent groups—one driven by oppression and the other by greed. Particularly dangerous to the nation's survival was the demise of the small farmer, America's backbone, the harmonizer of conflicts and contrasts. The tiller of the soil was neither rich nor poor, big nor small, exploiter nor exploited. A family man who worked alongside his hired hands, he retained the human touch. He owned his land and was thus independent—especially of the capitalists. In addition, the pre-Civil War farmer had been white, Protestant, and native born. Ruralism embodied the traditional values. It was all that contemporary America was not, the only hope for stability and moderation, the last chance for peace and survival. *Caesar's Column* is a bitter chronicle of the passing of agrarian America. Donnelly saw the new conquering the old, the city eclipsing the country, agriculture being swept away by industry. The intensity of his attack reveals his fear that Arcadia was passing— never to be recalled—and this despair generated Donnelly's cataclysmic tale.

Xenophobia was one manifestation of Donnelly's pessimism. The man who had once defended immigrants now joined the ranks of doubters and attackers, those who felt the nation was not big enough, rich enough, or strong enough to accommodate the newcomers. "The overpopulation of the globe will come soon enough," warned the author of *Caesar's Column*. "We have no interest in hurrying it. The silly ancestors of the Americans called it 'national development' when they imported millions of foreigners to take up the public land and left nothing for our own children." As the Immigration Restriction League registered Brahmin despair over lost status, so Donnelly's antipathy reflected agrarian alienation. He even mirrored the racism of displaced bluebloods. Gabriel, while visiting the proletarian quarters, is reminded by "the slant eyes of many, and their imperfect, Tartar-like features" "that the laws made by the Republic, in the elder and better days, against the invasion of the Mongolian Hordes, had long since become a dead letter." Like his unacknowledged Boston brethren, Donnelly lost faith in America when it appeared that his group would be swept aside in the nation's advance. He who had once glimpsed infinity when he gazed west now wondered if there were enough acres for his own people. He who had once championed the cause of all persecuted minorities hid his frustrations behind the fear-ridden prejudices of the racists.

The self-reliant pioneer who had once impatiently demanded that "every tub should stand on its own bottom" became a relic of the past along with the defender of the downtrodden. In his place was a frightened soul like a speck of dust in the universe, buffeted this way and that by forces over which he had no control. Donnelly's sense of feebleness reflected his isolation. He belonged to no religion or fraternal organization that could interpose itself between him and mass society. Alone in a hostile environment, stripped of any protection, he faced community-wide pressures. Personally frustrated by adversity, Ignatius concluded that all humanity was at the mercy of elements far beyond its power. His tale of the "Oligarchy's" rise is not unlike his explanation for his own fall. Society was enslaved by a bankers' conspiracy, which seized wealth and power by duping the farmers into giving up their rights and returns. Through "subtle combinations, 'rings,' 'trusts,' as they called them," financiers cunningly "transferred the substance of one man into the pockets of another, and reduced the people to slavery." The farmers were beaten in a foul fight by trickery and corruption. Only through violating that basic American ideal of fair play had the "Plutocracy" been able to win.

The triumph was due to neither strength nor courage, nor did it sustain itself by those virtues. Prince Cabano, the cabal's leader, is a physical coward who flees from Estella's knife. "The money power," by eschewing "all ideas of national glory," reflects its commander's cowardice. So unmilitary is the coterie that even its armed forces must be bribed for their support.

Conspiratorial government continues because of the money power's cravenness and fear of imminent class conflict. Meeting clandestinely, the group plans to crush the forthcoming rebellion. To forestall any proletarian surprise, it infiltrates their organization with spies. The height (or depth) of conspiracy is reached when the Oligarchy, fearing the independence of the air fleet, decides to liquidate the commander after the uprising is repressed. Government by stealth, violating hallowed canons of honesty and democracy, is the ultimate perversion of American character.

The conspiracy theme reflects Donnelly's belief that society had played him false. A paranoid conviction that he had been robbed of wealth, prestige, and political power led him to think of contemporary civilization as a vast swindle. Failure could be rationalized by attributing defeat to criminal conspirators. If these operators had conquered the whole society, how could Donnelly alone be expected to prevail?

The notion of conspiracy explained Donnelly's own inability

to realize his youthful potential, but explanations are not enough to neutralize the guilt and anxiety generated by failure. The frustration of defeat manifests itself in aggression and withdrawal—the attempt to grab what has been denied or the flight from competition due to lack of confidence. Projecting conspiracy serves both these moods. By branding the established order illegitimate, it justifies hostile aggression in the form of cataclysmic conflict. The envisioning of clandestine groups is, at the same time, a form of flight from society. But withdrawal and aggression can at best only externalize self-alienation. Visions of impending doom do not facilitate adjustment to the community, and belief in secret organizations intensifies anxiety by strengthening feelings of betrayal.

Oligarchical conspiracy must be answered by conspiracy from below. The "Brotherhood of Destruction" is also a secret organization. Vicious overlords create such fear and passion for revenge that a "desperate and bloody . . . conspiracy" has been formed. The Brotherhood borrows cloak-and-dagger tactics from the Oligarchy, and for the same end—obliteration of the enemy. The proletarians intend to accomplish their aims through barbaric brutality that matches the plutocrats' shrewdness. For, as the rich have grown hard-hearted in their pursuit of wealth and comfort, so poverty and tyranny have turned the masses into savages. Whipped into a vengeful frenzy and capable of nothing but destruction, they are about to destroy Sodom and Gomorrah in one wrathful day of judgment.

The Brotherhood captain personifies these traits. Caesar Lomellini is an Italian-born giant, a great brute of a man reduced to bestiality after creditors have seized his land and a lawyer has seduced his daughter. Brute that he is, the chief difference between him and the bankers is that "they are brutes who are in possession of the good things of this world; and Caesar is a brute who wants to get into possession of them. . . . they are polished and cultured brutes, and Caesar is the brute natural." [33]

Lomellini's history is a microcosm of America. He is the noble yeoman made savage after being stripped of his land and dignity. Donnelly drives this point home with obvious symbolism. The seduction of Caesar's daughter signifies Populist resentment of exploitative laws and deceitful legal minds. The very name "Caesar" suggests Rome, a republic that was destroyed by wealth, luxury, corruption, and class conflict.[34]

Gabriel makes a valiant attempt to prevent the forthcoming clash, but his failure only emphasizes the futility of individual effort. Donnelly's political activity had been a crusade to save

society, and Weltstein also becomes a would-be rescuer of civilization. As society's rejection of the author was evidence of its
suicidal tendency, so his protagonist's failure is a prelude to doom.
Gabriel is Ignatius fictionalized, come from pastoral Uganda to
preach the gospel of agrarianism to a sinning world, in much the
same manner as Donnelly came out of Minnesota to convert the
backsliding East. In fact, the name Gabriel was taken from the
archangel who called for Christianity to awaken nations slumber-
ing in vice.[35] Gabriel fails, however, as Ignatius had failed, and, in
a sort of perverted wish fulfillment, the catastrophe following
Gabriel's defeat takes the edge off Ignatius's own disappointments.

Weltstein twice tries to convince the belligerents that conflict
will end in disaster. First, he implores the Oligarchy to prevent
the bloodshed of revolution and repression. Gabriel begs them to
"yield a little of your superfluous blessings; . . . [to] save the
world from such an awful calamity!" But the Oligarchs reject his
plea because they want a "tremendous massacre" that "will strike
such terror into the heart of the canaille that they will remain sub-
missive to our will, and the domination of our children, for
centuries to come."

Gabriel represents one aspect of Donnelly's thought, the
principle of altruism—eventually Weltstein will reign as a benevolent patriarch in Uganda. Maximilian Petion, the secondary hero,
embodies another of Donnelly's convictions. He is a leader of the
Brotherhood and seeks revenge against the oppressive Oligarchy.
The action of Petion, and other victims of injustice precipitates the
uprising that enables Weltstein to found his utopia—and allows
Donnelly to become, vicariously, a statesman.

The dichotomy between Max and Gabriel is the American success formula. Achievement depends upon being well liked, and
Gabriel is certainly lovable, but affection unreinforced by respect
often leads to exploitation. Fulfillment also depends on a realistic
and aggressive quest for power. The shrewd and combative Petion
supplies this quality. All his life Donnelly had vainly sought that
balance of respect and love, that admiration that is the prime
requisite for success.

The rejection of Gabriel and the revenge of Max both explain
and justify the coming cataclysm. Revolution will occur because
the downtrodden want vengeance and because the rulers refuse to
modify their evil ways. By damning the established order, this line
of thought legitimizes its destruction.

Thwarted by the money power, Gabriel tries the proletarians.
At one of their meetings, he asks for peace and good will. This

gathering is interesting because it reveals another aspect of Donnelly's defeatist fatalism: the belief that individual effort can no longer save the nation because the disease is too critical. The remedy, therefore, must be basic and radical. Such half-way measures as education or the promise of salvation in heaven merely aggravate the evil.

One speaker at the workers' assemblage claims that universal education would solve society's problems. In his more sanguine years, Donnelly himself had subscribed to this notion. But this panacea had been discarded during the period of dissent. Now he argued that education was too superficial. It "is right; it is necessary," says Gabriel, "but it is not all-sufficient."

After the argument over education subsides, a gentle clergyman suggests that workers ought not to seek justice in this world but to purify themselves for the next. Weltstein disagrees with this plea for deferred happiness. To preach other-worldly bliss while ignoring earthly conditions is an invitation to further tyranny. He would substitute the social gospel for the gospel of "turn the other cheek": "What the world needs is a new organization—a great world-wide Brotherhood of Justice. It should be composed of all men who desire to lift up the oppressed and save civilization." [36] Love for their neighbors is, however, as alien to the oppressed masses as to their haughty masters, and they prefer unity for destruction to Christian brotherhood.

Donnelly's belief that only a divinely inspired "Brotherhood of Justice" could save the world came from his personal creed. God, for him was a "general intelligence behind nature," men "his [sic] agents to perform his [sic] work." It was characteristic of Ignatius to reject organized religion in favor of a universal prime mover. He despised all contemporary institutions for perpetuating the sins of modern civilization. Traditional sects were simply one more form of conspiracy against justice and happiness. In this manner, he painted the twentieth-century church and its up-to-date minister. Indeed, his entire chapter on the viciousness of religion in 1988 reflected an opinion that "religion . . . chloroformed poverty while vice robbed it." Hating all organizations sustained by respectable opinion, he charged religion with being "the half-brother of tyranny—the moral police force of the murderers of mankind. . . . preach[ing] submission to oppression and send[ing] billions of human beings through wretched lives to shameful ends." [37]

Imagining himself to be the champion of virtue against organized vice, Donnelly exalted the inspirational and ethical aspects of religion, the side of the prophets like Gabriel over ritualized sectarianism. For Donnelly—and for Donnelly's God—the sole condition of salvation was altruism.

Denial of Christianity was one more departure from traditional America, still another example of how industrialism had corrupted national spirit. Modern capitalism, bringing with it strange gods of change, progress, adaptation, and relativism, converted many to the new faiths of evolution and pragmatism. Donnelly, ever looking to the past, opposed these novel beliefs with the simple absolutes of the Sermon on the Mount. He asked Americans to remember the Christian morality of their primers and Sunday schools and to cast down these new idols.

Society's rejection of Christianity made the conflict absolute. Not only economic opportunity and political justice, but virtue itself, was at stake. The struggle between the farmer and the banker was no longer catastrophe; it was cosmic tragedy. Religious absolutism polarized the struggle. Gabriel and the conspiracies incarnated good and evil. If Gabriel triumphed, the Kingdom of God would be established; if not, civilization would be consumed. Absolutism was thus an impetus to cataclysm, for the angel and the devil's agents could never compromise, and an unrepentant society was doomed to a dismal end.

Traffic with the devil does not earn credits for the Day of Judgment, and those who flirt with Lucifer cannot be saved by a reformer's good will. Indeed, so vile is the state of things that even the criminal leaders cannot really be blamed. They live "in the culmination" of the "misdeeds" of our "blind, indifferent, heartless" ancestors. Donnelly removes the stigma of personal blame, thus underscoring the futility of forgiveness and making it still more imperative and still more inevitable that society be totally destroyed.

When Donnelly finally arrives at the cataclysm, he has had it both ways. He had been the messenger of peace and forgiveness; now he comes as an avenging angel. With the self-righteous anger of an unheeded prophet, he cries: "Two hundred years ago a little wise statesmanship might have averted the evils from which the world now suffers. One hundred years ago a gigantic effort, of all the good men of the world might have saved society." But now it is too late, "Now there is but one cure—the Brotherhood of Destruction." The nation shall pay for rejecting Gabriel, and Donnelly can derive vicarious satisfaction for his own years in the wilderness. Any lingering guilt about portraying national disaster or about his desire for revenge has been lulled by the Christlike failure of Gabriel. Thus Gabriel Weltstein-Ignatius Donnelly can look on in Christian horror, while ex-Congressman Donnelly, the embittered Populist, enjoys his grim retribution.

The debacle in *Caesar's Column* was conceived by a mind obsessed with violence. The conflicting forces are incapable of composing their differences within the system. Instead of seeking compromises, the rivals feel compelled to eliminate the opposition in order to save themselves. This cataclysmic impasse came from a personality torn by unresolvable contradictions. Donnelly's existence could seem meaningful only in a world divided by antagonistic forces: submission or mastery, deprivation or satisfaction, aggressiveness or passivity, survival or surrender, impotence or grandeur. Years of defeat gave rise to his paranoid perception of life. In his world, persecution was reality and any defense legitimate; vengeance became virtue and violence reason. The shame of having lost could be mitigated, the futility rising from alienation could be given direction. Even failure might be phantasized into victory, if the conquerors were also destroyed.

The holocaust begins when the commander of the air force is bribed to deliver the planes to the Brotherhood. Since the planes control the balance of power, victory has been decided before the first shot is fired. Fittingly enough, the Oligarchs are defeated by the same methods with which they first triumphed. Cunning and corruption are not steadfast allies; they can be turned against those whom they have long served.

The army, unaware of its betrayal, confidently marches into a trap set by the insurgents and the fliers. Strangely, Donnelly describes the handsome ranks of regulars as "a splendid sight." They are "the very efflorescence of the art of war—the culmination of the evolution of destruction—the perfect flower of ten thousand years of battle and blood." Their "banners, and uniforms and shining decorations" make a vivid "contrast with that gloomy, dark, ragged, sullen multitude." Donnelly's admiration for the soldiers reveals his yearning to be part of the established order. It is the secret longing of one who has struggled mightily, but unsuccessfully, for legitimate power. Underneath this praise, however, lurks a sadistic desire for revenge, a barely suppressed eagerness to see these splendid serried ranks torn to pieces by the enraged mob. How delicious is the destruction of respectability to those who have sought it in vain! A few pages later, and Donnelly has slaked his thirst for vengeance. The magnificent army lies crushed and bleeding as "dynamite bullets exploding in the soldiers, [tear] them to pieces, like internal volcanoes," while the traitorous pilots rain bombs upon them from above.

Despite Donnelly's vindictiveness, it is not without misgivings that he surveys the rout of the money power. Bad as the Oligarchy was, it had at least maintained order. This point did not escape the attention of a small property-owner like the Nininger farmer. Indeed, one reason he admired the army was its ability to restrain the mob. Consequently, once the threat from above has been eliminated, Donnelly dwells on middle-class fears of proletarian confiscation. Victory unleashes anarchy, pillage, murder, and rape by "a foul and brutal and ravenous multitude . . . dark with dust and sweat, armed with the weapons of civilization, but possessing only the instincts of wild beasts." The poor have triumphed.

Caesar Lomellini's brief reign is inaugurated by an orgy of horror and destruction. In a blend of sadism and retributive justice, Donnelly selects a few highlights from the host of atrocities. Prince Cabano, shot and slowly dying, uses the remainder of his fortune to bribe a thief to end his misery. Maximilian Petion makes flaming torches of the judge and perjured witnesses who sent his father to jail. The most blood-curdling scene of all, however, is Caesar's drunken inspiration to pile up the dead into a ghoulish monument of cemented skeletons. Called "Caesar's Column," this macabre monument symbolizes the ideals and accomplishments of the revolution. Lomellini asks Gabriel to inscribe it. His dedication is an indictment of society present and past:

IN

COMMEMORATION OF

THE DEATH AND BURIAL OF

MODERN CIVILIZATION

It is composed of the bodies of a quarter of a million human beings who were once the rulers, or the instruments of the rulers . . .

They were dominated by leaders who were altogether evil.

They corrupted the courts, and the juries, the newspapers, the legislatures, the congresses, the ballot-boxes and the hearts and souls of the people.

They formed gigantic combinations to plunder the poor; . . .

They used the machinery of free government to effect oppression.

. . . They degraded humanity and outraged God.

They were the culmination of centuries of misgovernment,

and they paid an awful penalty for the sins of generations of short-sighted and selfish ancestors . . .

From this ghastly pile let it derive the great lesson, that no earthly government can endure which is not built on mercy, justice, truth and love.

Violence does not end with the annihilation of the rich, however. There is also treachery among the Brotherhood leaders. The second in command, "a nameless Russian Jew," flies to Palestine with the booty of victory. The mob, now suspicious of the remaining leaders, kills Caesar and almost murders Max and Gabriel. Undisciplined without commanders, the revolution has degenerated into anarchy. During the "dreadful night" after they have deposed their captains, the rabble "invaded the houses of friend and foe alike, and murdered men, women and children. Plunder! Plunder! They had no other thought." Freedom withheld so long becomes license when finally won, and deprivation makes men mad with desire.

The uprising purges an evil civilization, but once society is demolished, the brutal masses are incapable of replacing it with something finer. The future holds naught but strife, starvation, and savagery. As the virtuous fly to safety, Max sketches the dismal existence awaiting the miserable masses. "After about three-fourths of the human family has died of hunger, or been killed, the remainder, constituting, by law of survival of the fittest, the most powerful and brutal, will find it necessary for self-defense against each other, to form squads or gangs." The "greatest fighter" among them "will become chief. . . . Then the history of the world will be slowly repeated" through centuries of slavery, commerce, and war. "And so, step by step, mankind will reenact the great human drama which begins always with a tragedy, runs through a comedy, and terminates in a catastrophe." As in *Ragnarok,* civilization is viewed as cyclical and man as irrevocably bound to the wheel of history. In his most sanguine moments, he can laugh, but he ends in doom.

The money power that has enmeshed Western civilization has dragged Europe, as well as America, into the holocaust. Donnelly, however, writing a didactic novel for an American audience, emphasized internal problems. Europe's involvement is hinted at only when the airship carrying the heroes to safety passes over the charred remains of the continent. Only Africa and Asia, which have not joined in the mad race for profits and progress, have been spared.

The survivors land in idyllic Uganda, the pastoral paradise

from which Gabriel started out. Here Donnelly creates a utopia, returning to his more characteristic role of reformer. But the disaffection pervading the cataclysmic portion of *Caesar's Column* influences even the most positive section of the novel. The location of utopia in the remotest possible place from America revealed the author's estrangement from his surroundings. Equally alien to contemporary conditions was the type of commonwealth established. Weltstein begins by invoking "Almighty God," source of all beneficence. Next he secures the foundations of "a republican form of government" by establishing universal suffrage and lodging political power chiefly in the rural middle class. The producers' prominence is reinforced by social safeguards. Universal, compulsory public education is provided to eliminate prejudice and ensure unity. Another measure to prevent the growth of an aristocracy is the limitation of possession of land and money. Equalization of opportunity is further guaranteed by abolishing interest and making paper money legal tender. In addition to all the other precautions against rebirth of the money power, urbanization is prevented by making each citizen a landowner. The government ensures social welfare, as well as equal opportunity, by ministering to community needs through state ownership of vital industries and regulation of working and living conditions.

Although professing democratic beliefs, Donnelly, as is made clear in Uganda's constitution, was an agrarian élitist. This disparity between republicanism and élitism is only one of many contradictions between denunciation and desire in Donnelly's mind. He attributes aggressive hostility, destructive urges, and dictatorial pretensions to the capitalistic cabal. These accusations, however, were projections of his own drives. He thirsted for violent revenge on those who had rejected his bid for power and, in portraying the people's uprising, showed as much contempt for the masses as had the Oligarchs. The holocaust is a prelude, not to an autonomous society, but to a community dominated by Gabriel Weltstein. Once again, Weltstein has acted as surrogate. Through his creature, Donnelly has at last assumed the leadership so long denied.

In *Atlantis* and *Ragnarok*, a golden age is destroyed by holocaust, and civilization must again struggle to the heights of a previous period. *Caesar's Column*, on the other hand, ends in utopia after disaster. But this pastoral paradise is also a glorification of the past. It is the type of society that Max looked back on when he spoke of a "golden age in America—an age of liberty, of comparatively equal distribution of wealth; of democratic institutions." [38] The two earlier works still hold out the hope of progress

—even if it is only hope for rebirth from disaster. But the future in *Caesar's Column* is really the past—it is the author's own youth recreated. He went west to fashion a community of happy yeomen, and, in Uganda, he vicariously realizes this wish. There is, however, one crucial difference between the anticipation of 1856 and the remembrance of 1889. The former mood was part of youthful ambition, of a conviction that the world was full of promise; the latter was a device to forget failure. Donnelly came to Minnesota expecting to carve a grand career. In his early years, he believed that status could be achieved through individual effort and sought to open up opportunities for the oppressed. *Caesar's Column,* however, is quite another story. Success is now the condition of villainy rather than virtue, and such underprivileged groups as foreigners and urbanites are dismissed with racist remarks and portrayed as anarchist mobs. These forces for social mobility have become accessories to civilization's downfall. The once progressive youth has become the most conservative of all cataclysmists with values, goals, and roots firmly planted in pre-Civil War America. The ideal state is a Populist paradise where the government ensures equality by excluding social and commercial aristocracies and prevents insidious urban poisons. It is a yeoman-centered, God-fearing republic in which rights, duties, and desires do not conflict. It is also however, a society in which nostalgia reigns and the past has triumphed over the forces for change.

Donnelly destroyed the present because it had betrayed him. Destiny refused him greatness, and defeat left him in despair. Unable to cope with his own age, he clung to an antebellum America. Reversing the course of history by proclaiming the ascendance of agriculture could scarcely, however, comfort a man whose life had been a constant pursuit of success in his own time. Donnelly's vision was rather a desperate avoidance of reality. He reveled in a double phantasy: the cataclysmic phantasy of destroying a society that denied his expectations and the utopian phantasy of a community in which they were realized.

Uganda was created out of memories of Minnesota in the 1850's. Those were days when Jacksonian slogans still had some meaning. Someone had said, "Go west, young man," and Ignatius Donnelly went West; someone had said "any man can be President," and he entered politics. As the years crept on, however, the slogans turned to mockery, and the fires of youth left behind the ashes of defeat. The dream of success had become the nightmare of failure.

MARY ELIZABETH LEASE

A sharper and shriller voice than Ignatius Donnelly's echoed from the plains and prairies in the 1890's. It belonged to that Populist Cassandra Mary Elizabeth Lease. Tall and spare, appropriately clad in black, she was hailed as "an orator of marvelous power and a phenomenal psychological force." [39] Time and again she ascended western platforms to exhort the farmers to "raise less corn and more hell." With blazing rhetoric she blasted capital, "the Vampire . . . [fattening] on the blood of the people," and warned that "the tendencies of the times are revolutionary." There would be a day of reckoning, she promised, because "the law of retribution enters into the lives of individuals as well as the history of nations." [40] An extraordinary woman was this Kansas fire-eater, invoking the wrath of God against those who would destroy the virtuous.

Mary Lease's childhood was somewhat similar to Donnelly's. She was born in Ridgeway, Pennsylvania, in 1853, six years after famine had driven her parents from Ireland. In 1873, after being graduated from a New York academy, she went to Kansas to teach in a parochial school. There she married a drug-store clerk named Charles Lease, and they tried to make their living homesteading. Farming proved quite unprofitable, and poverty drove them to Texas, where Mary took in wash to make ends meet. When the Leases came back to Kansas after ten years of struggling with the soil, their wealth consisted of four children.

Despite the burdens of poverty, family, and her sex, Mrs. Lease studied law and was admitted to the Kansas bar in 1885. It was at that time that she began to speak in public. Her first talks were for a cause also espoused by Donnelly—Irish freedom. It was but a step from agitating for the Irish to arguing for American farmers. Mrs. Lease became a member of the Union Labor Party in 1888, and the next year she worked with the Farmer's Alliance. These agrarian-labor organizations prepared her, as they did so many other Populists, for the great insurgence of the Nineties. By 1890, Mary was in great demand as a Populist lecturer. Within two years, she was prominent enough in the Peoples' Party to be given the honor of seconding the presidential nomination and accompanying Weaver on his campaign tour.

After the election of 1896, Mary came to New York City as a correspondent for the New York *World*. In this capacity, she attended the Democratic National Convention of 1900. Her fiery report of the proceedings indicated that she had dropped the agrarian cause for that of imperialism. She predicted that the Democrats would be defeated in the presidential campaign because the party was "on the wrong side of the expansion question." For someone who believed it was "as natural for us to take the Philippines as it was for our forefathers to take the thirteen colonies," anti-imperialism looked like political suicide.[41] Although Mary had now moved away from the concerns of her Populist days, she still regarded her Populist years as well spent. "My work was not in vain," said Mrs. Lease in 1914. Living in the heyday of Progressivism, it seemed to her that agrarian ideals were being realized, that "the seed we sowed did not fall on barren ground." [42]

Mary had not always been so tranquil. In the days when the West blazed with hate, "Mary Yellin" was a fire-brand helping to spread the conflagration. She voiced the fears, prejudices, and ideals that Richard Hofstadter calls the "folklore of Populism." For this virago, the farmers' struggle was a crusade, in which the forces of the Lord stood in battle array against the devil's battalions. Political and economic issues faded before this religious crusade. Through "moral evaporation the guilt has been ascending until we stand today beneath a dark cloud suspended in the heavens, surcharged with the electricity of the coming storm." [43] Mrs. Lease was fighting to make America once more a Christian nation, to end "the present condition of affairs [which] is a parody on the religion of Jesus Christ." [44]

In her crusading zeal, she pictured the opposition as much more than a group whose interests clashed with those of the farmer. The enemy had organized a "government of Wall Street, by Wall Street and for Wall Street" to enslave the "common people" and make "monopoly . . . the master." Wealth had humbled the "West and South . . . before the East," and "clothes rascals in robes and honesty in rags." [45] This conspiracy was master-minded by "the Rothschilds of England," charged Mrs. Lease in 1896, "who are but the agents of the Jews." [46] The virtuous, however, would not go down like wheat before the scythe—the yeoman at bay was still a formidable foe. "We will stand by our homes and stay by our firesides by force if necessary," she cried, "let the blood-hounds of money who have dogged us thus far beware." [47]

In 1895, Mary Elizabeth Lease added another occupation to her already formidable array of professions. She became, in addition to a reformer, lawyer, lecturer, politician, and state official, the author of *The Problem Of Civilization Solved*. This book was designed to present her ideas in more complete and permanent form to a wider audience than she had reached with the verbal thunderbolts hurled from Populist podiums.

The Problem Of Civilization Solved begins with the usual agrarian complaints against modern capitalism. In the opening pages, Mrs. Lease criticizes industrialism and its evil offspring—poverty, maldistribution, class conflict, and urbanism. If class legislation, inequitable distribution, metropolitan pauperism and crime, and capitalistic oppression of labor continued unchecked, America would face a crisis. Mary's cure is as familiar as her diagnosis of the disease. She prescribes the traditional agrarian nostrum of political and economic reform mixed with a generous dose of fundamentalism. Her "remedy" for industrial ills "lies in first removing the cause of extreme poverty by giving every toiler access to the soil." Even more than concrete measures, however, "earnest and fiery zeal" is needed. The farmer must lead America back to the path of righteousness. He must "introduce the ethics of Christ in the politics of the nation and revolutionize the world."

Since Mrs. Lease was champion of a native American movement rooted in the most isolationistic region of the country, one would expect her to follow this airing of agricultural grievances with a tragic tale of domestic disaster. This Kansas Populist diverges from the well-trod path of agrarian criticism, however, and launches into an argument for imperialism. She does suggest that a national catastrophe may rise from the evils of modern capitalism, but domestic debacle will be only one aspect of a possible global cataclysm, and class conflict will be only one cause of the disaster. "Our grand civilization is menaced today" by two great perils, warns the author. One danger "is that mal-formed creature, born of Intelligence and Poverty—whom we call the Anarchist," the other "that dread semi-barbarian from the cold North, the Russian Empire, which is pressing down upon Europe." Once the Slavic bogey has been raised, Mrs. Lease mutes the Populist rhetoric and emphasizes colonization to counter the foreign threat. For the first time, Populist ideas of conspiracy, conflict between producers and parasites, cataclysm, and agricultural utopia are projected onto the world scene and incorporated into the new framework of racist imperialism.

Being both Populist and imperialist, Mrs. Lease is caught in ambivalence. As a Populist, she harbors the old agrarian grudge against Britain for holding "the world in financial thralldom." Anglophobia leads her to impute all sorts of clandestine schemes to the British. In what is perhaps the most far-fetched Populist fear of conspiracy, she charges that English agents sought to weaken France by murdering Lee, McClellan, and Alexander of Russia.

These mysterious machinations were part of "the power of British gold," "that one mighty influence—secret, profound in its cunning, or wisdom, [which] with its vast ramifications, sways the human family, to the remotest confines of our globe." Britain must be stopped before her activities "inaugurate a reign of anarchy that in its throes, will surely subvert all modern civilization."

Mary's hatred for England, however, is tempered by her belief in American imperialism. She fears that her dreams of national empire will be turned into nightmares of Russian conquest. The Tsar can be halted, however, only with British assistance. Consequently, Great Britain, bad as she is, must keep control of the world's commerce. Russia is aiming to wrest this dominance by eliminating the British Empire and replacing London with Constantinople as the world's "center of exchange." Such an accomplishment would be a tragedy for Western civilization, for "from out of this chaos would emerge a hideous nightmare, the Universal Russian Empire, and thus for a second time in history civilization would be trampled under the hoofs of the Northern barbarian in his modern guise of the Cossack."

Anglophobia was one factor that kept most Populists from becoming racist expansionists by depriving them of that great rationalization for imperialism—preserving Anglo-Saxon culture. Mrs. Lease, therefore, had the problem of accommodating agrarian anglophobia to imperialist beliefs. She resolved it by the strange assertion that Russia and England, which threatened society's existence, would be pacified if the Caucasian race, encompassing Slavs as well as Anglo-Saxons, were to rule the world. White supremacy, rather than Anglo-Saxon hegemony, became the racial standard for this prairie expansionist. With divinely endowed "gifts of personal beauty, . . . physical perfection . . . prodigious mentality, . . . Ambition, activity, soaring intelligence, and a keen enjoyment of the refinements and comforts of life, . . . [and] its crowning grace of Christian virtue," Mrs. Lease expected this majestic race to "dominate the world."

Caucasian domination would guarantee utopia. Western nations would be relieved of the overcrowding that causes urban evils, class division and exploitation, militarism, immigration, anarchy, and foreign rivalries. Inferior races would also be better off because conquest would place them under the "Christianizing guardianship of our institutions." White supremacy, oddly enough, would make them "recognize the brotherhood of man." Contact with the white man's gods and the white man's ways would bring the blessings of civilization to heathen savages.

Arcadia was to appear first in the Western Hemisphere because American democracy would facilitate the new allocation of human resources. All the plantations would be governed by Populist policies —Free Silver, nationalization of utilities, and direct democracy. Land, power, and wealth would be taken away from the Jews and bankers, and given back to the people; city-dwellers would be dispersed through rural areas. Most important, Christianity would triumph. Mary had begun her book with a prediction of impending doom, but she ended it on a note of mystical Christian optimism. Above the chaos of history, she discerned "the hand of God guiding and directing the destinies of man." Divinely "destined" America is "to be the refuge of the world's oppressed—a true republic." As Christ's steward, the nation's mission is to "introduce the ethics of Christ," to make Christian brotherhood the law of all the lands.[48]

The Problem Of Civilization Solved abounds with paradoxes that reveal the cross currents of Populism and imperialism. Mrs. Lease wanted the white race to cooperate for conquest, but at the same time she did not advocate real Caucasian unity. The world was to be cut into separate spheres controlled by their respective Caucasian nationalities. America, then, could retire within her realm in undisturbed isolation. Mary's imperialism was not the externally oriented expansion of the post-1898 period. It was rather the old West speaking, the antebellum belief in the "course of empire," which conceived of the American continent as farming land for the settler.

Having resolved one contradiction in favor of Populism, Mrs. Lease was guided by imperialistic considerations in structuring the empire. It was to be an agrarian utopia with no American farmers. Mary Lease may have been championing the party of the yeoman, the party that glorified man's labor, but her racism implied a master race—and those who commanded could not also work with their hands. Still another inconsistency lay in her traditional portrayal of this nation as divinely ordained to be the democratic "refuge" of the world's oppressed." In a curiously aggressive formulation of this old ideal, Mrs. Lease asked that the republican refuge export its superior race to snuff out all but pure white liberty.

Despite her confusion of purposes and ambivalence of values, Mary Lease did adhere to three basic tenets of agrarianism. She aimed to preserve the moderately endowed from the threat of the property-destroying anarchist or the property-expropriating trusts in the form of Russian or British empires, and her program was designed to implement ruralism and Christianity.

More interesting than her adherence, however, is Mrs. Lease's divergence from the agrarian creed. Why did she not share in the more humanitarian views of most Populist leaders? Why did she concern herself more with racism and territorial acquisition than with the internal problems of financial exploitation? The answers to these questions can be found in her age, her poverty, her sex, and her family life.

Mary Lease was born a generation after the older Populists like Weaver and Donnelly. She grew up after 1860 and did not experience, as they did, an America of prosperous and respected farmers. When bitter poverty overwhelmed agriculture, she had no residue of the sympathy for persecuted minorities, which older reformers had learned in their youth. No such early memories helped to forestall the paranoid xenophobia of those in her generation who like herself lived with failure. Destitution also helped to dissipate generous feelings toward other groups. Mary's poverty was of a different order from Donnelly's occasional financial embarrassment. The squire of Nininger City was a gentleman farmer, but the Leases desperately roamed the country to make some sort of stake for themselves. They were poor, dirt poor, as only a homesteader of that era could be. Those whom Mary held responsible for her deprivation seemed much more vicious to her than to associates who were not so hard hit by the depression. Furthermore, she had no cushion of intimate family life to soften the blow that society had dealt her. She could not, as Donnelly could, obtain relief at home from the failures, indifference, and hostility she experienced in the outside world. Her unhappy marriage did not provide a reserve of tenderness to be expended on the needy. Being a woman caused further frustration. She suffered all the rebuffs aimed at the Populists, in addition to the prejudices and indignities directed at a woman trying to make her way in a man's world. For these reasons, she was more warped than other Populists. Fear, hate, and failure had a stronger hold on her, and she sought no explanation or redemption for the enemy. They were bankers, conspirators, and devilish Jews who were drawing blood from the toiling farmers. Mary Lease's hostility to other races and other people was based on the belief that the farmer had to take care of himself or go under. If securing a livelihood meant oppressing others, it could all be rationalized by the claim that such measures were taken to spread Christianity in a brutal world. What a great deal of bitterness must have scarred a life that saw justice only in revenge and progress only in racial domination!

7

Populist Perspectives

CURRENT INTERPRETATIONS of Populism differ over the relationship between farmers and social change. Historians have divided on the question of whether the movement was a romantic-atavistic gesture to recapture the past or a realistic-progressive attempt to cope with modern times. Two aspects of the farmers' ferment—anti-Semitism and the conspiracy theory of history—have been the chief points at issue. Populist prejudice and fears of clandestine expropriation also found expression in predictions of doom. A study of these attitudes as manifested by the agrarian cataclysmists should therefore provide insights into agricultural insurgence in general.

An awareness of the varied and sometimes contradictory characteristics that constituted Populism must serve as a guide in analyzing any of its components. There is a fundamental division in Populism, as in all great movements, between the inspirational and the organizational, the idealistic and the pragmatic. To uncover all these strands and weave them into a coherent whole would take an intensive and extensive study of the various leaders and groups within the movement. A brief examination of the Populist élite will show the complexity of the task and the difficulty of putting agrarians into any one particular category. Some leaders, like Mary Lease and Pitchfork Ben Tillman, were given to prophetic poses, but there were also such practical and sober reformers as William V. Allen and William A. Pfeffer, who did not utter revolutionary imprecations or dwell on impending doom. Then there were men

like Donnelly and Weaver, who dwelled in both camps, The Populists came from different regions; some were southerners, others
western, and several were born in the East. These diverse geograph-
ical origins played their part in increasing of heterogeneity of the
movement. Differences in education and occupation—many were
lawyers and college graduates rather than simple sons of the soil—
also caused cleavages in the ranks. Even disparity in age had an
influence. Donnelly and his generation were reformers of pre-Civil
War vintage for whom free silver was merely one article in a varied
creed of dissent. On the other hand, Populists of Mrs. Lease's type
had grown up in the agricultural depression, and their convictions
were bound to differ from those who had known a youth of confident plenty. Finally, there were those who turned "soft" and embraced free silver, while the hard-core "middle of the road," represented by Donnelly, kept the earlier reform program and, after the
brief Bryan interlude, controlled the party.

Since Donnelly shared both moods, since he was both an unrealistic seer and a hard-headed politico, it is rewarding to examine
Caesar's Column as a product of these attitudes. Its conspiratorial,
cataclysmic, and absolutist elements are irrationally idealistic. Donnelly suggests a conspiracy theory of history, brands the money
power as absolutely evil, predicts complete destruction of a godless
society, sees no discrepancy in achieving individualism through
government interference, proposes a radical political framework
to maintain a reactionary economic system—and offers as a twentieth-century panacea a Christ-dominated, antebellum, rural paradise. Because Donnelly was more than a hysterical hayseed, however, his book is also more than the primitive response of an
innocent rustic.

Donnelly's dualism is most apparent in his treatment of Jews.
He uses many irrational anti-Semitic stereotypes. The Oligarchic
leader, Prince Cabano, is a Jewish banker whose real name is Jacob
Isaacs. In fact, the whole governing class, "the aristocracy of the
world is now altogether of Hebrew origin." To be under the heel
of an un-Christian foreigner is the ultimate degradation of traditional America. A Jew is also prominent in the Brotherhood. He is
second in command and flees with the booty of victory to recover the
kingdom of his people in Judea. These two leaders comprise the
classic anti-Semitic image. The Jew is both rich banker and proletarian anarchist; he threatens society and its backbone, the independent middle class, from both above and below.

Another example of this type of bigotry is Donnelly's charac-
terization of the Jew as a crafty coward—the typical anti-Semitic

charge that the Jew makes up for his lack of straightforward man-
liness with supple shrewdness. Both commanders are physical failures. The revolutionary is crippled, and Prince Cabano is a coward,
but they compensate for their inadequacy with great cunning. The
"cripple" is "the brains of the Brotherhood," and Isaacs maintains
his position by wit. They also exhibit the other attributes of superior
intellect associated with Jews—mystery and treachery. The head
of the Oligarchy tries to trick his military aide, and the other Jew
sneaks away to Palestine with the Brotherhood's plunder. Both men
surround themselves with mystery. Isaacs changes his name to
Cabano and always acts secretly, and the "Vice President" of the
Brotherhood is "the nameless Russian Jew."

Uncleanliness and lechery are two more traits supposedly representative of Judaism. Accordingly, "the Cripple" in "his person was
unclean," and Cabano lusts for the Anglo-Saxon Estella Washington.[1] Another Semitic vice manifested by the two antagonists is an
unscrupulous and infinite hunger for wealth. Isaacs is willing to
slaughter millions rather than give up some of his riches to forestall an uprising, and the Jew of the Brotherhood absconds with its
entire treasure. Finally, Donnelly manifests the basic anti-Semitic
fear: the fear that the Jews, a people without a country, are ever-
wandering aliens subversive to all societies. The cripple symbolizes
this Jewish failure to assimilate by fleeing to recreate the only home-
land to which the Hebrews have ever been loyal.

It is not difficult to find an explanation for Populist anti-Semitism. The Jew was alien to everything that the farmer held most
dear. He lived in the city, usually did not perform ennobling manual labor, spoke a strange tongue, and dressed exotically. In addition, he was history's eternal criminal, a member of the sect that
had been guilty of mankind's greatest betrayal. In view of his sinful
past, he became a ready suspect for any horrendous conspiracy.
Christ's murder had not sated the Hebraic appetite for evil, and
now the descendants of Jesus's killers were plotting to wipe out
those who still lived in His image. Farmers were sure that the
international cabal of Jewish bankers, typified by Rothschild and
his American agent, the Jewish banker and Gold Democrat Perry
Belmont, were trying to crucify them economically, as their ancestors had done physically. Fortifying these suspicions of conspiracy
was the aura of mystery through which Americans saw the Jews.
Rabbis were rumored to have powers of divination, Jewish detec-
tives were supposed to have an occult "second sight" in trapping
criminals, and the theme of the mysterious Jewess ran through much
of American fiction.

The Jew became a man of mystery, part of a secret coterie aiming to steal the hard-earned property of the farmer. This belief alone would have been enough to stir agrarian anger. The villain's role in this rural drama, however, rested on far more than one evil. The Hebrew was foreign and unassimilable, as well as greedy. His refusal to be integrated into other cultures branded him an incurable alien. Surviving all assimilation schemes indicated superior powers—since he could resist change himself, the Jew had the power to change others. Thus, in *Caesar's Column,* he has transformed the United States. These superior powers, the means by which he conquers other societies, were associated with wealth, the East, the city, and business. Semitic strength was the power of the mind, or so thought the agrarians. Superior cunning was used to victimize the sturdy but simple yeoman. It mocked his upright virtues while using them against him. The farmer felt that he was being destroyed by such chicanery, and the Jew became the symbol of this duplicity. Since no American could be responsible for his decline, it must be a foreign conspiracy that was corrupting the nation and robbing the farmer of his birthright. Only Jews had the craft and the will to destroy the nation; only history's greatest betrayers could commit this greatest of betrayals.

Despite the plausibility of this explanation and the common use of anti-Semitic imagery, the facts are that Populists did not originate American anti-Semitism; that they were no more antagonistic toward Jews than toward other groups; and that, even though individual Populists may have disliked Jews, the movement as a whole was not anti-Semitic.

Here is the evidence for the allegedly anti-Jewish nature of Populism. The New Jersey Grange in 1892 warned of candidates who represented "Wall Street and the Jews of Europe;" an Associated Press reporter noticed as "one of the striking things" about the Populist Convention at St. Louis an "extraordinary hatred of the Jewish race!" Coin Harvey and Gordon Clark slurred Jews in their free silver pamphlets; during the campaign of 1896, some Populists made anti-Semitic remarks; one foreign bigot did not deny that Bryan allegedly agreed with him; *Puck* and *The Police Gazette,* which contained unfavorable Jewish references, were widely read in the hinterlands; and Donnelly and Mrs. Lease frequently criticized Jews.[2]

This evidence, sparse in quantity, looks even thinner when examined qualitatively. There were scarcely any Populist references to anti-Hebrew feeling before 1896. Thus almost a generation after its birth and several years after agrarianism had become a tidal wave of dissent, the movement showed no signs of hatred for Jews. There was some documentation of anti-Jewish attitudes during the campaign of 1896, but even a student seeking to prove that Populism was anti-Semitic apologizes for the paucity of "anti-Semitic references." [3] Furthermore, most of the evidence for this feeling, except the statements by Donnelly and Mrs. Lease, was taken at second hand from Jewish periodicals, reform magazines, and the anti-Bryan press. If the Populists were indeed anti-Semitic and if they came from a region where such prejudice was welcome, it is indeed surprising that it did not appear in their own press.[4] No other movement with an appreciable amount of anti-Semitic bigotry was ever so reluctant to express it.

A close look at the facts makes the allegation of Populist anti-Semitism seem even more specious. Citing anti-Semitism in the New Jersey Grange and alluding to the wide western circulation of *Puck* and *The Police* Gazette contradict rather than confirm the argument. All that these references prove is that this bigotry was not most at home in the West. New Jersey was hardly Populist territory, and *Puck* and *The Police Gazette* were published in the East, where they had a far larger audience than in the West. The same erroneous reasoning is evident in pointing to anti-Jewish remarks made by Populists in Louisville, Pennsylvania, Michigan, Indiana, and Florida. None was a center of agrarianism, and one looks in vain for evidence of such sentiments in Iowa or Kansas. As for Coin Harvey and Gordon Clark, they were Free Silverites, not Populists. Harvey was born in West Virginia; had mining and real estate interests in Colorado, Utah, and California; and was only briefly associated with the Populists in 1893-1894. Clark's anti-Semitic pamphlet, *Shylock As Banker, Bondholder, Corruptionist And Conspirator,* was printed, significantly, not by a Populist house but by the American Bimetallic League in Washington, D.C. It is not surprising that anti-Semitism existed among the bimetallists. This group, committed to the silver cure, would fear a "Jewish dominated gold conspiracy" much more than Populists whose diversified program was not tied solely to the money issue. It may be granted that agrarianism was temporarily allied with the bimetallists. The People's Party made many alliances, however, and in politics, virtue is rarely measured by one's bedfellows. Using Mrs. Lease and Donnelly, two of many Populist leaders, as evidence of the movement's deep vein of religious prejudice is typical of excessive generalization from scanty evidence. It proves only that some of the leaders were bigoted people, as are some individuals in any organization. To judge a group on the basis of a few members' personal traits smacks of guilt by association, hardly a valid historical method.

To ascertain what agrarians really thought about Jews, it is necessary to compare western feelings with national attitudes. Students of anti-Semitism place the upsurge of this prejudice about the time when Joseph Seligman was refused accommodations at the Grand Union Hotel in Saratoga Springs. Exclusion at summer resorts, numerous articles about the Jewish question in periodicals, and the barring of Jews from the Union League Club in New York City revealed burgeoning anti-Semitism in the 1890's.

These acts, showing that the East as well as the West was coming to look with disfavor upon Jews, indicate that this prejudice was not induced by Populism. Before 1890, when there was little bigotry, there is no proof that agricultural reoganizations disliked Jews. Afterward, when anti-Semitism became nation-wide, there is no evidence that it was greater in one area than in another, nor that one region spawned and another merely caught the disease. Indeed, some of Mary Elizabeth Lease's anti-Jewish statements were made in New York City and, according to the New York *Times,* were greeted with cheers.[5]

One historian, claiming that there was significant anti-Semitism in Populism, has explained away the scarcity of unfavorable references toward Jews as stemming from lack of publicity because the country was not sensitive to tolerance.[6] This explanation does tie in with the growth of religious prejudice at the end of the century, but it is a self-refuting argument: If the entire nation accepted bigoted campaigning, it can hardly be claimed that anti-Semitism was exclusively, or even predominantly, western. Furthermore, we may conclude that this insensitivity—far from being the reason why the greater number of such remarks went unpublicized—was actually the cause of many of these epithets. Insensitivity may imply lack of preoccupation with, as well as intolerance of Jews. When the farmers uttered the terms "Shylock" or "Rothschild," they may have unwittingly been using colloquialisms that had no real reference in their minds to the Hebrews. One Jewish magazine, commenting on slights in Populist rhetoric, observed that "ofttimes when attention is called to public speakers and the press of the injustice and wrong of thus creating religious prejudice, the offensive words are explained in other ways, withdrawn, and a promise given never to use them again; seldom is the virulence pressed." [7] Prominent Populists like Pfeffer, Allen, Weaver, and the young Watson never, to this author's knowledge, expressed any anti-Semitism. They blamed their plight on the English and the East, more specifically on the money power in Wall Street and Lombard Street, but never were the Jews accused as culprits. If these men attacked other foes, would they not have singled out a group much feebler in numbers, resources, and political power? At worst, it can be claimed that farmers were beginning to use stereotypes that would eventually become the bywords of anti-Semitic groups. Certainly, hatred of Jews was neither a Populist obsession nor part of its basic ideology.

An analysis of anti-Semitism is important because it throws much light on Populism and its cataclysmic thinkers. In the case of *Caesar's Column,* for example, it would prevent the confusion of agents with causes of catastrophe. More significant, however, is what this prejudice reveals about Populism. Anti-Semitism has never been part of any widespread and respectable political movement in the United States. It has always been the creed of demagogues, like Gerald L. K. Smith and Father Coughlin, who hover on the fringe of American politics. Most Populists, on the contrary, were not rabble-rousers leading a half-crazed mob. They were sincere and sober men, many of whom had grown old, if not prosperous and wise, fighting for the underprivileged, and the party to which they belonged was not a quivering ganglion to be motivated by any irrational stimulus. Proof that the Peoples' Party was made of substantial stuff can be seen by a glance at its platform. Treasury loans on stored crops and federally controlled elastic currency are not the principles of a primitive political organization and do not suffer when compared with the Manchester mutterings of the gold-standard academicians. Populist ideology was much more than stale slogans mouthed by paranoid bigots.

Tolerance was not only due to the realistic, progressive side of agrarianism. Populism was an American agricultural crusade and differed from European peasant uprisings in that religious prejudice was not a part of the traditional legacy of the middle-class American farmer. Tender-minded traditionalism, even more than tough-minded pragmatism, may very well have been the source of the farmers' tolerance. Certainly Populists were traditionally oriented. Donnelly, to take one example, hoped that God would "give us back the simplicity, the purity and the prosperity of the early days." [8] This group, like the Jacobins, was economically conservative and sought to protect small property-owners, yet it found itself forced into radical political action. Unlike the Jacobins, however, Populists hungered for the old days and remembered best the old values—values of an independent and prosperous era, of an ascendant middle class that was confident of itself and the nation. Populist prejudices can be traced to the insecurity born of crushed hopes, vanishing opportunities, and declining status. But America before 1865 was the land of promise with plenty left over for alien groups. In those days, there had been little bigotry among farmers; people cared more where you were going than where you came from. If that was the past the farmer desired, if that was part of the agrarian myth, did it not have a mightly influence on his thinking? Would not the old faith of tolerant democracy be more a check than a spur to anti-Semitism?

The conspiracy theory of history is another idea that revealed both perceptive and paranoid elements in Populism. Although this vision sprang from suspicions of intrigues aimed at destroying the farmer, it also inspired intelligent suggestions for alleviating his plight.

Agrarian writers saw society dominated by a vast cabal seeking to transfer wealth from the laboring classes to parasitic bankers. Conspiratorial phantasies rose from suspicions of being victimized by a great swindle. Singling out a mysterious and evil coterie was a convenient defense mechanism to externalize feelings of failure associated with loss of prosperity and status, and it justified socially unacceptable reactions like violence and revenge.

The conspirators supposedly directed the Wall Street and Lombard Street international "money power," which gathered the world's wealth while crushing its producers. In 1895, Party leaders William V. Allen, James H. Kyle, Jerry Simpson, and James B. Weaver stated, in the "Populist Manifesto," that "as early as 1865-6 a conspiracy was entered into between the gold gamblers of Europe and America to . . . fasten upon the country the single gold standard of Britain, and to [give] . . . banking corporations . . . the sovereign control . . for the issues and volume of all supplemental paper currency." The signers found "every device of treachery, every resource of state craft and every artifice known to the secret cabals of the international gold ring . . . being made use of to deal a blow to the prosperity of the people and the financial and commercial independence of the country." [9]

The conspiracy theory was based on the idea that a parasitical minority had seized the reins of government and was digging its golden spurs into the mass of producers. This "money power" embodied all that the farmers feared and despised in the new industrial era. It was foreign (British) and urban (London and New York); it achieved wealth and status through mental rather than physical labor, and it represented the remote and mysterious world of finance, commerce, and industry. The alien nature of the gold cabal made the struggle between producers and parasites seem deeper and far more dangerous than any previous contest. On its

outcome rode the future of the republic. "The contest opening in
the United States," thought Farmers' Alliance member Leonard
Brown, "narrows down to the individual contending against corporate power for the 'rights of life, liberty, and the pursuit of happiness'— the inalienable rights of man." [10]

Convinced that the gold bugs threatened national prosperity
and republican institutions, the farmers concluded that catastrophe
could be averted only by immediate action. Dismal prognostications
by such agrarian leaders as James B. Weaver and Tom Watson have
been alluded to above. Other powerful voices joined the chorus of
doom. Leonidas Polk, President of The Southern Alliance, said
that "retrogression in American agriculture means national decline,
national decay, and ultimate and inevitable ruin." [11] W. Scott Morgan, author of one of the most widely read accounts of the Alliance,
felt that the machinations of the government produced "cracks in
the foundation," which revealed "the whole substrata of the social
structure . . . in commotion." Morgan reminded bankers that in
1776 and 1789 "the wrongs of the people [were] wiped out in the
blood of the patriot." Revolution, he warned, would happen again
"if our statesmen persist in ignoring the encroachments of organized capital upon the rights of the people." [12]

Despite the frequency of its expression in Populist thought,
belief in conspiracy was no more restricted to agrarians than was
anti-Semitism. Other reformers, even those who identified with the
established order, were haunted by visions of wily subversives.
There was, however, a distinction between Populist suspicions and
the immigrant, anarchist, or Populist conspiracies imagined by
defenders of dominant groups. Agrarians and other disaffected
critics regarded conspiracy as a symbol and cause of evil trends that
were destroying society. Ruling élites and their spokesmen, on the
other hand, saw conspirators as foreign obstacles impeding the
normal harmony of social forces. They blamed evil individuals who
sought to wreck a sound social system. Their conspiracy fears, instead
of inspiring reform measures became an argument for conservatism.
These conservatives explained away grievances by attributing them
to agitators and substituted moralizing for reform.

Fears of conspiracy were more than persecution phantasies that
distorted reality. Feeling that he had been duped by a malignant
and brilliant cabal enabled the farmer to face his own weakness.
To be vanquished by a superior and unscrupulous foe made defeat
less humiliating. By shifting responsibility for his failure, the yeoman could admit his inability to cope with modern forces. Recognition of his decline led the farmer to devise remedies to redress the

imbalance of strength. Although the conspiracy theory of history distorted the farmer's analysis of his plight, it also provided a foe against whom to rally. "Gold bugs" and "Rothschild" may not have been the chief sources of agrarian troubles, but focusing on these enemies forced farmers to examine their situation and even inspired some sound monetary policies that were later adopted by the major parties.[13]

Keeping the Populist dualism between realism and distortion in mind, we return to Donnelly. Certainly Donnelly fired his share of emotional broadsides at a stronghold that could be taken only by modern organizational methods. His ideological flabbiness is apparent. It manifested itself in his use of stereotypes, theories of conspiracy, and predictions of doom. The epithet "Prince of Cranks" was not totally unmerited by him. This Prince of Cranks had another name, however, which signified another aspect of his character. Ignatius Donnelly, the "Sage of Nininger," was respected for his learning, his sympathy for the unfortunate, and his experience as a reformer. Because of these qualities, *Caesar's Column* does not represent the raving of a demagogue; it is not surface without substance. In place of the free silver elixir, Donnelly suggests a diversified program in which fiscal policy is only one of several remedies. The same touch of realism conditions his belief in a conspiracy theory of history. The accusation of conspiracy in *Caesar's Column* is no mere accusation of deviltry charged to men who are evil incarnate, nor does it rationalize the simple revenge of the outraged rustic. Experience and wisdom made Donnelly go deeper than aimless vilification. He sought the system, not the man. "There were some among these men whose faces were not bad," says Donnelly when he introduces the reader to the Oligarchy. "Under favorable circumstances they might have been good and just men. But they were the victims of a pernicious system."

Donnelly's attitude toward the Jews best brings out the process of a complex and intelligent mind coping with its prejudices and emotions. Donnelly, who portrayed the Jews unfavorably only in *Caesar's Column,* had a reputation for minority tolerance. He had many of the character attributes associated with bigotry, however. His life was a long, painful record of humiliation, frustration, and failure. He reached his pinnacle before forty, then watched his career waste away. Hence, his natural sympathies for the downtrodden conflicted with the very human desire to find a scapegoat for his own misfortune. Out of this conflict came ambivalence toward Jewry. It is an attitude full of Jew-baiting on the one hand, but, on the other, it reflects dissatisfaction with the easy epithets of anti-Semitism. Having undergone hardship himself, Donnelly sympathized with a people that was persecuted, humiliated, and denied respectability. In these passages, the Jew is the yeoman of yesteryear; his history foreshadows the destiny of the western farmer. He is persecuted rather than persecutor, victim not victor. The Hebrews, "originally a race of agriculturists," were turned into rootless and ruthless capitalists by centuries of oppression. "Christianity fell upon the Jews, . . . and forced them for many centuries, through the most terrible ordeal of persecution the history of mankind bears any record of. . . . Only the strong of body, the cunning of brain, . . . survived the awful trial." Now "the Christian world is paying, in tears and blood, for the sufferings inflicted by their bigoted and ignorant ancestors upon a noble race." [14] The Jews had become oppressors, but they would suffer the fate of all oppressors. History was a cycle, and oppression always brought with it a thirst for revenge to be sated only by cataclysm. Soon the Jews would be destroyed, but they would be sacrificed as the victims rather than the creators of the evil society over which they ruled.

Caesar's Column is a book of contrasts. It demonstrates, as did its author, all that was good and bad in Populism: doubt and despair conjuring up scapegoats and conspiracies; bitterness and frustration dwelling upon envy and revenge; the futility of the present half-concealed in the shrouds of adoration for the past; and the once brave words of the noble yeoman turned into the somber tones of a dirge. But there is more to Caesar's Column, as there was more to the author and the group from which it came. There is the sense of justice and equality, the ingenious proposals for mankind's hope and happiness. But most valuable is the throbbing pulse of humanity beating through the book, its writer, and his movement—the idealism that envisioned a world where innocence would triumph and virtue rule.

Ignatius Donnelly and Mary Lease were only two figures in the Populist gallery, a collection of many faces revealing a multitude of thoughts and expressions. More accurately, we can say that there is really only one portrait—an image more faceted and shaded than many observers perceive, a mind dwelling on reforms, and a heart longing to retreat into an eden-like past. We can discern a line of radicalism here and a stroke of reaction there. A glint of hatred merges into a glow of humanity, and a smile of victory becomes a grimace of defeat. But there is one central element in this sketch: Tragedy is etched in it so deeply that no eye can miss it. It is the tragedy of all failures that have a touch of nobility in them: the tragedy of great expectations that are not realized.

8

Uneasy Aristocrats

POPULISTS CANNOT BE CONFUSED with patricians, and no farmers tilled Boston soil in 1890; nonetheless, cataclysmic thinking among agrarians and Brahmins had many common elements. Social change had shaken both groups, and both were sustained by glorious memories. The Populists echoed Jeffersonian slogans, while the Brahmins recalled their Federalist heritage, but history taunted as well as comforted. The legacy of agricultural or aristocratic hegemony betrayed those who clung to it in an age that ignored their demands and deprecated their values. Alienation and a sense of futility eroded self-confidence, as the present no longer responded to cues from the past. These two declining élites defined legitimacy in terms of history; new leaders therefore seemed anarchistic upstarts. Loss of traditional status gave rise to persecution feelings and, in some farmers and blue-bloods, to a pessimistic fatalism about the future of a society that denied the worthy.

Common motives and common moods did not result in common ideology. Although the agrarians may have been unconscious élitists, they belonged to the middle class and were committed to the *bourgeois* value of social mobility. The farmer, therefore, retained a modicum of faith in the American credo that change meant progress and often brought success. The strength of this belief was exhibited by Populist concern over economic obstacles that prevented farmers from getting ahead. Even a negative reaction to social change such as is visible in *Caesar's Column* still contained Algeristic elements. The catastrophe described in this work was to have occurred a century after Donnelly's era. By then it would be too late to save civilization, but in 1890 a voluntary conversion could still reverse the dangerous course of society. Personal accomplishment involved individual will, and the author's conception of national success was straight out of Alger—it depended upon the will of the people. The utopian ending of this novel was also influenced by the success myth: Uganda represents a wish-fulfillment for Donnelly, who realized vicariously his aspiration to become a respected statesman.

The Brahmins, because their status was inherited, were much further removed from the typical American dream. As aristocrats, they abhorred equal opportunity because they believed social position must be a matter of birth and education. An open society would necessarily be characterized by vulgarity, corruption, and irrationality and would eventually engulf all distinctions. Patrician success notions revolved around holding on to what had already been achieved—an idea completely at odds with Algeristic conceptions of change and progress. Mugwumpery, the characteristic upper-class reform movement, reflected this static belief. In their opposition to the corruption of immigrant bosses and business-oriented politicians, the Brahmin reformers were attempting to destroy the bases of the success of those who had deposed them. They sought a true aristocracy, government by the best, but their ideal government would curb social mobility by cutting itself off from the dynamic areas in American life. Mugwump officials would be free of the urban masses and from need for commercial contributions. They would have the virtues, but also the remoteness, of independence.

Disbelief in any relationship between change and progress made Brahmin predictions of cataclysm even more despairing than those of the agrarians. Brooks and Henry Adams could never get ahead because they had long since arrived. Consequently, their ominous expectations could not be relieved by vicarious accomplishments. Dreams of success gave Donnelly a means of escaping catastrophe, but there was no Uganda for the Adamses. Those who could not rise had a barren future. In a sense, they had already perished and now merely awaited the debacle that would destroy the empty husks of their lives.

Bostonian, Harvard man, Unitarian, Congregationalist, old family—these had been the signs of power, wealth, and prestige proudly worn by the New England aristocracy. As the nineteenth century came to a close, however, newcomers had wrested leadership from the old order. The mercantile élite was eclipsed by a more vulgar and perhaps a more unscrupulous—but also a more ingenious, daring, and progressive—group of industrialists and bankers. By the end of the century, even the Brahmin stronghold of Boston had been stormed. National policy too was now largely determined in Wall Street or Pittsburgh. Each year the new tide rose higher, washing away the power and privileges of the Brahmins and leaving them an isolated island of aristocracy cut off from the mainland of middle-class America.

The bluebloods reacted to their displacement in a variety of ways. Some foresook national affairs for aesthetic pursuits. Others, swallowing the vulgarity and corruption of the new age, sought to regain political leadership. Those whose sensibilities were too tender for the rough-and-tumble of ward politics tried to move behind the scenes as king-makers or advisers. Political issues were as divisive as political attitudes. Many sons of old families, forgetting their fathers' creed, enrolled in the anti-immigrant crusade of the Immigration Restriction League or sought to check the power of the foreign-born through the Municipal Reform League. Expansion was another issue that caused friction among patricians. Those following the course of empire into the Pacific fought others who made a crusade of anti-Imperialism.

This study is concerned, however, not with the manifold reactions of the upper class, but with those of its more extreme wing, with those who were so despairing and so disgusted at their decline that they discerned national destruction in the process. To them the new America was so vulgar, so humiliating, and, above all, so indifferent that pride prevented their acceptance of it.

Aristocrat Charles Eliot Norton was keenly aware of his place in society. Born into one of Massachusetts's first families when one Adams was still in the White House and another scarcely in the grave, he followed a typical patrician path through Harvard College, the editorship of the *North American Review,* and a long-term professorship at the college from which he had been graduated.

Norton, however, was the gilt son of a golden age. As early as the 1850's, he had substituted Know-Nothingism for the self-confident tolerance of the older generation. By 1888, the changing nature of the country "swept [him] along with irresistible force" into a confusing world whose "precise character" was "undefined," since "old landmarks" and "high" culture had disappeared.[1] During the 1890's, Norton decried other elements of the new America. Immigration and its attendant evils of bossism and "materialism" were undermining "the vitality of the republic." These developments, he was sure, would lead to corruption, national purposelessness, jingoism, and "the steady growth of disrespect for rightful authority." Appalled by this vulgar disorder, he wondered "whether our civilization can maintain itself, and make advance, against the pressure of ignorant and barbaric multitudes; whether the civilized part of the community is eventually to master the barbaric, or whether it is to be overcome in the struggle." [2]

Even Norton, however, unable to be completely pessimistic in those years of America's emergence, took solace in the rapid growth of the national economy. He was willing to hang grimly on for that "considerable time to come [when] there will be an increase of lawlessness and of public folly" because "the calamities resulting from these conditions are to be slowly beaten out on the anvils of time." [3] Although his class was destined to be one of those anvils, it might not be wholly disastrous because the process that was enfeebling the aristocracy was also raising "the lower classes . . . from degradation into comparative civilization and comfort." [4]

This thin reed of optimism broke in the storms of Populism and the Spanish-American War. Norton regarded the Chicago Convention of 1896 as "a miserable spectacle of the willfullness of misguided ignorance and selfishness; an alarming spectacle to everyone who believes that free institutions rest securely only on the intelligence and moral sense of the mass of the people to whose guardianship they are committed." [5] When the nation escaped free silver only to be captured by imperialism, the Harvard professor testily declared that only fools could be optimistic. He himself was convinced that "America has rejected her old ideals, turned her back on her past, and chosen the path of barbarism." [6]

The new century did not inaugurate an era of promise for Norton. The fears of his last years far outweighed any lingering legacy of national faith. "New questions have arisen and new perils threaten us," he wrote in 1902, to which "no lover of his country can look forward without anxiety." Imperialism, belligerency, free silver and protectionism were symptoms of "the ignorance and the consequent lack of morality of a large part of the people of our republic." Future survival, was at best, "a long, a difficult, an uncertain task . . . the fight of civilization against barbarism in America." [7]

America's future looked bleak to this aging aristocrat, who found himself a misfit in modern times. The past seemed to him so much happier, especially when colored by the nostalgia of an old man's memories and the poignance of an old man's loneliness. The Cambridge of his youth, when "the intermixture of foreign elements was so small as not to affect the character of the town," had offered an idyllic existence in which "everybody knew not only everybody else in person but also much of everybody's traditions, connections, and mode of life." But that had been the past when everyone had a place and when having a place still meant something. Now those days merely served to make more poignant Norton's awareness that "it has been a pathetic experience for me to live all my life in one community and to find myself gradually becoming a stranger to it." [8]

Moorfield Storey was another uneasy patrician. Storey had an American gentlemen's education, having been graduated from Harvard in 1866. In later years, he became an outstanding Boston lawyer and was President of the American Bar Association in 1895. He is remembered best, however, as a civic leader. This Brahmin gadfly in the guise of a Mugwump spent a lifetime goading his class into facing its responsibilities. "Free government must fail," he warned, if we continue "to leave the work to be done by the ignorant and the base. The complex problems of modern society are worthy of the best thought and the best efforts of the best men in the community." [9]

To Storey, who never spoke to Henry Cabot Lodge after Lodge refused to bolt for reform in 1884, "the insidious influence of general corruption" was the great peril facing America. "Populist movements, Coxey armies, Chicago, Homestead and Pittsburgh strikes" were symptoms of mass anger at bought legislatures that could not give the people relief in hard times. Although sure that "when things get bad enough, we shall find and apply the remedy," he wondered "how much lower must we sink before we begin to rise?" If corruption corroded public institutions, there would come "a time when the only remedy is revolution," and then "the fate which has befallen other republics" would claim America.[10]

Alarmed as he may have been by the union between immigrant "bosses" and the *nouveaux riches,* Storey was even more frightened by expansion. Turning from Mugwumpery to anti-Imperialism after the Spanish American War, he fought against those who would trade democracy for a few islands in the Pacific. "Will you now deny the truths which for more than a century we have called self-evident?" he asked. "Will you abandon the ideals of free America, and approve the principles and practices of despotism?" [11] It seemed a given probability that a policy of territorial acquisition would "result in the overthrow of self-government in this country."[12]

Storey fused belief in clean government with anti-Imperialism, linking corruption and empire to the same root. The great web of business interests that for years had strangled aristocratic enterprise on the mainland now sought to throttle it with colonialism. Thus in

1913 he charged Rockefeller's National City Bank, "the very citadel of the interests which have so long sought to influence the
government of the United States for their private gain," with
financing the Imperialists.[13]

Fundamentally, imperialism imperiled America because it was
a "New Departure," a rejection of "The Declaration of Independence and the Golden Rule" for "the pagan dogma" that "might
makes right." [14] Such abandoning of tradition boded ill for the
nation. In order "to meet our problems here . . . we need a deeply
rooted faith in our institutions, a passionate love of justice." The
habit of empire, if not renounced, would so undermine American
ideals that "when some crisis occurred we might find our people
as glad to welcome a strong man as the French were to receive a
new Napoleon." [15]

As the twentieth century unfolded, Storey grew more morose.
He pictured the Progressive Convention as a horrible affair with
a Mirabeau-like Theodore Roosevelt presiding over a mob of howl-
ing radicals. Despairingly, he wrote to Charles Francis Adams,
another pillar of the *ancien regime,* that "the situation seems almost
worse than in 1861. Then we faced division, but . . . Now, what
with labor unrest, the progressive movement, and the rest, the
danger is dissolution and a very serious and dangerous change in
our political fabric." [16] Two years later, when war began, Storey
realized that it was the end for his kind. No matter which way the
contest went, "the world that you and I have known and loved," he
told T. S. Perry, "seems likely to be destroyed." [17]

Barrett Wendell also had a conventional career, having graduated
from Harvard in 1866 and later becoming a distinguished professor of English literature at his *alma mater.* There, at the podium
and in print, he steadfastly defended New England pre-eminence
in American culture.

Along with fellow Brahmins, Wendell feared the emergence of
new political forces. "If American democracy turned tyrant," he
asserted, by "implacably favoring either the many or the few in
the tyranny of privilege which both seem attempting to exert, that
faith [American democracy] must perish in the whirlwind, or the
morass of such catastrophe we have never known—the full reality
of American Revolution."

Wendell was another alienated aristocrat who looked upon the
new wealth as corrupting national ideals and threatening solidarity.
Failure to check finance capitalism, he declared, might mean "the
end of our ancestral democracy—the abandonment of all that our
conservative revolution won us with our independence while we

are struggling amid the confusion and the violence of the radical revolution conceivably to come." A commercially inspired uprising could only end in "anarchy" or "empire," and, therefore, it would "be a confession or a proclamation, as you will, that democracy, too, has failed." [18]

The triumph of the newly-risen commercial élite turned Wendell from fears that democracy would fall to a hatred of democracy itself. In an address to the Harvard Phi Beta Kappa Society during World War I, he cast doubts on the very ideal for which the nation was fighting. True, Germany was idolatrous and "irresponsible," but might Americans not "be hard pressed, if called on to explain why our American ideal of omnipotent, irresponsible democracy, is altogether different?" And then came the inevitable Brahmin cavil: "The disease which kills popular government by diverting its energies from public welfare to vulgar gratification, . . . [is] named democracy." [19]

Thomas Bailey Aldrich was not born in Boston and did not go to Harvard. Despite these handicaps, however, he became, as editor of *The Atlantic* from 1881 to 1890, the arbiter of aristocratic taste, and he shared all the prejudices and fears of his adopted class. Aldrich's account of an anarchist meeting in 1892 may be taken as a model for the mixture of class fear and patrician disdain with which many Brahmins approached social problems:

> I looked in on an anarchist meeting the other night, as I told you, and heard such things spoken by our "feller citizens" as made my cheek burn. These brutes are the spawn and natural result of the French Revolution; they don't want any government at all, they "want the earth" (like a man in a balloon) and chaos. . . . A hundred and fifty years from now, Americans —if any Americans are left—will find themselves being grilled for believing in God after their own fashion. As nearly as I can estimate it off-hand, there will be only five or six extant—the poor devils! I pity them prospectively. They were a promising race, they had such good chances, but their politicians would coddle the worst elements for votes, and the newspapers would appeal to the slums for readers.[20]

Worsening social and political conditions intensified Aldrich's doubts. By 1894, he foresaw "bloody work in this country some of these days, when the lazy canaille get organized. . . . In about twenty years." [21] His apprehension about popular rule did not subside after the troubles of the 1890's ceased. "Personally," he confessed in 1899, "I have never been very deeply impressed by the administrative abilities of what we call the lower classes." Popular sovereignty, Aldrich feared, was liable to lead to something very much like "the reign of terror in France." [22]

Cataclysmic thought was not an obsession with Aldrich, Wendell, Storey, and Norton. They had misgivings about the future but were never so consistent or so convinced as Brooks and Henry Adams that it would all end in catastrophe. The more saturnine tendencies of the Adamses can be explained partly by their origins. The Adams family had long been considered unconventional and introspective, given to feelings of insecurity and fits of depression. Their painful self-awareness was characteristic of the first of the famous clan, John Adams, who was constantly on guard against his own vices. This sense of inferiority engendered the ubiquitous Adams pessimism, which often tended to view personal disappointment as national catastrophe. [23]

John Quincy Adams inherited his father's sobriety. He early realized, as did his father, that Americans infrequently responded to Spartan virtue. Few things make a man more morose than rebuffed righteousness, and Adams spent his last days in the White House brooding over the "combination" that had been formed "against me, and is now exulting in triumph over me, for my devotion of my life and of all the faculties of my soul to the Union, and to the improvement, physical, moral, and intellectual of my country." [24]

Defeat made John Quincy lose faith, as it had the older Adams, in a fickle populace that was swayed by "demagoguery the besetting sin of popular government." The family propensity toward magnifying private lamentations into public disasters had once again appeared. Would the ship of state founder without an Adams at the helm? [25]

The elder Adamses' influence lived on in the esteem accorded to them by their descendants. Continuity of generations is one of the great themes of *The Education of Henry Adams* ("He [Henry Adams] belonged to the Eighteenth century, and the Eighteenth century upset all his plans"). [26] Brooks Adams, too, was most reverent, ranking John Quincy "as possibly the most remarkable mind ever produced in America" and "the highest product of our civilization." [27] Ancestor worship also manifested itself in Brooks's retention of Adams values, principles, and characteristics. Family traits and family beliefs had a way of lasting through the ages.

Of the four sons of Charles Francis Adams, Sr., only Henry and Brooks became cataclysmists. John Quincy and Charles escaped, possibly because they were men of the world, one being active in business and the other in politics. For the two youngest brothers, however, who had no vocation except for Brooks's desultory law practice and Henry's short term of teaching at Harvard, there was a lifetime to be spent brooding over the nation's destiny. Mutual interests and a mutual mood drew the two brothers together, and each reinforced the other's attitudes. "We are too much alike, and agree too well in all our ideals," said Henry of Brooks.[28] On his part, Brooks worshipped Henry. "I am fonder of you than of any living man," he wrote Henry in 1915. "You always were the best of us four brothers . . . good or bad the best part [of my life] has been yours since I was a boy. And now, as an old man, I look at your worth and thank God that you have redeemed our generation." [29]

After serving as his father's private secretary during the Civil War, Henry had come back from England ready to assume an Adams place in state and society. He dallied first at Newport to regain his social bearings and then threw himself into the slough of politics confident that Adams honor would prevail even amid the muck of Grantism. In those simple, hopeful days, "political corruption" was the "whole root of the evil," and Henry belonged "to the class of people who have great faith in this country and who believe that in another century it will be saying in its turn the last word of civilization." [30]

National destiny reflected the promise of Adams's own existence. He was one of Washington's brightest social butterflies, entertained high hopes of political success, and, in 1872, made an extremely happy marriage. Those years were confident ones, when there could be "no such thing as failure" unless "a young man . . . fails to support himself." [31] He even imagined that "I am myself, with my fellow gelehrte here, the first faint rays of that great light which is to dazzle and set the world on fire hereafter." [32]

Even in those happy times, however, Adams's horizon was not cloudless. As a young man, restless at the embassy in London, impatient with Englishmen who opposed the North and feeling a little guilty at not being in the army with brother Charles, he sometimes "lost faith" in the future of his "truncated life." [33] These despondent moods occasioned speculation that foreshadowed the pessimism of his later years. "Before many centuries more," he once wrote from London, "science will be the master of men." Then "the human race [may] commit suicide by blowing up the world." [34] A decade later, similar despondency was generated by reverses in the reform movement. Grant's victory, gained in spite of Henry's greatest efforts, made him fear that the "family [was] buried politically beyond recovery for years" and, as a consequence, that "he was becoming more and more isolated." [35]

Although Adams disclaimed political ambitions, he could not entirely reject the family career of three previous generations. Early in life, he recognized that "two things . . . seem to be at the bottom of our constitutions; one is a continual tendency toward politics; the other is family pride; . . . " [36] There can be little doubt that Henry also felt keenly the reverses of his fellow Mugwumps. Such defeats convinced him that America had retired his family from political affairs. At any rate, even though he cast off the family vocation, he retained the family character. Like his grandfather and great grandfather before him, retirement turned Henry into a disgruntled observer, both of himself and of the nation.

His withdrawal was gradual and relatively painless until 1885. In that year, Marian Adams, his wife, committed suicide. After her death, seclusion, far from gratifying, "bores me and scares me." Even when he returned to society, it never produced in him the elation it once had—he was now a spectator rather than a partici-pant.[37] Alienation through personal tragedy was intensified by the Panic of 1893. Family fortunes were the economic basis of the aristocracy, and, when the Adams Trust was shaken, Henry feared, not only for himself, but for his entire class. The threat of financial ruin at the hands of upstarts made him feel ever more irrelevant and feeble.

Faced with economic and political impotence, Adams turned to the last refuge of the aristocrat, that combination of aesthetics and etiquette known as "fastidiousness." No longer able to hold his own in the primary power centers, Henry, like the feudal lords who were transformed into fourteenth-century chivalric knights, became an arbiter of taste. Taste was the only area where aristocratic standards still held sway. Here the patrician could justify his leader-ship, not only to himself, but to others as well. Those who con-trolled the real power centers deferred to aristocrats in these matters because of lack of time, lack of background, and their desire to gain entry into the old upper class. Postbellum businessmen and politi-cians could not allow patrician principles to govern their quest for wealth and power, for aristocratic exclusiveness and traditionalism resisted the emergence of new élites. Such traditionalism and ex-clusiveness in matters of taste, however, are usually accepted by the *arriviste*. They guide his behavior in his new social position and help to distinguish the successful from those still struggling to reach the top. Consequently, only through fastidiousness could a Brahmin muster what was left of his influence and, at the same time, maintain proper distance from upstart groups. After the shocks of 1885 and 1893, Henry frequently made remarks about the disappearance of old society and the tastelessness of the new. He consciously assumed the function of enunciating aristocratic values. "We are still in power, after a fashion," he asserted. "Our sway over what we call society is undisputed." Society was determined by who excluded and who was excluded. Adams bolstered his position by barring from his circle the great symbols of the modern era. No Jew ever passed the sensitive scrutiny of blueblood Henry Adams.[38]

A major function of setting standards in aesthetics and etiquette is to give the aristocrat something to occupy his leisure. Such a role especially fitted Adams, since he had plenty of time and was a self-confessed "man of contemplation" who, unable to play "the game . . . lost himself in the study of it. . . ." [39]

For Henry, taste-making served still another purpose. It provided a criterion for social criticism and indicated the causes for civilization's demise. He was fascinated with the Second Law of Thermodynamics. Study of the degradation of energy supported his theory that society, like a clock, was running down. Adams's subtle mind could not be satisfied with a pyrotechnic catastrophe like Donnelly's.

The end of civilization had to be part of a philosophical order that had ramifications throughout the universe. Decadence, for example, had affected art. Aesthetic deterioration was manifested in society's dullness and lack of artistic response, by an "atrophied," "passive" American mind whose imaginative faculties had been drained through a "levelling down" of culture.[40] Thus Henry, by articulating aristocratic consciousness, was able to attack his problem from two directions. By setting standards, he maintained his own position; by criticizing the criteria of others, he derived some solace for his class's vanished hegemony. Displacement of aristocratic values, to this Brahmin, would eventuate in the destruction of the successor society.

Fastidiousness, however, is weak stuff to compensate for loss of leadership. At best, it can palliate bitterness and resignation with pride and nostalgia, or it can help to repress realization of being unwanted by providing a means to snub the dominant clique. Matters of taste cannot forever satisfy a mind like Adams's, which in earlier generations would have been occupied with public affairs. He sought other outlets for his bitterness at his failures in life. The Jew, eternal scapegoat and embodiment of all the forces alien to Adams, served the purpose admirably. In 1888, he wondered "why the German Jew should be the aim and end of our greatest triumphs in science and civilization." [41] During the debacle of

1893, he became more outspoken. The depression emphasized the obsolescence of his class, "total ruin" appeared "to be now only a question of time for all of us survivals of a misty past, who know not the tricks of money making." [42] Adams believed he was the victim of a conspiracy, which had made him an anachronism; of the "infernal Jewry" which turned his "brothers and their contemporaries" into "old men," and put him "more than ever at odds with my time." He wanted "to put every money-lender to death, and to sink Lombard Street and Wall Street under the ocean." [43] Henry was hurt, hurt because he knew that the bluebloods had broken their last lance, that America's aristocracy had finally surrendered to the modern era.

Financial ruin on top of personal desolation had been too much. After 1893, Adams declared war on his age. He believed that business was "a society of Jews and brokers, a world made up of maniacs wild for gold." Estranged from such a society, he envisioned himself "helping the London mob pull up Harcourt and Rothschild on a lamp-post in Piccadilly." [44] Science, which had seemed a force for unity and progress to "the confident child of Darwin and Lyell in 1867," now seemed to promise despair and confusion. "In 1900 he entered a far vaster universe, where all the old roads ran about in every direction, overrunning, dividing, subdividing, stopping abruptly, vanishing slowly, with side paths that led nowhere, and sequences that could not be proved." Every year, science became more of a blind alley as each discovery doubled and quadrupled "its complexities," while human ability to comprehend correspondingly diminished. But the worst was still to come. Science, formerly only confusing to man, soon would enslave him. "The new American" was the "child of steam and the brother of the dynamo," a standardized "product of some such mechanical power" who had become "the servant of the powerhouse." [45]

Politics looked equally dismal. Democrats and Republicans seemed at best unable to cope with America's decline and at worst in league with commercial interests: "The gold bugs have resumed their sway," he wrote to Brooks in 1895. "Cleveland and Olney have relapsed into their normal hog-like attitudes of indifference, and Congress is disorganized, stupid and childlike as ever. Once more we are under the whip of the bankers." [46] The Republicans, crushed under the "intellectual imbecility of McKinley and his Ohio-Philadelphia following," were scarcely any better. The established order would lead to corporate domination, and "Bryan's success would mean chaos, and general ruin for a time, and probably a great breach with Europe." [47] Even a victory for respectability would lead to revolution. "Hanna," Adams expected, "will drive us to Bryan—and then!" A victory of the have-nots would be even more intolerable than the rule of privilege. "Much as I loathe the regime of Manchester and Lombard Street in the Nineteenth century," he wrote to Brooks, "I am glad to think I shall be dead before I am ruled by the Trade Unions of the Twentieth." [48]

Foreign affairs seemed to be disintegrating as rapidly as was the domestic situation. Adams feared "an immensely strong and concentrated Germany," and, during the Russo-Japanese War, he was "in terror about Russia." [49] By 1911, the entire world seemed near "a general debacle," and he expected everyone to "be running for caves before long." [50]

No matter where one turned, complete collapse was inevitable. "From top to bottom the whole system is a fraud," he assured his younger brother, who needed little convincing on that score. "The best we can any of us now do is just to keep our tempers, and try to make the machine turn without total collapse in a catastrophe, so that it may rot out quietly by its natural degradation." The "only question" now was "whether it will break down suddenly, or subside slowly, after a long lapse of time into motionless decay." [51]

Now that it was only a matter of time until the combination of business, class struggle, loss of energy, and foreign conflicts made everything disappear, the game became one of dating the end. At first, Henry was relatively optimistic, foreseeing "more than two-hundred years of futile and stupid stagnation." [52] But his own advancing age made doom seem more imminent, and, by 1903, this estimate had been lowered to "1950 as the year when the world must go smash." [53] As time passed and age made existence still more forbidding, disaster seemed to creep closer. Alarmed by the foreign situation, he wrote to Elizabeth Cameron in 1905 that "nine years have swept away men and empires and upset science. Another such ten years will set us on our heads and knock all our social systems silly." [54]

Ominous expectations engendered mixed emotions. After all, catastrophe would merely terminate an ugly civilization. Consequently, Adams often affected indifference to the coming event, cloaking his deep dissatisfaction with a half-jocular, half-defiant attitude. In this vein, he wrote Elizabeth Cameron that "only my brother Brooks makes me cheerful; he sees the times worse than I and is deadly serious. At least I don't care if the world has gone to the devil. Serve it right!" [55] He mocked his brother's concern for a "world . . . going to the devil" and tried "to console him by the assurance that it went there at least ten years ago." [56]

Sometimes Henry's assumed unconcern was conveyed (or betrayed) in his pose of resignation. Here, as usual, the more obviously and passionately committed Brooks was his foil. He scolded his younger brother for taking it all too seriously: "As I have often told you, I have but one ideal left, and that is to get out of the world as soon as I can. Your forebodings do not affect me at all." [57] Frequently, however, anger burst forth, tearing away his mask of indifference and laying bare Adams's hatred for the system that had beaten him:

> None of you dare touch the essential facts; and since 1893, I dare not touch it myself. The whole fabric of our society will go to wreck if we really lay hands of reform on our rotten institutions. All you can do is to vapor like Theodore about honesty! Damn your honesty! And law! Damn your law! And decency! Damn your decency! From top to bottom the whole system is a fraud,—all of us know it, laborers and capitalists alike,—and all of us are consenting to it. [58]

But when the depths of his personality were sounded, there appeared at bottom the stark fear of a lonely old man, confused and weak in the face of forces that had passed him by and beaten him down. He was "scared as a rabbit, . . . on the brink of my . . . own precipice of anarchy, my knees shak[ing] and my tongue rattl[ing] against all my false teeth." "Why is one ever sixty-six years old!" he wailed. "Why is not one shut up in an asylum?" [59] An even more pathetic account of this lost life was a letter he wrote to Charles in 1911, full of regret that there had been nothing to grasp, nothing to sacrifice for.

> As I look back on our sixty years of conscious life, I have to search hard for a word of warm satisfaction. Again and again we pinned our hopes to some figure, but it always got drowned in the mud. . . .
> If they had existed I should have attached myself to them, for I needed them bad. As life turned out, I am dying alone, without a twig to fall from. I might as well be a solitary woodchuck on our old Quincy hills as winter comes on. We leave no followers, no school, no tradition. [60]

The self-proclaimed dotage of Henry Adams reflected an inner image of futility and rejection. The world had been unkind, and he had failed to make his way in it. Early in life, Adams had aggressively demanded his legacy of leadership, but later he had sought acceptance through submission and withdrawal. He was an old man resigned to adverse fate, a twentieth-century pilgrim seeking shelter in the Middle Ages. His existence was hopelessly divided between the mechanistic, changeable present of the "dynamo" and the permanent protective past of the Virgin. Adams's weakness drew him to power centers, and the adoration of Mary seemed to him a compelling force. His identification with power did not impel him toward the masterful male figure, as did Jack London's, nor the aggressive destructiveness of *Caesar's Column*. Impotent, passive, and resigned, he eschewed the defiance of Donnelly and London for submersion in the maternity of Mary.

The self-image of this feeble old man was an evasion, as well as an admission, of responsibility. His weakness mitigated his guilt. How could the helpless be blamed? There was even a certain nobility in bowing to fate. His denial by destiny made the lonely old man a martyr to his age, a victim of its insensitivity.

But Adams did find a figure to which he could cling. Although the present might be empty, there was meaning in the past. As Henry withdrew behind the cover of aristocratic sensibility, he found himself belonging more to past ages than to his own era. Of course, being a relic had its drawbacks: "The Eighteenth century upset all his plans" and made him feel anachronistic. But if history had betrayed him, it was also his salvation. After a lifetime of failure, he turned to medieval Christianity, finding there everything that modernity lacked and that he needed so desperately. In those centuries, "man held the highest idea of himself as a unified universe." [61] All forces were united in one concept, one faith, and one aesthetic, and everyone was moving in the same direction. Without Jews, science, or business to fragment society and accelerate its disintegrative momentum, "vital energy" had had its greatest "intensity." Even more important, this energy was "stated in its two highest terms," in terms most appealing to a patrician's consciousness—"religion and art." [62]

The Middle Ages fascinated Adams and not alone because its heart beat in his own tempo. Nor was he solely attracted by the medieval manifestation of energy. Part of the era's appeal lay in its irrelevance to modern times. It was a field "deserted" by the *bourgeoisie;* like taste, it was an area where Adams would not be challenged, where "us old people" could "play . . . undisturbed." [63]

The unity, nobility, and even the tragic irrelevance of the Middle Ages were symbolized in the Virgin. Whatever else the twelfth century meant to Henry Adams, it was chiefly the age of Mary, the "woman of Chartres," Magna Mater, woman—eternal, warm, protective, and sympathetic. "Her chief joy was to pardon, her eternal instinct was to love; her deepest passion was to pity!" Even an Adams could find relief here, drawing a curtain of love between him and the outside world. Mary and Henry shared the same moods and tastes; the Virgin's weaknesses were Adams's weaknesses, her prejudices his prejudices. "She disliked Jews, and rarely neglected a chance to maltreat them"; she rejected money-makers and "had a very rudimentary knowledge, indeed, of the principles of political economy as we understand them, and her views on the subject of money lending or banking were so feminine as to rouse in that powerful class a vindictive enmity. . . ." In matters of taste, Henry trusted her completely. She was "always the greatest aristocrat," the "Queen" whose "manners were exquisite" and whose "art" was "so true that everything else shades off into vulgarity, . . ." [64] Through her, the tired, cynical, and bewildered old man could once again "feel the energy of faith." [65] To Henry, dessicated, weak, and thirsting for direction, Mary was the fount of vitality and unity. She imposed order on the anarchy of science and the meaninglessness of modern times. Her reality was not "a raft to which limpets stuck for life in the surge of a supersensual chaos; she conceived herself and her family as the centre and flower of an ordered universe which she knew to be unity because she made it after the image of her own fecundity." [66] Above all, however, Mary was the champion of the alienated individual, of an Adams seeking to rise above his fate, his law, and his society. Concentrating "in herself the whole rebellion of man against fate; the whole protest against divine law, the whole contempt for human law," the Virgin reversed that degradation of energy that mirrored Henry's own sense of impotence and decline. Adams saw her as the great emancipator—Mary enabled him to "hope that . . . man had found a door of escape." [67]

As a young Mugwump, Henry had been motivated by New England morality. Age and defeat made him retreat into an aristocratic past. He became a devotee of medieval Catholicism, a philosophy of hierarchy and permanence rather than of equality and change. Twelfth-century Christianity attracted him by its tolerance even more than by its defense of established order. The Puritan ethic of his fathers demanded retribution for sin and preached the activism of constant reform. But Adams was already buckling under a mountainous burden of guilt due to personal failure and the passing of his class. A Calvinist conscience was simply one more burden to a man already rejected by himself and his age. Beaten and tired, Henry sought the softer and more passive tolerance of the old Church. He craved the mercy of Mary, not the justice of Jehovah. Mary could do for Henry what he could not do for himself—forgive him for his wrecked life. A frightened Henry Adams, hemmed in by an ugly society and haunted by an irrevocable fate, reached out his hand through the ages to grasp the meaning and sympathy that had been denied him in the insane, cold, modern world.

The final tragedy of Henry Adams's life is that he could not embrace the Virgin. His eye and mind subdued his heart, and Mary was lost amid Gothic beauty and twentieth-century complexity. Henry always realized that it would not work; he always knew that Mary was too much like Mrs. Lodge or Mrs. Cameron or all the other women with whom he sought refuge. As for the period during which the Virgin reigned, Adams was "inclined to think that if it were not for our troubles, we should find the immersion in the twelfth century less alluring." [68] That was the trouble with Adams's aristocratic consciousness. No matter on what path it led him, he always knew it was an escape route, that would end in his own heightened awareness that, for those trapped in their age, there was no exit.

9

Brooks Adams

BELLIGERENT BRAHMIN

IT WAS BROOKS ADAMS'S MISFORTUNE to be born in 1848. Had he lived a generation earlier or later he would have been a far happier man. Adams would then have escaped the frustration of estrangement from American life, the painful memory of decaying Brahmin prestige and power, and the obstacle of an unadaptable aristocratic outlook.

Patrician privilege, however, was still undisputed when the youngest son of Charles Francis Adams was born. Old families still counted, Irish immigrants had not yet overrun Boston, and Peter Charendon Brooks, the lad's merchant grandfather, was one of the richest men in the area. Massachusetts Whiggery, whether Conscience or Cotton, wielded a mighty influence, and Sumner and Webster were still names to be reckoned with. The Adamses too retained their public position. It was only a few years since old John Quincy had won fame defending liberty in the House of Representatives, and his son bid fair to take his place. Intellectually, Boston was the national hub. Transcendentalism was in its prime, and Lowell, Longfellow, and Parkman had barely embarked on their great careers. The great tragedy of this fourth Adams generation was that it was born into such a society and forced to make its way in a world where New York bankers, western writers, and urban politicians held sway.

Brooks Adams grew up unaware that he was enjoying the

Indian summer of his class, with no hint of his later irascibility and despondency. Charles Francis Adams regarded his son as a "good . . . boy . . . with a very fine disposition." [1] Brooks fully reciprocated this paternal pride and affection. Even late in life he retained fond memories of his father and thought him "the most remarkable man I have ever known."

Adams's only really difficult boyhood experience was living at an English private school. Most of his classmates, sons of aristocrats, were Confederate sympathizers and did not welcome the American ambassador's son. Many years later, he remembered experiencing "their feelings in all their crudity" and hearing "the North vilified or ridiculed, . . ." [2] This unfortunate sojourn among the young "gentry" may have influenced his dislike for England and his contempt for European aristocracy.

In 1866, like the scions of most other prosperous and prominent Bostonians, Brooks Adams enrolled in Harvard College. He was quite similar to hundreds of other undergraduates, and certainly his college days indicated no later moroseness. Adams rowed in regattas, played in the productions of the Hasty Pudding, was admitted to the highly coveted Porcellian Club, and indulged in several collegiate pranks. As a senior, he looked back on those days and could not "help thinking how lucky I have been."

While at Harvard, Brooks developed the interests and attitudes that marked his mature years. The Adamses' testy individuality appeared early; even in college he wanted to go his own way. He complained about living with his brother Charles because "I am second fiddle and I like to play my own fiddle my own way. . . ." [3] Another family trait, passion for self-improvement, developed during his undergraduate years. "I despise an idle man, or rather clubmen, more than any being I know," he wrote to his father in 1868, "and would rather be anything than that." [4] Lasting intellectual interests, particularly in medieval history, were formed in these years. Politically, too, Brooks was absorbing ideas that would determine his future course. Taking a Brahmin's dim view of Andrew Johnson's administration, he commented sardonically that "our politics seem to me to be getting more and more muddy and beautifully worse, and hold out rich promises of, in the end, managing to bring us to the ardently desired point of having no politics at all." [5]

In 1874, after having been graduated, taking a law degree, and acting as his father's private secretary at the Alabama Claims Arbitration, Brooks Adams made his political debut. He started out as a conventional patrician reformer, becoming active in the

Commonwealth Club, a Mugwump organization run by his brother Henry and made up of young bluebloods like Henry Cabot Lodge and Moorfield Storey. During the next several years, the fledgling reformer conscientiously fought the good fight and followed his elders out of the Republican Party.

Brooks was orthodox in those days. Like many other young aristocrats, he saw himself as a Brahmin St. George entering politics to slay the dragon of corruption. Certainly there was plenty of evil to combat, and who else but an Adams should lead the crusade? In July, 1874, he wrote an article for Henry's *North American Review* expressing the views of the conservative reformers. "Grant-ism" represented the ultimate corruption, the national nadir, as a witless President and a lawless Congress plundered the country. The blame, this young élitist thought, lay in "the naked rule of numbers" through which "majorities are manufactured by dema-gogues craftily manipulating the least intelligent portion of society." To Mugwump Brooks Adams, "a government by a corrupt civil service, with demagogues manipulating caucuses, is ruin!" In the nation's dire need, he proposed to "cut the evil at the root." These were brave words, but in reality his solution did not differ from the superficial suggestions of other genteel reformers. The "root" was a shallow, if troublesome, growth of a "feeble executive, a corrupt civil service and the caucus system." His cure, therefore, was correspondingly bland. Measures like the election of a strong president to curb Congress, the end of rotation in office, and the protection of minorities from demagogic "thralldom" were to bring America again to full bloom.[6] During these years, Brooks was the blueblood reformer. Mugwumpery was to him, as to Henry, a vehicle for asserting aristocratic élitism by fighting the influence of business and numbers in politics.

Although his political opinions later changed, Adams formu-lated some permanent principles in this period. A glimpse of things to come was contained in his review of James Fitzjames Stephen's *Liberty, Equality, Fraternity*. In this article, he exhibited his pref-erence for the realist—"Mr. Stephens . . . an active, ambitious lawyer, accustomed to deal with men and facts as they actually exist, [who] looks on life as a long struggle, in which the prizes are to the strong and wise,"—to "Mr. Mill, the highly trained, speculative philosopher, with a passion for doctoring society of all its ills, real and imaginary, [who] was apt in his great longing to bring all the world to something nearer his ideal to forget and ignore any practical difficulties . . . which might stand in his way." Adams fired away at the British liberal, maintaining that every "election [is] but an appeal to force." "Fraternity is simply a nauseous lie,—men are not brothers," he said, curtly dismissing the Christian ethic that he felt underlay Mill's politics. Much sounder, Brooks thought, was the doctrine "that in the end the battle must always be to the strong, and the race to the swift; and that the strong man will always rule the weak; by persuasion if possible, but if necessary by force. Nothing can alter the order of nature." [7] Darwinian pragmatism, the foundation of Adams's emphasis on *realpolitik* and of his contempt for muddle-headed, sentimental liberals, appeared even at the heyday of his membership in a group with more than its share of the visionary and the tenderhearted.

Other blocks in the Adams edifice (perhaps sepulchre is a better word) were added during these years. In 1879, he first suggested a cyclical theory of history. This idea, later to become his explanation for the rise and fall of world empires, appeared in rudimentary form in his "plague on both your houses" attitude toward class conflict. "The rich man," he wrote Henry Cabot Lodge, "has had his fling for a thousand years and while he was the stronger he led his poorer neighbors the devil's own dance, and if they didn't like it, he struck an iron spike into them." But "he prodded once too often, and . . . the poor man got the rich man by the throat and cut his stupid head off, and served him right." Since the French Revolution, however, we had completed the circle, and now the poor man was growing as "greedy and silly as the nobles did." [8]

These somber thoughts, which he refined in the next several years, generated Adams's theory of social revolutions. His old belief about ruling groups establishing themselves by force became the basic premise of a class-conflict theory. Revolutions were caused by the "drifting of power from class to class, and the effort of the new class to assert itself." [9] This analysis was the embryo of future works. Perhaps already lurking in Brooks's mind was the notion that the passing of his own class might lead to such an uprising.

Changes in Adams's personality occurred concomitantly with conceptual developments. A bitter, quarrelsome adult replaced the agreeable youth. Charles Francis noticed as early as 1877 that his son was "singularly brusque in his manners." [10] Outsiders also saw the change. Mrs. Duncan Cryder, who had known him "as a young boy, when . . . he was friendly and pleasant," now found him "full of gloom." [11] Some of his acerbity was due to his hairline defeat for the state legislature in 1877. No doubt the decline of Massachusetts Mugwumps and his father's death also contributed to the transformation—and there were rumors of a broken romance. Brooks seemed aware of what was happening to him and com-

municated some of this negativism in a letter to Lodge. He wondered how he could ever have "enjoyed the life" of travel. Musing
on his present dissatisfied state, he concluded that "after all the
years make a difference in the way a man looks at the world." [12]

Disappointed in politics and dissatisfied with himself, Adams
turned scholar. The first fruit of his new vocation was *The Emancipation of Massachusetts,* a study of the Bay Colony Puritans. His
purpose in this, as in all future, works was "to set forth a scientific
theory of history" by applying "certain general laws to a particular phase of development." [13] Thus, in 1887, he began his lifelong quest for "general laws" based on historical facts. Ultimately it would lead him to view history as a cycle in which all
civilizations were doomed to catastrophic ends.

The law investigated in *The Emancipation* was the motive
power of fear. In seventeenth-century New England, a "spiritual
oligarchy" buttressed its position with "superstitious terrors." When
the Puritan ministry was threatened by eighteenth-century ration-
alism, it became bigoted and reactionary. Progressive enlightenment
and reactionary prejudice then locked horns in "the fiercest battle of
mankind; the heroic struggle to break down the sacerdotal barrier,
to popularize knowledge and to liberate the mind." In Massachusetts, free inquiry, "that constitutional system which is the root of
our national life," triumphed. So complete had been the victory
that "wheresoever on this continent blood shall flow in defense of
personal freedom, there must the sons of Massachusetts surely be."

Adams outraged fellow Brahmins by calling their ancestors
"cruel bigots," men who shrank "from no deed of blood to guard
the interests of their order." [14] He claimed, contrary to everything
his class had been taught, that only in spite of their Puritan forefathers had liberty found a refuge in America. Despite Brooks's
rejection of the past, however, he had not yet broken with the
present. Behind his ancestral scorn lay an optimistic belief in the
inseparability of progress, virtue, liberty, and truth and in the
destiny of America to be their champion.

Despite its patriotic ending, *The Emancipation* was taken to task
for bias and inaccuracy. Unfortunately, criticism drove the youngest
Adams to castigation rather than to investigation. Rejected by
readers and experts, he became contemptuous. Alienation expressed
itself in diatribes against the opposition. "My estimation of popular
intelligence has fallen," he defensively wrote to Henry. "I used to
think you were wrong for the language you used to use about popular criticism and popular estimations of work but I give in, you are
right." [15] The critical barbs sank deeply, intensifying his isolation.

Never again would Brooks write a book so hopeful about America. The turbulent Nineties gave Brooks a public cause on which to vent his personal bitterness. Trouble was in the air in 1892, and the always apprehensive Adams quickly sniffed it. Strikes, agrarian political insurgence, and the emergence of giant corporations made him doubt the future. "Between the tariff and the trust," he wrote, "we are approaching something akin to a social revolution; for government by capital must necessarily be government by a minority and a government by a minority is a reversal of what we have had hitherto." Plutocratic government, he warned, would result in class conflict. Such a "state of affairs" could last, at best, "twenty five years," and then "we shall be in a social revolution of which no man can see the end."

Adams's rhetoric was radical, but his message was still conservative. After all, was it not natural for a Brahmin merchant's grandson to attack the high tariff, and blame industrialists and bankers for social and economic unrest? Brooks's essential moderation can be seen in his election plea for 1892. Amid "the mutterings of the storm," he called for "the defeat of Mr. Harrison." Cleveland's victory was vital because it would destroy the tariff that "holds together the great moneyed combination" and draw labor and capital "into violent collision." [16] Revolutionaries do not flock to Mugwumps like Grover Cleveland, nor do they congratulate Republican friends on winning Senate seats.[17]

Despite Adams's faith, Cleveland did not save the nation. Within a year after his triumph, bankruptcy threatened the Adams family. Although failure was avoided, the brothers suffered considerable "care and anxiety." [18] Harrowing experience now reinforced Adams's inherited dislike for bankers and businessmen. After such painful personal proof of their determination to crush him and his fellows, he became their intractable enemy.

During the misery of 1893, Brooks Adams began the *Law of Civilization And Decay,* the first full statement of his pessimistic philosophy. Adams sought to trace the development and decline of society with scientific principles of force and energy. According to these principles, communal growth and decay involved "oscillations between barbarism and civilization, or what amounts to the same thing . . . movements from a condition of physical dispersion to one of concentration." In the primitive state of dispersion, fear is the major manifestation of human energy. Fear, stimulating the imagination, stems from the need for self-defense. Hence, "religious, military, [and] artistic" types characterize the initial stages of society. The advance of civilization entails a "consolidation of energy" by which "fear yields to greed, and the economic organism tends to supersede the emotional and martial." The degree and rate of centralization depend upon the abundance of energy in any given society. Thus the growth and scope of civilization is proportionate to the flow of energy.

Having analyzed the principles of progress, Adams went on to describe its process. Through this discussion, he formulated his doctrine of the rise and fall of civilizations. In daily living, a richly endowed society does "not expend all its energy," but stores a "surplus . . . in the shape of wealth." Wealth, however, is accumulated by conquest, and "a race must, sooner or later, reach the limit of its martial energy." These limits are reached when "surplus energy" preponderates "over productive energy," i.e., when capitalists triumph over priests, artists, and soldiers.

When capital prevails, economic competition is substituted for war. Soldiers and farmers, creators of surplus energy, are ill adapted to the new style of life and give way to the parasitical "usurer." Since businessmen, unlike martial types, do not produce, "the effect of economic competition has been, perhaps invariably to dissipate the energy amassed by war." Consequently, the rule of bankers is as temporary as that of their predecessors. If war does not destroy the pacificistic "economic organism," it sinks more slowly "because the energy of the race has been exhausted." Thus "by war, by exhaustion or by both combined, . . . disintegration may set in, the civilization may perish, and a reversion may take place to a primitive form of organism."

Although the Adamses had a dramatic and personal vision of doom not unlike those of Donnelly and London, they also formulated a philosophical system of catastrophe. Brooks Adams's doctrine of disaster rested upon an impossible attempt to combine three contradictory ideas. He explained social growth through Darwinian concepts but attributed society's destruction to the triumph of the fittest. The organism that would finally survive the struggle for existence would doom civilization by dissipating vital energy. Disintegration, however, actually would resuscitate the race and reverse the decline. Once civilization had fallen, energy-gathering types would reappear and initiate a new society, which would itself go through the inevitable cycle of development, deterioration, and destruction. Evolution became a popular way to explain the emergence of America and to rationalize the triumph of corporation owners. Adams, as an aristocrat, resisted the social implications of Darwinism because America's growth drew the nation away from Brahmin values and because the Algeristic myth of business success underscored his own failure to achieve life goals. Thermodynamics and the cyclical theory of history provided a framework with which to use evolutionary ideas while escaping their unfavorable implications. This fusion of theories enabled Brooks to reject the captain of industry as nature's fittest organism and to deny that archaic types hindered survival. According to his application of the Second Law of Thermodynamics, commercial organisms dissipated energy, and aristocratic types created it. Consequently, the victory of industrial titans involved the decline of civilization.

Adams derived only limited gratification from contradicting the theory that posited his class as atavistic. Although asserting the relevance of aristocrats to American society, he also accepted the thesis that the old must give way before the new. Brooks believed enough in evolution and the success myth to block his own wholesale rejection of these ideas. His thesis therefore, by admitting defeat, yielded only the negative satisfaction of withholding the spoils of victory. The triumph of his own class was impossible because it had not adjusted; the triumph of its displacers entailed society's disintegration. Only the theory of fatalistic cycles could resolve these clashing claims of relevance and legitimacy. Brooks Adams received some grim hope from seeing in the commercial élite's supremacy society's eventual reversion to a state of savagery where warriors and churchmen would prevail. In this way, the subjugation of the aristocrat would guarantee his return.

After conceptualizing his theory of energy cycles in general terms, Adams applied it to modern times. When Europe emerged from the Dark Ages, capitalism enabled men to accumulate surpluses and delegate their defense to others. Physical force was transmuted "into money and this process went on until individual strength or courage ceased to have importance." The mercantile triumphed over the martial way of life. The merchants, however, then gave way to modern bankers. These parasites who lived off other men's labor constricted the flow of currency so that money appreciated and "the borrowers had to part with more property to pay his debt when it fell due."

To Brooks Adams, Mayer Rothschild, the Jewish banker, epitomized the new group. According to Brooks, Rothschild's last words, uttered to his son as he lay dying, were: "You will soon be rich among the richest, and the world will belong to you." Nathan, who succeeded Mayer to the Rothschild empire, was sketched with the acid of an aristocrat's pen. He "had no tastes, either literary, social or artistic; in his manner and address he seemed to delight in displaying his thorough disregard of all the courtesies and amenities of civilized life; . . . . Extremely ostentatious, though without delicacy or appreciation." Adams was trying to even the score of 1893 by attacking with rapier finesse the business blunderbuss that had almost annihilated him.

With the bankers' victory, gold had become supreme. As a result, credit was "manipulated by a handful of men" who had financially enslaved the debtor. Even the triumphant capitalist system, however, "bears within it the seeds of its own decay." In their unquenchable desire for markets and cheap labor, the magnates had opened up the East. Easterners, once mechanized, could undersell western businessmen. Greed, which impelled capitalism's triumph, would destroy it.

Apart from economic strangulation, modern civilization was threatened with biological extinction. In a centralized capitalistic society, the family was losing its economic and social significance, marriage was no longer sacred, and children had become a burden. Consequently, reproduction was declining, and, since modern society had no revitalizing "supply of barbaric life," race suicide was a likely prospect.[19] For Brooks, the decline of that basic aristocratic institution, the patriarchical family unit, meant society's disintegration.

Adams turned history into a treadmill. There were stages but no progress, Darwinian conflict but no evolution to higher types. He acknowledged the financiers' success in the struggle for existence, but evolution did not seem to him a progressive process. Compared to previous aristocracies, the banker was dull, cowardly, and uncultured. Even though he disagreed with its positive conclusions, Brooks borrowed much from Darwinism. The human situation was conceived in terms of constant change, adaptation through necessity, and conflict for survival. Substituted for the tenet of growth to higher levels, however, was an endless repetition of triumph alternating with defeat. There was a ceiling to any society's development, and, when it was reached, the pendulum would always swing the other way. Decline, ending in disaster, would occur, and another civilization would rise to go through the inevitable cycle.

Doubtless Adams's portrayal of the financier was colored by a combination of his experience in 1893, a Brahmin bias against the *bourgeoisie*, and the traditional Adams animus for State Street. Like Henry, Brooks chronicled the emergence of the class that had displaced his own and took grim satisfaction in discovering the sources of its eventual disintegration. He, too, linked capitalistic deterioration with its divergence from the patrician style of life. Both brothers saw in the gross manners, pervasive materialism, and artistic inarticulateness of the businessman his ultimate destruction. To these aristocrats, taste meant energy, and sensibility meant survival.

There was another theme in Brooks's treatise, a theme far different in context, though not in content, from that of the alienated aristocrat. It was a long way from Boston to Nininger City, and an Adams could never be confused with a Donnelly, but nevertheless they shared a common grievance against commercial interests. Brahmin Brooks Adams agreed with the Populists in attributing to the financiers a tight money policy deliberately aimed at crushing producers. He joined the farmers in condemning "usurers" whose only activity in the economy was to destroy it by their own greed. The aristocrat and the agrarians held a common opinion of the materialism and cowardice of the dominant class. As members of disaffected groups, even their cataclysmic outlook was similar. They both predicted that the élite, through its insatiable greed, would doom itself and all civilization.

Adams did not restrict himself to deploring capitalistic depredations, however. He attemped by political agitation to redress the balance between Wall Street and Beacon Street and sought revenge against the bankers who had made him so miserable in 1893. In 1894, he fought business with bimetallism as earlier he had opposed it through the tariff. With Francis A. Walker, Brahmin economist and President of Massachusetts Institute of Technology, and Benjamin Andrew, President of Brown University, he formed the International Bimetallists, an organization that advocated the use of both silver and gold for an international money standard.

Brooks opened his campaign with "The Gold Standard," a pamphlet written in 1894. Devaluation of silver, he argued, had brought depression and dissension. If the silver solution was not immediately implemented, Adams characteristically foresaw catastrophe. Nihilism "in Russia, agrarian insurrection in Italy; anarchism in France and Spain; socialism in England and Germany" were warnings of what could happen here under the gold standard.[20]

Brooks Adams was becoming more radical. Even though he was a moderate silverite compared to the westerners, still the money issue, in the Populist context, was much hotter than civil-service reform or tariff reduction. Its potential explosiveness did not bother Adams in 1894 and 1895, and the campaign acted as a tonic. For years, he had "been preaching disaster and . . . suffering under the thing which is hardest to bear, the conspiracy of silence, and the being set aside as a harmless crank." But the popularity of "The Gold Standard" made people think of him as they did of other men. Approbation was particularly gratifying because it came from his own class. "I admit to being frankly more pleased at your letter," he told Lodge, "and one or two others I have received, than I have been at anything since Mrs. Adams told me she would marry me."

Although buoyed up by approval and resolving to fight hard, he remained convinced that the bankers would win. "Between you and me," he vowed to Lodge, "I think the end is near, but I am in the popular side of this fight and I mean to fight to the last." [21]

These were brave words, but Adams did not "fight to the last." Within a year of its unfurling, he hauled down his flag. In June, 1895, gratified at prospective recovery, he took comfort that "the bankers themselves are perfectly assured." Impressed by "Morgan's pool" which stopped the drain of gold, he admitted that "as for myself I am desperately anxious for the success of Morgan. Everything I am interested in hangs on that and I admit I cannot contemplate the collapse of the corner with equanimity." The possibility of another recession made "silver agitation . . . the worst thing for us, and the whole country. . . . If silver is to come it had best come naturally. . . . Not through a political, semi-revolutionary agitation, which would prostrate all values for several years." [22] Brooks, after all, was bound hand and foot to the master class. Whenever opposition got too radical or too threatening or whenever his own finances were in danger, he retreated behind the battlements of the bankers and rallied to the standard of the dollar sign. Henry was right, when many years later while commenting on his brother's cataclysmic predictions, he claimed that Brooks confused personal interests with political perceptions. [23]

An Adams, however, could not forever live in peace with a Morgan. "I can't disguise from myself that the victory of capital . . . will lead to anything but disaster to us," he wrote to Henry. "I can see no glimmer in the future, less than a year ago, far less than in 1893." [24]

With a vision of ultimate doom weighing on his mind, Brooks entered the campaign of 1896. At Chicago, he steered clear of both radicals and eastern bankers and supported the conservative silverite, Henry M. Teller. When Bryan was nominated, however, Brooks switched parties. Bryan's election, he feared, "would mean revolution and probably armed revolution." But Adams was not like other self-righteous McKinleyites who regarded the Nebraskan as the devil's latest disciple. If Bryan meant revolution and confiscation to Brooks Adams, McKinley meant oppression and depression. No matter who won, Adams would lose. Whether Bryan "is or [is] not [elected] appears to me to be the end of the Republic, or very near it." [25]

When the "Great Commoner" went down to defeat, there were no cries of joy or jeers of derision from Adams. McKinley was not his savior, nor had Bryan been an object of his hatred. Sensing an affinity of basic outlook and seeing another vestige of civilization destroyed by the modern machine age, he had a word of condolence for followers of a lost cause not unlike his own. Never had he seen so impressive a sight as this election—"a rising of miserable, bankrupt farmers, and day laborers, led by a newspaper reporter, have made the greatest fight against the organized capital of the world that has been made this century—or perhaps ever." [26]

When the brief elation of 1894 had passed, Adams reprinted *The Law Of Civilization And Decay*. The second edition, which came out in 1896, reflected his more pessimistic mood. A study of science and society had convinced him that man was but a plaything of fate. Determinism, the natural outgrowth of his worship for objective, scientific laws, was an admission of inability to cope with modern forces. This confession was emphasized by his personalized version of the Darwinian principle that anachronisms go under in the struggle for survival.

> Like other personal characteristics, the peculiarities of the mind are apparently strongly hereditary, and, if these instincts be transmitted from generation to generation, it is plain that, as the external world changes, those who receive this heritage must rise or fall in the social scale, according as their nervous system is well or ill adapted to the condition to which they are born. Nothing is commoner, for example, than to find families who have been famous in one century sinking into obscurity in the next, not because the children have degenerated, but because a certain field of activity which afforded full scope, has been closed against their offspring.[27]

What could Adams do? What could anyone born past his time do but wait for the inexorable laws of civilization to sentence him to oblivion?

Adams's pessimism, which culminated in the despair of 1896, was partly due to the cool reception of his books. Brooks's moods always fluctuated with his own image in the public eye. The great tragedy of his life, as in the lives of his ancestors, was his failure to receive plaudits from the populace. Rejection resulted in alienation, in the construction of a barrier between himself and humanity. Call it weakness, hurt pride, paranoia, or perverse self-isolation. However it is labeled, Adams's attitude defined his relationship with the world. Sometimes it appeared as self-pity, as when he wrote to Cecil

Spring Rice, then a comparative stranger, "My dear fellow, I'm a crank; very few human beings can endure to have me near them, but I like to be with you, and I suppose I like to be with those who are sympathetic, the more since they are so few." [28] Less hesitant with Henry, he unburdened himself of a mixture of pity and pride, of paranoia and outraged justice:

> I cannot disguise from myself, that for me too my race is run. I have nothing more to hope from the world. Here I am really an outcast. I hardly think you can appreciate not only how completely I am alone, but how I am shunned. I am treated as a man with a mark. As for a hearing I shall never have one, and now my strongest wish is to escape somewhere where I shall forget and be forgotten . . . this winter has been almost more than my nerves can stand; I am beginning to be frightened, . . .[29]

Sometimes the syndrome was dominated by anger. He raged at those who refused to accept him, and hell could have had few furies more bitter than Brooks Adams scorned:

> I don't care a damn for this country, or indeed for anything much except to get out of it at least for awhile, or at least out of Boston; Boston the modern Sodom. . . . Oh Henry; Oh my dear, what a bloody fool your brother has been ever since he was born, and he has lain in the gates of the rich like Lazarus. Why do I want to print a silly book that no one will read, and that I shall be cursed for, and laughed at for, by every chuckle headed gold bug who will be told by a reviewer that at last I have done the thing everyone was waiting for me to do. Proved myself insane.[30]

By 1896, with western radicals moving into the silver crusade, Adams had no more stomach for the fight on "the popular side." The allies of 1894 had departed leaving him "but one lonely man against whom all society is banded. . . . to crush me, to ridicule and suppress me." The "weight of this monied mass" was on him and all he wanted was "to escape from the whole thing." As Henry had been disillusioned with Grantism, Brooks discovered that "I am not made for this fight. It is folly in me to enter it." [31]

Defenseless and exposed, the silver moment having failed him, Adams could find no new source of strength, no belief behind which to seek shelter. "If I believed in a god, in a future, in a cause, in human virtue, right or wrong, in an ultimate transfiguration of the human race," he wailed to Henry.[32] But there was no cause and there was no belief—there was only loneliness.

Brooks inherited the family propensity for turning private reverses into cosmic catastrophes. If Adams had been crushed by money-grubbing philistines, then the whole world would share this defeat. Amid his own disappointment, "The country . . . seemed . . . utterly barren," without "one ennobling instinct." Society was "at the end," he thought, "and the one thing" he found gratifying was "that we have no children." [33] The Adams habit of amplifying personal setbacks into national crises deflected guilt by placing the burden of failure upon society. Seeking relief from defeat by reading global misfortune into unsettling experiences was a characteristic response among cataclysmists.

Mutual moroseness made Henry and Brooks partners in misery. Having similar values and reactions, they pooled their emotional resources to compensate each other for wounds received from an unfeeling world. One conviction they held in common was a dislike for Jews. Brooks matched Henry's bigotry, bitterly condemning Jewry as the embodiment of the master class. A bit of free-silver anti-Semitism must have rubbed off, for he thought "the pure Jew," a "pure concentrated gold bug," a villainous parasite living off the hard earned gains of the producing class.[34] Through "a vast syndicate," the Hebrews controlled London and thereby "the world."[35] This vision of the conspiratorial Jew holding the globe in his mercenary grasp revealed Brooks's alienation from the contemporary era. The Jew symbolized both betrayal and the advent of financial capitalism. In arguing that the Jews had become supreme, Adams proclaimed his own displacement by business.

His estrangement also manifested itself in a longing for the past. Medieval history had been Brooks's favorite period since his youth. He eagerly responded to his elder brother's interest now that Henry, drawn by a similar need, was immersed in the Middle Ages. "I am delighted to hear that you have been making a Gothic pilgrimage," he told his brother. "On the whole, the parts of my life which I look back to with the greatest delight are those I have spent among the churches and castles of the Middle Ages." Like Henry, he had been overwhelmed by the cathedral where he "really and truly did believe the miracle, and . . . sat and blubbered in the nave and knelt at the elevation." The "Gothic is the greatest emotional stimulant in the world. I am of it, I understand it, I know how those men felt, and I am in feeling absolutely one with St. Anselm, or Godfrey de Bouillon." [36] The twelfth century, an age unsullied by commonness, became a refuge for alienated aristocrats.

Despair drove Brooks Adams abroad in 1895, but his spirits were not raised by the trip, and he surveyed foreign lands with the same scorn as his own. A journey to India brought forth strident racism and an almost Nietzschean contempt for the weak. "To the Western mind, the mind of the conquering race, . . . The Indians are slaves." Instead of exhibiting the conquerors' vitality, they only "endure—endure beyond all belief." In Anglo-Saxon freebooters like Adams, pacifism invoked instinctive contempt. Even racism, which had compensated inferiority feelings in so many others, did not bring comfort, however. Inert India, for Adams, was an example to nations like the United States of what happens when "the fighting races, the manly, bold and noble races, the only men who have ever done anything worth doing, have been annihilated, evicted from their lands, wiped out, and their place . . . taken by a mixed mass of usurers." [37]

Adams's foreign trip initiated a crusade that occupied his remaining years. America's world position concerned him greatly, and he felt that the course of empire was the only route to national power. Geopolitics had fascinated Brooks for some time. As early as publication of *The Law Of Civilization and Decay,* he had believed that trade routes, access to markets, and ability to undersell competitors were the vital sinews of a country's strength. The visit to India, by awakening racism and expectations of an East-West conflict, stimulated his imperialist thinking. By January, 1896, he was sure that the United States was in a death battle for world supremacy that would end in defeat if the magnates continued to dominate soldiers and luxury to undermine Spartan living standards. Without soldiers or cheap goods, the West could neither conquer nor compete with the East. To Adams, the situation bore "every mark of premature decay." He gave Europe three generations and the rest of the "system" until the "twenty-first century" before total disintegration.[38]

After 1896, Adams embraced imperialism. The silver crusade had ended dismally, and there was no better way to regain public favor than to court the present popular passion. Furthermore, expansion not only had mass appeal but one's closest friends advocated it. Imperialism, however, meant something more to Adams than a vehicle by which to win congenial companionship and popular approval. It engaged his interests, embodied his ideals, and thrilled every fiber of his being. Initially opposed by business, it was, for Brooks, another way to combat commercial encroachment. Through the quest for empire, he idealized force and deified the warrior. Thus he hoped to reinforce those vital qualities that he saw being undermined in the modern era. In addition, belief in racist expansion compensated for patrician decline. If the Brahmin élite had been displaced, at least he could still be part of the sovereign race. The cause also appealed intellectually; it furnished a global program corresponding to the world outlook for which Adams pleaded. Finally, the belligerency inevitable in imperialism was a fitting climax to the conflict of a Darwinian society. In mind and in spirit, if ever a man was suited to an idea, Brooks Adams was suited to imperialism.

At first, Brooks treated foreign prospects as glumly as he had domestic problems. America's commitment to empire, the Spanish-American War, was greeted with the usual pessimism. "I am in despair," he wrote Henry, "to have this silly business forced on us, where we can gain neither glory nor profit . . ." He fretted about the nation's finances and military ability and about his own bank account.[39] As Brooks put it, however, nothing "lays me out" like a victory. Accordingly, after Manila, he adjudged "our world position" much improved.[40] But global strategy was not nearly as thrilling as the specific exploits of America's forces. Adams, brimming with pride over victory, retracted his long standing accusation that the country was under the golden thumb of the financiers. "I have often told you that the old tradition was dead," he said to his young niece, "that the world was the Jews and that State Street and ignominy were all that was left us now. I was wrong. The old tradition lives. Gentlemen still survive." [41] The war meant America's rebirth and Adams's own resurgence. "Taking Boston, in general," he gleefully remarked, "it is beginning, if you can believe such a thing, to trifle with our notions." [42]

The conflict intensified Adams's nationalism. Conscious of being on the popular side for once, Brooks proudly proclaimed that "I am an expansionist, and an 'imperialist,' if you please, and I presume I may be willing to go farther in this line than anybody else in Massachusetts, with perhaps, a few exceptions." [43] Victory made him wave the flag even more grandly. Prewar despair had disappeared, and the new century dawned optimistically on an Adams who believed the nation's pre-eminence to be at most only a few years away.

Adams's next book, *America's Economic Supremacy,* developed the argument for America's assumption of world power. The Panic of 1893, once a source of dismay, had actually brought about the nation's economic supremacy. Driven by depression to undersell Europe, America had turned the Continent into a market and had become leader of the western coalition against Germany and Russia. The outcome of the struggle between Orient and Occident would be decided in Asian markets. Due to recent territorial acquisitions, the

United States had only to drop its isolationistic traditions, and hegemony would easily be secured. The Teutonic-Slavic combination, once quite formidable, was, in Adams's *fin de siècle* optimism, bankrupt and obsolescent.

In order to sustain its position, the nation had to adjust to changing conditions. Success in modern life meant economy, activity, and centralization. Business, above all other contemporary forces, had met these demands. Corporate efficiency had enabled America to undersell other countries and capture international markets. Since empire was the political counterpart of the trust, Adams, by advocating one, had come to support the other. The combination of personal prosperity, the imperialist crusade, and capitalistic support of military conquests had caused him to repudiate his former antipathy toward the corporations.

Adams remained sanguine for the next few years. *America's Economic Supremacy* sold widely and was respected in the right circles. For once, Brooks was accepted by the influential intelligentsia. "Opinion is running . . . strong with the new movement," he wrote. "As I happen to be pretty widely identified with the new departure it naturally makes a change in my position; and to my intense astonishment, I find myself, for the first time in my life, growing actually popular." [44]

These already high spirits soared at Roosevelt's accession. With Theodore as President and Cabot running Congress, it seemed for a time as if the commercial tide had been rolled back, as if America's destiny was once again being guided by aristocrats who believed in action, imagination, and expansion. At last, Brooks Adams would have a hand in national policy. A lifetime of hungering for recognition, of being frustrated by issuing clarion calls that bounced back as empty echoes, seemed to be over. Only a few months before Brooks received his great chance, Henry attested to his brother's craving for power. He pointed out that his own displacement was as nothing compared to that of "poor Brooks," who was "the real sacrifice, for he was ambitious." [45] A truer comparison between the brothers has never been made. Henry had relaxed his grip on the twentieth century and was sinking into the passive romanticism of Virgin adoration, while Brooks still tried to make his way in this world. Long after one Adams had given up, the other, still driven by a Puritan conscience and a reformer's energy, eagerly grasped his final chance for power. At last, his ambition was to be realized. "Thou hast it now: King, Cawdor, Glamis, the world can give no more," Brooks cried perhaps a bit vicariously to Roosevelt. So inspired was he in his fight for Roosevelt that he lauded him as greater than the greatest Roman emperor. "Hail Caesar!" Hail Theodore!—"The President who began the contest for the supremacy of America against the eastern continent." [46]

Brooks was deliriously happy in the months following the inauguration. Anticipating a Roman triumph, he willingly forgot years of iconoclasm and embraced values upon which he had previously spat. Now "that we have the world at our feet," he was "for the new world. . . . electric cars, mobiles, plutocracy and all." After all, he reasoned, "I don't live but once, and when one is dead its for a long time and a nation is only great once. One might as well try to cut off a hunk of fat, even if you don't like a particular kind." [47] Adams, like Donnelly, was the marginal man—condemning what he really wanted and praising a way of life that was at best a consolation for what he could not have. Usually, he posed as the lonely aristocrat, the forgotten man martyred by his age, but when ambition beckoned, he became a modern man. How the tune changed when success was the piper!

America was the macrocosm of Adams' euphoria, and he wellnigh burst with national pride. America's "enemies were either foolish or bewildered." For the "first time," Brooks felt "that for us is the earth and the fullness thereof." [48] Utopia never meant much to Henry Adams. After Mugwumpery failed, he awaited an adverse fate. For activists like Brooks Adams and Ignatius Donnelly, however, resignation was impossible. As changes in personal fortune triggered elation or depression, their visions of the future fluctuated between wish-fulfillment and wish-destruction. In the all-or nothing-world of these cataclysmists, utopia alternated with disaster.

Adams's nationalism was not notable for its uniqueness. Like a thousand other patriots before and after, he called for a native culture and was thrilled by any display of national power. Military glory became more of an obsession than ever before. "As to me there is nothing so magnificent as the soldier's death," he said at a veteran's memorial service. "War may be terrible, but it is also beneficent, for it has given us the noblest type of manhood that, I believe, the race has ever known. It has given us the American soldier." [49] The man on horseback, whether twelfth-century knight or twentieth-century warrior, was always Brooks's hero.

Even those hopeful times, however, were not without problems. Believing war to be "the ultimate form of economic competition," Adams anticipated that America's prosperity would invite strife. Germany and Russia could not be squeezed out without violence, and, as a last resort, they would start a "war to the death,—a struggle no longer against single nations, but against a continent." [50]

The danger of impending conflict seemed to escape most citizens. By being woefully unprepared, inadequately armed, and pacifistic the people indicated that they had not "maturely considered" their position in the power struggle and were still hampered with "old prejudices" against making war and conquering territory. The worship of force that led Brooks Adams to admire uniforms also convinced him that an "opulent, unarmed" America was putting a "premium" on European aggression.[51]

Another weakness was our decentralized and disorganized government. Survival depended upon organizing for cheap production, but even in a hopeful mood Adams doubted whether there could be such consolidation to capture foreign markets. Although the country's industries were expanding, "administrative power does not grow with the mass." Haphazard organization was unable to manage the unprecedented mass and accelerated energy created by science and competition. Already "society is quivering under the strain," a "social reorganization must take place, or something would give way." [52]

By 1904, these doubts had undermined Brooks's confidence. Business, once the force behind national greatness, now symptomized administrative inefficiency. In order to establish an adequate measure of government control over commerce, he re-engaged the vested interests. Adams's campaign for railroad rate regulation was carried out in the same moderate fashion as his previous reform efforts. Brooks did not cross the Rubicon of radicalism by demanding state ownership, but, in true Progressive style, he rapped errant corporations across their greedy hands with the rule of law. He asserted that transportation should be regulated by government because travel on highways is a "public trust" and railroad monopolies were setting "arbitrary" rates that taxed people far in excess of a fair return. Therefore, the railroad was violating one of the most sacred Progressive canons, "equality before the law." But for Adams, "sovereignty" was even more important than equity. If the government did not act, private corporations would encroach upon its powers, subvert the law, and seize control of the nation. Then the state "will have become a formal instrument serving as a mask to protect a sovereign oligarchy," and the capitalists would absorb "the whole national wealth." These two essentials of Progressivism, equality before the law and the public sovereignty, had to be maintained— otherwise "constitutional government" would be destroyed. On its ruins would arise the bugaboo of all middle class reform—the threat of violent conflict between those who had too much and those who had nothing. "The worst convulsions which have rent society," he warned, touching Progressivism's most responsive chord, "have been caused by the effort of the weak to free themselves from unequal exactions imposed by the strong." [53]

Brooks was thoroughly imbued with the spirit of New Nationalism. He recognized the value of trusts and even advocated more economic concentration, but he never forgot the difference between good and bad corporations. He worshipped neither Adam Smith nor Andrew Carnegie. If free enterprise would destroy our economy because it was inefficient and antiquated, monopoly would strangle it through greed and corruption.

Adams regarded his skirmish with the railroads as part of a general offensive Roosevelt had mounted against the vested interests. Although victorious in his own battle, he was disconsolate because the campaign on Capitol Hill seemed lost. The honeymoon of 1901-1903 was over. Capital had vanquished even his idol, the Lochinvar of the upper class, Theodore Roosevelt. "The magnates have won," he told Henry. "You are now to have Mr. Morgan and his hired hands owning the Senate, the Senate really naming the judges, and the judges executing the orders of the Senate." Anticipation of business rule awakened cataclysmic thoughts dormant since Roosevelt's accession. Once again, Adams doubted the duration of "this system." [54]

Underlying the gloom of these years was keen disappointment at being denied the recognition he so eagerly desired. "Ten years ago," Brooks once remarked, "I admit, I should have liked to hold office, but a man cannot be young forever, nor can he be Jack of all trades." To this disclaimer, however, he added, "I have turned toward writing, not from choice, but from necessity." But even if he is taken at his word about holding office, there was still the attraction of moving behind the facade of titles to grasp real power. By 1902, any hopes along this line had also been dashed. After having "had a good look at Washington," he was sure that, although "they are willing enough to use me, and take my ideas when convenient . . . they don't want me about." [55] Deprivation of a long awaited and ardently sought after reward raised old suspicions of persecution. Others would "steal" from him, they would get "money" and "fame" properly his.[56] Being shunted aside just when he expected his hour to strike brought back the old depressing sense of worthlessness. Once more he felt "nothing one does matters very much one way or the other." Effort made no difference in an "age notable for the way it could ignore." [57]

Depressed by Roosevelt's failure to halt business, disappointed at not having an official role, and watching his contemporaries disappear through the attrition of old age, Adams sank into cataclysmic thoughts. As a result of Russia's defeat in 1905, he was sure Europe would collapse, thus precipitating the final "struggle." [58] In 1906, he set the date for international catastrophe in 1925, but two years later, after being "shaken most uncomfortably," he doubted whether disaster would hold off that long.[59]

As the present grew more forbidding, the past became more precious. Increasingly conscious of the passing of his class, Adams indulged in a sentimental requiem with his equally nostalgic brother: "Almost the worst is that I feel as if we were the last of it. I'm afraid the next generation knows little and cares less for the things we cared for." [60] Brooks spent summers in the "Old House" at Quincy and decided to turn it into a memorial. He collected all the Adams memorabilia and, in a fit of ancestral possessiveness, prevailed upon his brothers to prevent family papers from being scrutinized by eyes that were not Adamses.' Adoration of the past extended to early heroes like Washington but concentrated chiefly on his own famous forebears. One offering of this worship was a biography of his grandfather. In such esteem did Brooks hold John Quincy, however, that, always prejudiced against family studies and doubting whether his own did full justice to its subject, he withheld publication.

A deep urge to establish continuity with the past is readily apparent in this work. John and John Quincy Adams are portrayed as having the same values, suffering the same slights, and enduring the same emotional anguish as their descendant. They, too, led thoroughly miserable lives, and their discouragement stemmed from the same source—popular rejection. Brooks saw his grandfather very much in his own image. To him, John Quincy Adams was the last of a species, the vestige of a vanishing society. John Quincy "belonged to a dying civilization," an era that "cherished antiquated standards of right and wrong." These virtues made him ineffectual against "the Jacksonian faction" and so he was swept aside in the triumph of a corrupted democracy.

Beliefs, as well as moods, were shared by the men. John Quincy had had little use for businessmen and was so resented that "the wealthy manufacturers of the North. . . . thought him a semi-demented incendiary." As an expansionistic Secretary of State, he had had the astounding foresight to realize that "the equilibrium of human society" was moving acros the Atlantic. The Adamses, agreeing on national destiny, were also in accord on the means of its implementation. John Adams and his son had advocated a strong military establishment. They represented "the nation militant," basing "their whole theory of life upon the necessity of the use of physical force."

The author's feelings of persecution were projected on the figures in this biography. His grandfather and great-grandfather appeared as the innocent objects of vicious opprobrium. Criticism against John Adams must have been "engendered by personal malice, since no one any longer attempts to dispute the purity or wisdom of his acts." His son, John Quincy Adams, despite great vilification, "was the last and perhaps the extremest specimen of an illustrious race of patriots and statesmen."[61]

Brooks now completely identified with his ancestors. Writing to Henry in 1909, he said of their grandfather and of themselves: "No one ever understood him, no one will ever understand us—but he was right and we are right." "Adams was heavy, I am heavy. We are what we are, we cannot be changed." In the defeat of John Quincy Adams, he read the doom of America: "Washington and he were the only two men who conceived of America as a unity and tried practically to realize their ideas. They failed and with them our civilization has failed." [62] Eighty years after that misfortune, another family failure had occurred. Once again, an Adams was scorned when he tried to point out the road to salvation. Indeed, one wonders to which Adams Brooks was referring in 1909.

Brooks had previously been ambivalent toward the past. His early book, *The Emancipation of Massachusetts,* was filled with ancestral criticism. At times, when he seemed to be moving in harmony with the dominant modern forces, Adams praised the present. But now that his star had definitely set, comfort lay only in the past. Unfulfilled ambition made only those things never contested seem worthy of winning.

Advancing age and contemplation of family tradition made Adams more conscious of class ties. He was even pained by the death throes of foreign aristocrats. A Tory setback in the elections of 1910 occasioned regret that England's "landed aristocracy" had not lasted "for my time." Their defeat meant "that the whole world is to be swept away before my eyes." It saddened him to realize that all is "gone, everything I love or understand or respect, is dead with the wild animals, and the country and poetry, and color and form." For him, perhaps, it was also "time . . . to die." [63] America's failure to halt business encroachment made him feel even more strongly the deposition of "an old ruling class whose power is broken, whose privileges are being taken away, who is facing an economic position with which they admit they cannot deal, and who is half wild with fear of attack." [64] It was the twilight of the gods for Brooks, as he praised Oliver Wendell Holmes for being "the last of the great race who have had at once the taste and the power to do them [make speeches] perfectly. Like poetry it dies with us."[65] Even taste, that last refuge of the patricians, was being destroyed by the onslaught of the ascending class.

Disappointments in the Roosevelt era turned the aggressive seeker after power into the victimized old man. Feebleness partly excused failure, and guilt was neutralized by a withdrawal from society. Nostalgia for the past and martyrdom in the present—such self-dramatization was all that remained after a life of defeat. The passing of his class convinced Brooks that disintegration was imminent, and he vied with Henry for the most pessimistic formulation of the Second Law of Thermodynamics. "I have reached precisely your conclusions," he wrote, "except that I incline to think that energy is absolutely lost and that it is not degraded." He was morally certain that "men are losing energy—mental energy I mean and very fast."[66] "The only question" now "is one of time," and even twenty-five years was "too long."[67]

Adams's cataclysmic mood varied. At times he felt himself yielding "to the depression of age." Catastrophe had become a "fixed idea," and he began "to fear lest . . . it makes me doubt my own balance. I talk and think of little else."[68] Unfortunately, these fruitful introspections disappeared as others came to share his outlook. As always, acceptance dissolved his self-doubt. Gratified at being "actually accepted as orthodox and conservative," Brooks suddenly discovered that "I have more than I ever deserved."[69] He had become "an exceptionally happy man, . . . happier than I have ever been," even if "the atmosphere about us is so charged with an indescribably sickening decay that it is very hard to resist depression." Though the old crowd was dying, and "we have not much further to go," Adams found "this satisfaction, thank God! At least I have lived. I have known the old world. I have loved, and hoped and believed . . . the deluge may come—but we have lived."[70]

Did this euphoria amid disaster mean that his gloomy prophecies had been a pose? Brooks's intimates sometimes thought so. "I have known you for sixty-odd years," wrote Henry, "and since you were a baby I've never known you when you weren't making yourself miserable over the failings of the universe. It has been your amusement, and a very good one."[71] Such an estimation is substantiated by his chameleon moods, in which somber expectations alternated with personal elation. But, even if Adams was not above gilding the lily or using the world as a stage for his own tragedy, a genuine atmosphere of despair hung about him. There was nothing of the *poseur* in these words of regret at his inability to commit himself to an ideal or cause:

> I wish I could have faith in Christ. It is sad to have no inner light as we near the end and I have none. I cannot care, as you do, for the race in general. I am no philanthropist. My nature, my race, my blood confines my affections and bounds my interests. If they are doomed I care not for the future. It is too cold for me. For me, the world dies with them. Very seriously, I envy you who can find consolation in the stars, as I envy men like Newman, who can find rest in the Church.[72]

While in this somber mood, Adams wrote *The Theory Of Social Revolutions*. In his other works, he had debated the people's willingness to administer energy released by modern science and business. In the new book, a veritable graveyard of abandoned hopes, he questioned whether "finite minds" ever have the capacity to organize such boundless forces. The discrepancy between organization and production of enegry, only a danger in 1904, had already enabled the capitalists to seize "sovereignty." Once in command, the magnates had shown themselves unscrupulously greedy, bankrupting debtors and twisting the laws to serve their ends. To protect themselves from corporate servitude, workers had formed unions. Now the two groups were squaring off for a battle that "may at any moment, shatter the social system; while under our laws and institutions, society is helpless." At one time, he had believed there was a chance capitalists could apply economic centralization to administration; now he conculded that specialization would prevent them from functioning outside of business. Paradoxically, the very specialization that had enabled captains of industry to seize power might be their undoing. Unless the vested interests became more responsible and adapted to new social demands, they would go the way of previous élites. Brooks warns that "the experience of the English speaking race" included a violent upheaval "about every three generations." [73] According to his calculations, capitalists had taken control around 1865, approximately two generations before. There was little time left.

In the *Theory Of Social Revolutions,* the final formulation of Brooks Adams's philosophy, Progressivism is fused with Darwinian determinism. Unlike Henry, who emphasized the laws of thermodynamics, Brooks clung to the Darwinian framework throughout his lifetime. Perhaps the younger Adams held onto the doctrine of evolution because he still struggled to survive in the modern world long after his brother had surrendered. Since business had failed to adapt, it must abdicate sovereignty or be annihilated. Some power must be found to mediate between management and labor, to suppress revolutionary forces by establishing the supremacy of law. To Adams's Progressive mind, only government could ensure equity. Roosevelt's Square Deal offered society its last chance to avoid becoming a jungle in which the struggle for existence could only go against its unfit leaders.

World War I confirmed Brooks's conviction that catastrophe was inevitable. In this cataclysmic mood, Adams published an article designed to crush the false illusions of our civilization. "No society," he asserted, "ever has succeeded or ever can succeed, in realizing any ideal or abstraction whatever, because, . . . the interposition of the flesh makes impossible the fulfillment of the law. And yet to-day our democratic society gravely proposes to cause infinite nature to permit man to live in peace." "Unable to reconcile himself to the calamities of his lot" the selfish American dreams "that he may escape self-denial and hardship by omitting those duties which entail a sacrifice." Brooks demanded that these delusions cease and that mankind face up to the fact that it was an atom of "measureless space . . . never being at rest, never in perfect equilibrium, but assuming forms which have the aspect of competing selfishly with each other." In such a cosmos, man could never achieve any goal, let alone the ideals of peace and freedom.

Adams vented his distaste for modern America by bitterly assailing democracy. Popular rule was actually a conspiracy of "recklessness and self-complacency" against "the common safety." It exalted "the individual" over the necessity for community cooperation. Without discipline, "even an approximation to order, justice, mercy, peace, or any of the ideals is impossible." [74] Even survival was impossible in a society atomized and immobilized by the centrifugal force of human selfishness. Shortly, Brooks expected, a "more cohesive and intelligent organism . . . shall spring upon us and rend us as the strong have always rent those wretched . . . feeble creatures who are cursed with an abortive development." [75]

Disgust for democracy was consistent with the Calvinist creed that attracted Adams in his later years. Submersion in family history and a confession of faith at the First Parish Church on November 11, 1914 (an adherence to an Old Puritan custom), were signs of his tapping of ancestral roots. Henry fled to history in order to escape his conscience, but Brooks embraced the past to reaffirm a rigid moral code. The elder brother pleaded for mercy; the younger demanded retribution. Brooks embraced the communitarian and even the authoritarian aspects of Protestantism. "No society like anything which we or our ancestors have known, can cohere without a faith in revealed religion," were the words of his confession.[76] "Perfection," to the new saint, presupposed "a code of moral standards" that would provide barriers against selfish irresponsibility. Sensual desire offered one challenge, but the real task was to overcome the sin of pride. Adams echoed his stern-visaged Puritan fathers by declaring that man's "greatest enemy is always his own vanity and self esteem," his refusal "to admit his own intellectual impotence in the face of the infinite, and endure with resignation his destiny. He is always aspiring to dominate nature and is always suffering defeat." "Democracy," reveling in "personal liberty," encourages rebellion against proper restraint and enables lust and pride to master men.[77] What could be more reminiscent of Governor John Winthrop's distinction between "Civil Liberty" and "Natural Liberty" than Brooks Adams's "Can War Be Done Away With?"

Adams's antidemocratic diatribe reflected his alienation from contemporary America. A "growing reluctance to express my views in public," evidenced the distance between him and his fellow citizens. "So far sundered from most of" his countrymen did he find himself, that he shrank "exceedingly from thrusting on them opinions which will give offense, or more likely still, excite derision." [78] Brooks was reluctant to express himself because the country's basic ideal was the source of all his problems. Democracy created an open society, which permitted the wrong people to eclipse the Brahmin élite. By substituting change for permanence, individualism for community, and anarchy for order, popular rule upset aristocratic calculations and turned patrician virtues into weaknesses.

The war was not a pleasant period for Adams. In 1915, his brother Charles's death triggered another wave of despondency. "Good luck has followed him to the end," he wrote Henry. "I wish I dared to hope that a like passage might be mine." Death in the family accentuated the emptiness of life. As Brooks looked "back through the long series of years," he wondered "more day by day what it has all been about and why I am here at all." [79] His depression was so overwhelming that the old stimulants failed to raise his spirits. America's triumphs did not "lay him out" as lesser victories had done twenty years earlier. Even long-awaited election to public office—that of delegate from Quincy to the Massachusetts Constitutional Convention of 1917-1919—failed to encourage him.

In 1918, Adams was struck an even more crushing blow in the death of Henry. When his brother died, he wrote to Holmes bemoaning the loss that "nothing can ever . . . make good." From boyhood, Henry had "filled a place in my life which was all his own and now, I frankly admit that, reason with oneself as I may, I cannot pull myself together at all—I do not suppose I ever shall be able to." [80]

Adams entered his last productive year with a heavy heart. His first venture was a new edition of *The Emancipation of Massachusetts*. The preface to this reprint sharply pointed up the differences between the old man of 1919 and the youthful optimist of 1887. Adams professed amazement that he had once maintained "the Twelfth and Thirteenth centuries" to be "as contrasted with the Nineteenth, ages of intellectual torpor." The venerable pessimist was startled by "the self-satisfied . . . finality of my conclusions." He renounced an earlier confidence in progress and repudiated any past belief in the order of the universe or the unity of science. In a passage similar to Henry's *Education* he recanted his former faith: "Each day I live I am less able to withstand the suspicion that the universe, far from being an expression of law originating in a single primary cause, is a chaos which admits of reaching no equilibrium and in which man is doomed eternally and hopelessly." As society sank deeper into directionless anarchy, an acceleration of energy was hastening our doom. Signs of disaster abounded. Imminent defeat by Asia, disorganized administration, and the triumph of desire over discipline all indicated that "democracy in America has conspicuously and decisively failed" and that "capitalistic civilization, . . . is nearing an end." [81]

Brooks's last publication was, fittingly, an introduction to Henry's *Degradation Of The Democratic Dogma*. Henry's work on the cataclysmic implications of the Second Law of Thermodynamics was in keeping with his mood. Characteristic also was Adams's lengthy discourse on the family. In this last projection of himself onto the past, he portrayed his grandfather as a tragic hero betrayed by the "Democratic Dogma." John Quincy embodied all the noble ideals, he was enlightened, rational, scientific, patriotic, and incorruptible. Yet in the end, these very merits led to his rejection. Trapped by virtue, he was lost in a struggle with slick charlatans who capitalized on the common man's selfishness. To Brooks Adams, John Quincy was a lion amid jackals. But a whole pack of jackals is too much even for a lion.

Brooks Adams was sure that in resisting the allurements of the harlot democracy, he had avoided his grandfather's failure. He too had "inherited a belief in the great democratic dogma" but had "learned . . . to look on man, . . . as a pure automaton, who is moved along the paths of least resistance by forces over which he had no control. In short, I reverted to the pure Calvinistic philosophy."

Fortified by Calvinism, Brooks skirted the pitfalls of his ancestor. He realized "that the strongest of human passions [are]—fear and greed," and he put no more faith in chaotic science.[82] Above all, Brooks was wary of democracy. This system, the child of idealism, science, and free will, had inherited all their faults. It was steeped in chaos and complexity. Democracy had deified competition and surrendered to selfishness. Adams could take pride in the fact that he had not yielded to the blandishments of popular rule. But even an arid pride is not satisfied by avoiding defeat, especially at the price of not entering the fray. His was still a Calvinistic pride to be gratified only when the millennium arrived. On that glorious day, when "the ultimate conclusion came," when "social war, or massacre" would end democracy, Brooks Adams and his kin would sit at the right hand of God.[83] In spite of this grim triumph, however, the grandson shared in his grandfather's downfall. It was clear that he too had been beaten, for he would hardly demand vengeance for a defeat that he had not suffered. Nonetheless, Adams called for the judgment day and claimed justice. He did not really, however, want them at all, for in his innermost heart, a voice plaintively cried for mercy.

Oliver Wendell Holmes once said that, although "I have known him [Brooks Adams] from boyhood. . . . yet I still don't quite know what to think." [84] These words are heartening to those who study Brooks Adams and also do not "quite know what to think." From the complex personality and the diverse moods, however, some basic emotional patterns do emerge. Clearly, his doubts about himself and his country rose out of status anxiety. Adams, keenly aware of belonging to a declining class, evinced the self doubt and ineffectuality that often accompany social displacement. A life that did not fulfill the promise of its birthright of national leadership must have been a nightmare of failure. Out of such feelings came the authoritarian conviction that man could neither master his fate nor be autonomous without sinning. The dead weight of the past was a staggering handicap for Brooks, and his whole life was a struggle to prevent himself from buckling under. Restlessness and *ennui,* anti-Semitism and imperialism, escape through Calvinism or cataclysmism were all attempts to lay down this burden. But Adams was too proud, too sensitive, and too intelligent to forget his legacy, and through the pathetic rationalizations and self-deceptions there frequently flashed insights that revealed painful awareness of his predicament. "I apprehend that I approach pretty nearly being utterly without a use in the world I live in," he told Henry in 1901. "It is a sign that the blood is exhausted, and that we have come to the end. Apparently our generation was all right. We seemed to have ability, energy and opportunity, and yet we all have tried and have not suited ourselves or anybody else." [85]

It was one thing to admit ineffectuality, but it would be asking too much of any human being that he shoulder full responsibility for a lost life. Brooks admitted to being an anachronism, but he never forgave the society that had made him one. Of all human conditions, irrelevance is the hardest to bear and the most difficult for its sufferer to forgive. The longer Brooks was ignored in his own time, the more he professed to scorn the present and to admire the past. When the present grew so unbearable that the divergence between the two could no longer be spanned, it followed that the modern era had to be destroyed. Lacking virtue, which meant not appreciating an Adams, twentieth-century society could not survive. The bitterest charges, the most dire accusations, were hurled against the pre-emptors. The Jew, the banker, and the industrialist were held responsible for society's miserable state because they typified contemporary culture. They had driven the Adamses from their perch; they were interlopers destroying America's native aristocracy. Not knowing the past, not having shared in building the present, their ravenous hands mercilessly tore civilization apart. But Brooks, angry at being displaced, would be revenged. In his own alienation, the new leaders became aliens; his own guilt for failure would be purged by society's destruction.

Since Adams had been born at the juncture of the present and the past, since he existed in the twentieth century but really lived in the eighteenth, he was deeply divided. Inability to come to terms with himself and his age caused contradictions in his thought and behavior. He could plead for centralization, expansion, and adjustment while claiming that preindustrial traits were necessary for adaptation. Ultimately, despite his commitment to modern times, he chose the past and rejected the magnates in favor of aristocrats like George Washington, John Quincy Adams, and Theodore Roosevelt. Great discrepancies also appeared between his diagnoses of radical social ills and his prescriptions for superficial nostrums. Despite his cataclysmic predictions, Adams was almost as much a Mugwump while he called himelf a Progressive as when he agitated for civil-service reform in the 1870's. The challenge of science also stirred irreconcilable notions. Brooks argued repeatedly that the application of scientific principles to social problems was our only salvation. Yet, at the end of his life, he embraced Calvinism and claimed that science was leading us to chaos.

Adams's values were as much at war as his ideas. Although

asserting aristocratic obsolescence, he trusted only Roosevelt and Lodge. Professing to be a rigid determinist, he spent his life trying to divert the nation from its fate. Thus despite his claim of amoral pragmatism, he wound up condemning America for its sinfulness.

His conflicting moods, values, and ideas were the results of a divided personality. A lifetime of dismal prophecy did not prevent his friends from thinking him something of a *poseur*. Nor did frustration at not being taken seriously prevent him from playing the "crank." Rather, it led to a transparent disdain for humanity that showed that he had been cut to the quick by lack of recognition.

Interminable contradictions were created by a deeply dissatisfied, doubt-ridden existence. In desperation, Brooks sought solace by suppressing the warring elements within him. Authority in any form, but chiefly military or religious, promised peace. Democracy, on the other hand, was feared and hated because it preached autonomy for one who craved discipline to curb his clashing emotions. Even the relief of losing his individuality was denied him, however. Adams was unable to fall back on the religion of his forefathers athough he had made a confession of their faith. How could one believe in a god who escaped his responsibility by allowing "young men to grow old?" How could one love a god who left one's life in "a devilish turmoil." [86] That was life for Brooks Adams— "a devilish turmoil." He was at war with society and at war with himself, and his great tragedy was that he could achieve neither victory nor peace.

Jack London

"THE STONE THE BUILDERS REJECTED"

JACK LONDON WAS UNIQUE among the cataclysmists. A generation younger than Adams and Donnelly, he had known no agrarian innocence or secure aristocratic position. The memories that others made into causes were absent in his life. He was not involved in the defense against industrialism, nor did he share the frustration of identification with declining groups. On the contrary, judged by the standard of social mobility, London would have been a fitting hero for an Alger novel. He climbed out of the anonymity of poverty to become one of the wealthiest and best known writers of his day. If he was spared the bitterness of fighting for lost causes, however, he was also denied the warmth and purpose of even quixotic crusades. Neither his freedom from birth-ties to the declining élites or success in his own time lessened his susceptibility to the debilitation and disappointment that the new era had inflicted upon the others. Bound to no group, having no ties with the past, London was a rootless individual. He was the romantic adventurer who blazed a path without guideposts—a path that came from nowhere and led to nowhere.

The romantic adventurer as a type is lonely and unstable. He eternally quests after life yet runs away from it; he seeks meaningful experiences but refuses to come to terms with existence in any but a fleeting and sensational way; he flaunts his individuality, dedicating himself to ego fulfillment, but he really has no coherent sef-image and in fact seeks to escape his self and the limitations its recognition would force upon him by constantly seeking new ties, new places, new thrills.

Even before birth, it seemed as if fate had conspired to give Jack London such a destiny. His natural father, William Henry Chaney, was born in Maine and went West intending to become a Mississippi river pirate. Instead, he became an enthusiastic astrologer. While pursuing his profession in San Francisco, Chaney met Flora Wellman, daughter of Marshall Wellman, a native born American who had risen from pioneer to wealthy Ohio canal builder. Any hope for a normal life had been lost to Flora after an attack of typhus. It had marred her looks and, according to some, unhinged her mind. She constantly quarrelled with her family and, after one particularly severe dispute, left home. Chaney, something of a ladies' man, lived with her for awhile. Under his tutelage, she became a spiritualist. Out of their union, unblessed by clergy, Jack London was born in January, 1876. Chaney had deserted Flora six months before the birth. When he left, she attempted, or faked an attempt at, suicide, and the whole affair was luridly reported in the San Francisco *Chronicle*. London never met his father, although in the shock of learning about his illegitimacy, he once communicated with Chaney to establish his parentage. Eight months after giving birth, Flora married John London, formerly a midwestern farmer and carpenter and, now a widower with two small daughters. Jack was closer to his stepfather than to his mother. John London gave his son the affection, concern, and trust that Flora withheld.[1]

Unfortunately, the family was dominated by the unstable mother rather than the affectionate and steady father. Flora was hardly a model parent. When Jack was a baby, he was nursed by a Negro woman, Mammy Jenny, and she and his stepsister Eliza raised him. Eliza remembered a time when she and Jack had had diphtheria as small children. After their case had been diagnosed as hopeless, Flora asked whether "the two of them" might "be buried in the same coffin . . . to save expenses?"[2] Flora's restlessness, as well as her indifference, unsettled Jack. The family moved from San Francisco to a truck farm in Alameda in 1880 and then to a desolate ranch in San Mateo where Jack "had no companions." In 1884, they moved to a farm at Livermore, and again the boy "was very much alone."[3] Finally, the Londons settled permanently in Oakland to run a boarding house. This constant uprooting affected Jack emotionally. He was never in one place long enough to make

friends and feel he belonged. Years later, London would recall
how frightened he had once been at finding himself alone in an
empty room filled with moving cases.

Jack resented his mother. Flora's spiritualism often drove him
from the house and undoubtedly contributed to his outspoken
materialism. As an adult, he claimed to have lost faith in his mother
when she once unjustly punished him. Previously, he had looked
upn her as omniscient. Now, at twelve, her "infallibility was
destroyed," and "henceforth I decided for myself as to the right
and wrong of things." [4] Obviously, this change was not the product
of the rational discovery claimed by Jack, but rather the action of a
child who could "not remember ever receiving a caress from my
mother." [5]

In view of London's reaction to his mother, it is not surprising
to find him remembering his childhood as extremely (and exagger-
atedly) bleak. He believed himself "born in the working-class,"
although his parents were *bourgeois,* and he remembered his boyhood as a period of great hardship. Since Jack had had to go to
work at ten, he later felt cheated of carefree youth. He told his
wife, Charmian, in a moment of stark self-awareness, "I never had a
boyhood and I seem to be hunting for that lost boyhood." A similar
conviction of deprivation was evident in earlier letters to a fiancée,
Mable Applegarth. Once he embarrassed his mother and sister by
claiming that he had never received enough to eat—another of Jack's
deprivation fancies, for whatever shortcomings Flora may have had,
she always kept a well stocked table.

Family financial reverses did, however, force London into back-
breaking labor, drudgery, and loneliness. Life seemed hostile and
people unsympathetic. He lived, like Wolf Larsen and Martin Eden,
in a world of conflict, deprivation, and persecution. Seeking the
sympathy he found lacking at home, he pictured himself to Mabel
as a man who, "from the hunger of my childhood," had been
looked upon with "cold eyes . . . or questioned, or snickered and
sneered." But Jack "calloused" his "exterior and received the strokes
as though they were not, as to how they hurt, no one knows but my
own soul and me." He had fought and was even now "fighting my
battle alone." London heroically posed as the romantic individual
relying on his own resources, making his way through life like a
meteor against a leaden sky.

Very early, Jack had begun to look at reality, at the stuff that
made up his life, as something from which to escape. While working at a cannery, he asked himself whether "this were the meaning
of life—to be a work beast?" Later he would tell his love that "if
I knew . . . that I was destined to live in Oakland, labor at some

steady occupation, and die in Oakand—then tomorrow, I would cut my throat and call quits with the whole cursed show." [6] Thus was born the resolution of the romantic hero—to liberate himself from dullness even if it meant suicide.

Jack fled his dismal childhood through books and imagination. His first significant reading experiences came when a teacher lent him works like Washington Irving's *Alhambra,* Paul du Chaillu's *African Travels,* and his favorite, Ouida's *Signa,* the story of a peasant's illegitimate son who rises from impecunious minstrelsy to become one of Italy's great composers. *Signa* broadened the lad's horizon and played on his eager imagination. It showed him, as he put it, what was possible if one dared. After the family moved to Oakland, London became a frequenter of the public library. His tastes ran to adventure tales, the literature of escape. Contrast between fanciful and real existence meant "a dual life"—outwardly "rough and tumble, happy go lucky, jostled by a score, a hundred rough elements," inwardly "reflective, contemplative, apart from the kinetic forces around me." [7] This dichotomy was never bridged, even in his maturity, for Jack was always torn between the frontier and the intellect, between domestic bliss and romantic thrills.

At fifteen, London took the first step toward making his exciting dreams come true by becoming an oyster pirate and petty hoodlum on the San Francisco wharfs. This adventure occurred as a result of contemplating the shabbiness of being a wage slave in the cannery. It was a decision between "money or thrills . . . between niggardliness and romance." [8] In his character, the adventurer eclipsed the family provider. Jack fled his responsibilities "to get away from monotony and the commonplace. I was in the flower of my adolescence, athrill with romance and adventure, dreaming of wild life in the wild man-world." [9] He was not disappointed, for the career of a bay pirate "was life raw and naked, wild and free." It raised the curtain on an existence full of spectacular experiences leading "out through the Golden Gate to the vastness of adventure of all the world, where battles would be fought, . . . for high purposes and romantic ends." [10] Youthful triumphs confirmed his romantic self-image. Years later he exulted in his boyhood of "raging through life without end like one of Nietzsche's blond beasts, lustfully roving and conquering by sheer superiority and strength." [11]

After several years of derring-do, climaxed by a sealing expedition to the Pacific, the pull of responsibility reasserted itself. London came back to San Francisco to support his family by working in a jute mill. Jack yearned deeply for the more settled life. Periodically a desire for domesticity would snatch him from some far frontier and plunge him into familial enterprises involving long years of

hard but remunerative work. A product of this desire for security
was the letter written to his fiancée during the Christmas season of
1898:

> And to-day is Christmas—it is at such periods that the vaga-
> bondage of my nature succumbs to a latent taste for domesticity.
> Away with the many corners of this round world! I am deaf
> to the call of the East and West, the North and South—. . . .
> A comfortable little cottage, a couple of servants, a select coterie
> of friends, and above all, a neat little wife and a couple of
> diminutive models of us twain— . . . an assured, the quiet and
> monotonous, future in prospect; a satisfied knowledge of the
> many little amenities of civilized life which are mine and shall
> be mine; a genial, optimistic, contemplation.[12]

Jack found his job in the jute mill the same kind of frustrating
labor as that in the cannery and decided to better himself by learning
a trade. He hoped to get ahead by becoming an electrician and
applied for work in a power plant. While he was discussing his
prospects with the manager, thoughts of brilliant business success
ran through his mind. "Thrift, energy and sobriety" would enable
him to "learn the business and rise from position to position until
he was taken in as a junior partner. After that the senior partnership was only a matter of time." The manager capitalized on London's dreams. He told the prospective partner that he must start
at the bottom by shoveling coal. After months of brutal labor,
London learned that he had been hired to do the work of two men
and that the manager had no intention of promoting him. Disgusted
at being cheated, Jack once more took to the road. He returned from
tramping resolved to court advancement in a more delicate manner.
No more would he start at the bottom and try to rise by hard labor.
"Brains period, not brawn" would be his means to success.[13]

In accord with his plan, he completed high school and entered
the University of California. With time out for an adventurous
interlude in the Klondike, he then worked hard to win success as an
author. This new life led him to aspire to Mabel Applegarth, a
genteel daughter of the cultured middle class. And he stuck steadfastly to his writing, despite a bitter apprenticeship of rejected
manuscripts and Mabel's termination of their engagement. Suppressing the romantic side of his nature, he disciplined himself to
the task of becoming an author. He even married Bessie Maddern
in 1900 to steady himself so that he could "devote more time to
work." [14] But it was not to be that easy. As Jack's imaginative and

restless mother had prevailed over his steady and solid father, he eventually answered the call of youth, the call of the wild.

There were two cataclysmic themes in Jack London's thought: race war and class revolution. In the former, he demonstrated his fear of foreign defeat and, in the latter, his fear of domestic disaster. These fears could have been held independently, there being no intrinsic connection between class uprising and ethnic conflict. In London, however, both stemmed from his early environment and were linked in his romantic self-image. The America of his day inspired adventurers either to crusade for Anglo-Saxon supremacy or to fight for freedom through socialism. Those causes emancipated people from the everyday drudgery involved in pursuing material success. Racism and socialism acquired their romantic aura by embodying a set of vague, universal, ultimate goals.

London's racism was a legacy from his mother. The daughter of Marshall Wellman had commanded some respect in Massillon, Ohio. After coming West, however, Flora had been humiliated by loss of social and economic status. Only by emphasizing the one obvious difference between herself and the people with whom she now lived could she save anything of her former position. Accordingly, when the Londons moved to the immigrant neighborhood of San Mateo County, Jack often heard his mother "pride herself that we were old American stock and not immigrant Irish and Italians like our neighbors." Flora harbored the conventional suspicions about foreigners. As Jack later put it, "My mother had theories. First, she steadfastly maintained that brunettes and all the tribe of dark-eyed humans were deceitful. Needless to say, my mother was a blond. Next, she was convinced that the dark-eyed Latin races were profoundly sensitive, profoundly treacherous, and profoundly murderous." [15]

Jack cast off other maternal teachings, but racism was one lesson he faithfully absorbed. "Yes, my name is Jack London," he told a friend, "rather an un-American heritage from a Yankee ancestry, dating beyond the French and Indian War." Beside being painstaking about establishing his own impeccable origins, he took great care to furnish his fictional characters with native pedigrees.[16] He was a self proclaimed "evolutionist, believing in Natural Selection, half believing Malthus' 'Law of People' and a myriad of factors thrown in," who hailed "as unavoidable, the Black and the Brown going down before the White." [17] Nothing esoteric or subtle characterized London's racism. He swallowed and then disgorged all the doctrines deduced from that fusion of science and fancy that passed for social Darwinism.

Belief in white superiority was central in London's early works. He made Alaska the scene of triumph over backward races. Conquest was symbolized by the pioneer's seizure of an Indian chief's daughter and his defeat of the braves who try to stop him. Another variation on the theme was the portrayal of old Indians remembering their past glory. Frequently he painted the Alaskan trapper or miner, subduer of nature and natives, as the forerunner of civilization. Thus, "The God of His Fathers" begins with a description of the Northland as a sort of ethnic no man's land: "On every hand stretched the forest primeval,—the home of noisy comedy and silent tragedy. Here the struggle for survival continued to wage with all its ancient brutality." Hard on the heels of Darwin comes Nietzsche: "Already, over unknown trails and chartless wildernesses, were the harbingers of steel arriving—fair faced, blue-eyed, indomitable men, incarnations of the unrest of their race." They were preparing the way "under the cold fire of the Aurora, as did his brothers in burning sands and reeking jungles," until "in the fullness of time the destiny of their race be achieved." [18] The frontier, whether in Alaska or the South Seas, was the place where the pioneer would roll back savagery to make way for civilization.

Even London's socialist belief in human brotherhood did not override the iron law of racism. Jack made propagandistic obeisance to this ideal in party tracts, but, when the doctrines of human domination and human solidarity clashed, he found "socialism . . . devised" not "for the happiness of all men; but . . . for the happiness of certain kindred races." Specious "laws" of "the brotherhood of all men" must bow to "the logic of events" that dictated that "certain kindred favored races" could survive and inherit the earth to the extinction of the lesser, weaker races." [19]

As early as 1898, while still convinced of Anglo-Saxon supremacy, London speculated about challenges to the dominant race. "The Question Of The Maximum" was heavily influenced by Brooks Adams's thesis of perpetual flux and competition. Phrases like "for any movement or development there must be a maximum limit beyond which it cannot proceed" or a "civilization which does not advance must decline, and so, when the maximum of development has been reached in any given direction, society must either retrograde or change the direction of its advance" indicated that London had copied Adams's thesis of perpetual, competitive change even to the point of using similar terminology.

Once again echoing his mentor, London forecasted a global conflict for commercial mastery. Economic growth and concentration would send "predatory capitalism . . . the world over, seeking where it may establish itself." As capital consolidation continued the search would grow more frantic and "competition grows keener and closer." Occasionally a touch of Jack's romanticism broke through Adams's *realpolitik*. London envisioned commercial conflict as "a new romance, . . . for the dazzling prize of world-empire will the nations of the earth go up in harness." But when contemplating victory, he reverted to his mentor's pedagogical prose. Those nations would triumph, predicted Brooks's disciple, who "adjust supply to demand, and eliminate waste to the last least particle." [20]

London borrowed still another Adams concept when he foresaw commerce contending for national sovereignty. Oligarchic rule, however, would not necessarily be catastrophic, for in order to maintain supremacy the élite would provide security and prosperity. Only in concluding on a Marxist note of eventual proletarian supremacy did London depart from Adams's previously charted course. But even at that early date, he believed the socialist revolution to be far from imminent. Especially noteworthy is London's conception of centralization and expansion as a bridge either to the workers' utopia or the racists' empire. It indicated their close link in his consciousness, as well as in his emotions.

In the expectation of world war, London searched for allies. Considering his racism, it is not surprising that he found "England . . . our greatest purchaser, and our greatest maker of markets, and the only nation which is not deep down hostile to us." In terms reminiscent of Brooks Adams and Mary Lease, he claimed that "the day England goes under, . . . sees sealed the doom of the United States. It's the Anglo-Saxon people against the world." But commercial considerations were secondary, they were "only a manifestation of the blood differentiations which have come down from the hoary past." [21] Not mere economic imperialism, but the more mystical, emotional, fundamental racial drive sent London's heroes in dogsleds to Alaska and in canoes to Tahiti.

At first, London was sure the Anglo-Saxons would triumph, but soon he spied a formidable challenge in "The Yellow Peril." There were many reasons for this fear. Prejudice against the Japanese and Chinese was widespread in California, particularly among white workers. Jack, always sympathetic to the unions, was quick to share. their resentment. In addition, he feared that China's land mass and human resources would overwhelm the West. China's potential, combined with Japan's industrial knowledge and strategic position at the heart of the world's most desirable markets, made him doubt the outcome of the ethnic conflict.

These general considerations were reinforced by his experience as a correspondent in the Russo-Japanese War. Jack was annoyed by Japanese treatment of him but awed by Japan's military might, and both impressions intensified his dislike. Having once "preached the Economic Yellow Peril," he would "henceforth . . . preach the Militant Yellow Peril." [22] For the first time the possibility of a real contest for global hegemony arose. This concern was apparent in that special note of urgency that marks the cataclysmist. "Affairs rise to conclusion," he said, "We shall not have to wait for our children's time nor our children's children. We shall ourselves see and largely determine the adventure of the Yellow and the Brown." [23]

Jack's nightmare about an Eastern victory was given full expression in "The Unparalleled Invasion." This tale takes place in 1976, by which time all his prophecies have materialized. Japan, after developing China, has been cast off as the Eastern colossus has assumed Asiatic leadership. China's enormous and ever-growing population has spilled into Indo-China. When France tries to resist this penetration, the French army is engulfed. Awakened to the danger, the Western nations call a convention to request China to stay within her own borders. These resolutions are ineffectual because any armed force sent to enforce them will be lost in China's "capacious maw." Finally a scientist devises germ warfare to combat the threat. Bacilli are dropped, plagues break out, and those trying to flee are cut down by Western armies massed on China's border. Starvation and cannibalism follow the plague, and the next winter the allied expeditionary force is sent in to mop up any survivors. After the original inhabitants have been completely obliterated, "a vast and happy intermingling of nationalities . . . settled down in China." [24]

Annihilation was the desperate conclusion drawn from irrational premises. London carried his Nietzschean-Darwinian doctrine of race war to its ultimate end. The struggle for existence would destroy the unfit. There could be no compromise between the blond beasts and those who would oppose their destiny. As Martin Eden cannot compromise with the middle class, Ernest Everhard with capitalists, nor Wolf Larsen with conventional decency, London could not come to terms with the Chinese. His fictional heroes are great individualists —they must destroy or be destroyed. The world had made power the arbiter of success; the greater the struggle the more intense the force required. In the basic conflict of race survival, defeat would mean annihilation.

At first glance, it is hard to believe that London considered himself a socialist for almost twenty years. Certainly, many of his notions contradicted the movement's basic tenets. Apart from being a racist, he abhorred manual labor and justified hiring servants by arguing, "Why tie my own shoes when I can have it done by someone whose business it is, while I am improving my mind or entertaining the fellows who drop in." [25] Moreover, his Nietzschean individualism ran counter to a cherished Marxian concept. He referred to himself as "a competitive beast," claiming to have been made for the battle of the primeval jungle 10,000 years ago rather than for the civilization of his day. Predator that he was, communitarian ideals meant nothing. He went for "the things I like." "Most of all," he craved "personal achievement for my own delight. It is the old 'I did it! I did it! With my own hands I did it!' " [26]

London's contempt for the people was another case in which his personal egotism ran counter to socialist doctrine. Violating the creed's most sacred canon, he asserted that "I grow, sometimes, almost to hate the mass, to sneer at dreams of reform. To be superior to the mass is to be the slave of the mass. The mass knows no slavery. It is the taskmaster." [27] The mass was static, as well as oppressive. Negating another Marxian axiom, he claimed, that mass "inertia" made "the evolution of institutions a slow and painful process." [28] Hatred of the herd also appeared in his fiction. He did not blanch at portraying the death of thousands in *The Iron Heel* or millions in "The Unparalleled Invasion."

Despite such attitudes, London was, at least consciously, a sincere socialist. Neither wealth nor prestige turned him from the party. He was one *arriviste* who did not become assimilated to those who raised his status. He contributed money to the socialist cause, gave free lectures, wrote without pay for party publications, risked his popularity on anticapitalist broadsides like *The Iron Heel,* and spoke out for such causes as the Haywood-Moyer-Pettibone Trial. Although the party did not have first call on his money, time, and sympathies, he nevertheless gave generously of them all, especially before 1908.

Jack gave several reasons for clinging to socialism. His well publicized proletarianism may have served to advertise his own phenomenal rise and thus stress his personal accomplishment. But such evidence for Algerism could easily have been displayed without maintaining his socialist associations. Actually, London claimed that his working-class attachments were formed as a result of being betrayed by the success cult. Whenever he had tried to climb out of poverty, he had been repelled by a cold, deceitful world that calculated human relations in terms of exploitation. Among his own kind, however, was "warm faith in the human, glowing idealism, sweetness of unselfishness." [29] Surely such warmth must have meant much to a boy fresh from the cruelty of the electrical plant and the loneliness of the road. Friends whom he met in the movement, like Herman Whitaker and Anna Strunsky, helped to assuage the bitterness of his alienated youth.

Jack's need for companionship made him join, but deeper ties kept him in the organization. There was, paradoxically enough, for all his Nietzschean rumblings and cruel fantasies of mass annihilation, a warm humaneness to the man. London remembered his gentle father, and many were his own kindly deeds. Upton Sinclair and a host of other young writers could have attested to his generosity with his time, criticism, and encouragement. In addition, he was an easy touch for old comrades or anybody else in want and an agreeable associate and employer. If he was capable of monstrous thoughts about some groups, he was sympathetic to others. The sight of lepers in the South Seas or the urban poor went to his heart. Collecting material on London slums for *The People of the Abyss* "blunted" his "nerves" and caused him much "suffering." [30] Jack might beat his breast and scorn the world, but he could also hear the whimper of the poor, the homeless, and the alone. On occasion, he sermonized like a minister spreading the gospel of Christian brotherhood. He pleaded for "understanding" and "sympathy;" for men to become "converted to the gospel of service" in order to "serve truth . . . kindness, . . . beauty." All people, he declared, should devote themselves to their "weaker fellows" by working to make them "into men rather than into slaves and beasts." [31]

Unfortunately, altruism was not the only factor in London's socialism. Marxism also provided the perfect framework for his paranoia. It gave him a rationalization for the feelings of persecution stemming from his mother's indifference and the hostile world of his childhood. He could claim that his alienation, now the alienation of a whole class, was caused not by anything within him but by the inexorable laws of history. His rejection had not been the result of personal failure; rather, it was due to the working out of objective economic forces. The manager who had swindled him was merely a cipher in a world where the swindle was the way of life. Jack was no longer alone; his experiences were part of science, part of history. Socialism gave him an answer for his empty youth, it purged him of any guilt he might have felt for his reactions, and, most of all, it gave him a group to which he could belong. He charged the capitalists with greed and mismanagement, thus escaping the responsibility for his antisocial youth. His greatest heroes are victims of this gigantic betrayal. Wolf Larsen is cheated by poverty and lack of opportunity to make something of himself. He is what Jack might have been if he had stayed on the wharf. Martin Eden is even more tragically trapped. He tastes success only to realize that the wine is vinegar and the cup soon empty. Fame, he discovers, is meaningless, for it comes not because of what a man does or is but merely because he has by chance become a popular idol. London escaped the lot of Wolf Larsen, only to share the greater pain of Martin Eden.

Socialism also appealed to Jack's romantic spirit. What better way to sneer at the time-serving, penny-pinching capitalists, to avenge their slights and thievery than to threaten them with expropriation? How could one show greater contempt for commercial success and such other pedestrian values than by assuring business-men that they would soon disappear? Where else would he find such a podium from which to castigate the capitalists as he did at Harvard in 1905, Yale in 1906, and in New York City? London challenged the master class to mortal combat by promising pre-emption. At Yale, he threw down the gauntlet, shouting, "The revolution is here, now. Stop it who can." [32]

One can easily imagine the satisfaction this Nietzschean egotist derived from tongue-lashing the privileged, from baiting his audiences by calling them bunglers, and from vicariously destroying them verbally. Eyewitnesses testified to triumphant scenes. At Harvard, Jack was observed giving "them unsparingly, all and more than they had bargained for, straight from the shoulder, jolting 'Revolution' into them . . . face set like a vise, and he hung over the edge of the platform, a challenge to their better part flaming from black-blue eyes and red, merciless tongue." [33] The relish with which Jack savored these scenes is indicated by the recreation of his New York speech in the famous "Philomath" chapter of *The Iron Heel*.

Marxist ideology also provided an outlet for London's tendency toward violence. Class struggle offered an ideal projective mechanism for inner conflicts, and the world revolution was the perfect battleground on which to vent destructive urges. Violence was particularly prominent in the movement's western wing, the group with which Jack was associated. The Western Federation of Miners and the I.W.W. engaged in industrial warfare born of the union between frontier violence and the class struggle. London, very much a son of the frontier, shared in this explosive mixture of foreign ideology and native belligerence. His contempt for the political gradualism of easterners like Morris Hillquit and Meyer London gathered intensity in 1907 after their theoretician, John Spargo, unfavorably reviewed *The Iron Heel* because "cataclysmic theory" repelled "many whose addition to our forces is sorely needed." [34] London's antipathy for the moderates led to an irreparable breach in his later years. He resigned "from the Socialist Party, because of its lack of fire and fight, and its loss of emphasis on the class struggle." The Party's "peaceableness and compromise," thought London, would prevent the liberation of labor. Unless workers would "rise up and by their strength of brain and brawn, wrest . . . liberty, freedom, and independence, they never in time can come to these royal possessions." [35]

Jack sensed that the growing respectability of the socialists left no place for the adventurer. What he really felt, however, was that he had become too old and too tired for the revolution. Beauty Ranch, the rural retreat of his later years, was now uppermost in his thoughts. More than anything, he wanted to leave "behind me a plot of land, which, after the pitiful failure of others, I have made productive." He even mouthed the Marxist heresy that "in the solution of the great economic problems of the present age, I see a return to the soil." Squire London had eclipsed socialist London. Perhaps it was only just, for his queer combination of individualism and altruism was much more akin to Tory paternalism than to submersion in a communist utopia. Agrarian paternalism obviously motivated his decision to turn the ranch into a self-sufficient manor where "the ranch people can have their homes . . . , trade . . . , be born . . . , grow up . . . , get their schooling . . . , and if they die they can be buried." [36] Jack had run the gamut from radicalism to reaction. He who quit the Socialist Party because of its conservatism was actually prepared to implement agrarian ideals whose feasibility even Ignatius Donnelly doubted.

The concept of proletarian revolution gave London his cataclysmic frame of reference. It satisfied his paranoid needs for violent revenge and his romantic desires for thrills. When Eugene V. Debs rolled up an unprecedented vote in 1904, Jack temporarily departed from his belief that the proletariat would triumph only through bloodshed, but this brief bubble burst after the abortive Russian uprising of 1905. In that year, Jack had already reintroduced the option of violence. Although the workers "love peace . . . they are unafraid of war. . . . If the law of the land permits, they fight . . . peaceably, at the ballot-box. If the law of the land does not permit, and if they have force meted out to them, they resort to force themselves." [37] For a time, London maintained the alternatives of peaceful transition or armed revolt. Even after writing *The Iron Heel,* he disclaimed "an attempt to prophesy" but "merely [warned] . . . of what might happen if the proletariat weaken in their fight and allow the enemy to make terms with them." [38] As the movement declined, however, he became convinced that bloody conflict was inevitable. *The Iron Heel* (1907), "When God Laughs" (1908), "The Dream of Debs" (1909), and "Goliath" (1910) all deal with social strife. By 1912, Jack saw "a hard time coming. We shall have a big fight, . . . The story of that struggle will be written in blood. The ruling classes will not let go until it is." Surveyed from the wreckage of his own life, labor's future looked bleak. London was now a self-confessed "pessimist" who saw "things dispassionately, scientifically." These rational ruminations convinced him that "the people are as bad off as ever," oppressed by "a mighty ruling class that intends to hold fast to its possession." All anyone could expect was "years and years of bloodshed." [39]

Jack London's first cataclysmic work, *The Iron Heel*, was begun during the summer of 1906 and completed in December. This somber tale of abortive revolt and bloody suppression did not spring from any immediate personal depression. Successes like *The Sea Wolf* and *Call Of The Wild* had already put an end to the years of poverty and anonymity, and the lecture tour of 1905-6 had provided thrilling triumphs. His "Long Sickness," the depressed state of 1904-5, had been cured by marriage to his second wife, Charmian. She dispelled the loneliness that had led him to contemplate suicide by "fighting with me shoulder to shoulder, fighting my own fight, in my own way!" [40] However much paranoia and an inclination toward self destruction may have motivated his depiction of disaster, at least he was happy while writing the book.

To sound the alarm was only one motive for writing the novel. As usual, Jack hoped to make money and, when the book did not sell, was quite disappointed. Although a commercial failure, the work vicariously fulfilled his need for revenge upon the enemy. "I am deep in the beginning of a socialistic novel!" he wrote to a friend. "Am going to call it The Iron Heel. How is that for a title? The poor futile little capitalist! Gee, when the proletariat cleans house someday!" [41]

London was distressed by the book's reception. He had trouble obtaining a publisher, and, when it finally came out, many reviewers found it "dull," "unconvincing," with "little to recommend it." Conservative magazines, after criticizing its literary qualities, condemned it for fomenting revolution. [42] Even liberal periodicals called the volume too incendiary. *The Arena* found it overly dismal and asserted that "all talk of forcible revolution is not only foolish, but it is bound to injure the people's cause." [43] The socialists' opinions varied with their radicalism. Spargo considered the novel ideologically antiquated and impolitic, but Debs, Haywood, and the left

wing thought highly of the work. Abroad, it received more approbation. Bukharin put it in his socialist bibliography, Trotsky was
impressed with "the audacity and independence of its historical foresight," and Lenin read London on his deathbed.[44]

Discouraging as was its original reception, *The Iron Heel* did
not disappear. On the contrary, world events increased its timeliness
and popularity. Many came to agree with Trotsky that "Jack London
already foresaw and described the fascist regime as the inevitable
result of the defeat of the proletarian revolution." [45]

As an anti-utopian novel, *The Iron Heel* has characteristics in
common with *Caesar's Column*. London and Donnelly dealt with
the same theme, an abortive uprising by workers against plutocrats.
Although chaos dominates both books, there are also utopian
elements. Gabriel Weltstein escapes to a Garden of Eden, and
London's horrible tale is discovered 700 years after the event in an
"enlightened age" so perfect that it cannot comprehend the facts.
In detail, as well as perspective, these works have an affinity. Both
disasters are projected into the future, but aware of the dramatic
impact of imminence, their authors' made them close enough to
impart a tone of urgency to the novels. Conspiracies, bloodshed,
mob action—attributes of a society dominated by brutality and
divided against itself—abound in both books. In short, these volumes are products of estranged souls who viewed society through
the distorted perspective of personal frustration.

The Iron Heel is more than a cataclysmic tale or a socialist tract.
It is a London novel, which means that the primary focus is on a
man rather than a cause. The main character, Ernest Everhard—five
feet nine inches tall, hard muscled, born into an old American
working family—rises to lead the proletariat because of his resourcefulness. If this story sounds familiar, it is not surprising, for it is
the story of Jack London. Jack, the eternal boy, spins a life of adventure from the wheel of his imagination, much as he had done when
he read *Signa*.

Ernest Everhard's basic trait, as his name implies, is his will.
Intellectually or physically he dominates everyone whom he meets.
"He was a natural aristocrat. . . . He was a superman, a blond
beast such as Nietzsche has described," declares his wife, Avis, after
their first meeting. Self-determination directs all his actions. He first
appears as a poor young socialist invited to Avis's father's house
to discuss social problems with a group of prominent clergymen.
The debate swiftly becomes a struggle, in which Ernest "with that
war-note in his voice," flays "them with his facts, each fact a lash
that stung and stung again. And he was merciless. He took no

quarter, and gave none." In this scene's construction, one can easily imagine London drawing on his early experience as an awkward academic neophyte in the Applegarth household. Ernest takes a genteel home by storm as compensation for those who once patronized Jack.

Avis, however, is not Mabel. She does not reject Everhard for his lack of respectability; rather, he makes a revolutionary out of her. In a reversal of the American success credo, Avis accepts proletarian status. Only after discarding *bourgeois* gentility, does she become a fitting mate. Ernest, no ordinary suitor, takes her by "splendid invincible rush" as would one of Nietzsche's noblemen.

Everhard's Darwinian individualism is even more starkly displayed at the "Philomath Club." In this scene, London relived his New York triumph of 1906. Jack had a theory that the primitive lurked very close below the surface veneer of civilization. According to him, natural man, was only barely suppressed and was ever ready to spring forth. Any struggle would bring out the savage, be it socialist revolution, trial in the northern wilds, or merely a heated discussion. Such moments would test courage, and London abhorred a coward. Hence, his description of the Philomath controversy does not differ greatly from the fights in *Call Of The Wild* or other stories. As Buck in *Call Of The Wild* or Humphrey Van Weyden in *The Sea Wolf* attains manhood through physical battle, so Ernest Everhard proves himself in the verbal jungle of the club.

Ernest's invitation to Avis foreshadows the evening's brutality. "If you come, I'll shake them for you," he promises. "I'll make them snarl like wolves. . . . If you can come, you will see the cavemen in evening dress, snarling and snapping over a bone." The subsequent struggle proves him right. Everhard undauntedly faces a hostile audience of the most renowned and redoubtable capitalists. He ridicules their incapacity, derides their morals, and finally sentences them to oblivion. This attack evokes "a low, throaty rumble . . . the forerunner of the snarl, . . . the token of the brute in man, the earnest of his primitive passions." Everhard, bearding the lions in their den, crushes their feeble defenses with pitiless logic and cold fact. Only Wickson, owner of a company notorious for cheating injured workers, answers him effectively. After disgustedly watching his compatriots banter ethics and economics with the young revolutionary, Wickson warns that the workers will be crushed by superior force. Everhard, realizing the gauntlet has been thrown down, cries "I am answered. It is the only answer that could be given. Power."

Unlike those in all the other cataclysmic works, London's debacle did not occur when preindustrial groups battle rising industrial élites. There was no struggle to the death between aristocrats and bankers, farmers and financiers, or godliness and materialism. London portrayed a Marxist conflict between modern groups of workers and capitalists for the spoils of the industrial revolution. It was emergence of the proletariat rather than nostalgia that would trigger the uprising.

By allowing Everhard to taunt the magnates into declaring war, London reconciled the blond beast with the class struggle. Revolution would legitimize the individualist's role in socialism. The adventurer could be instrumental in imposing proletarian order upon a crumbling society. London had created circumstances that met all his basic needs. Persecution suspicions were substantiated by the threat of violence from the enemy against the hero of the exploited. Violence and destruction, which would be justified in such an uprising, served the double purpose of paranoid revenge and gratification of London's death wish. Ernest's death and defeat are also psychically necessary. The romantic individual can have no place in the workers' paradise. Since he cannot subordinate himself to history, Everhard must be swept away in its course. Death and failure are also demanded by persecution drives and suicidal tendencies. They are the only conceivable results for a mind unable to cope with life. The cataclysm in *The Iron Heel* was thus a projection of Jack London's own twisted outlook, and it is not in the least astonishing that he foresaw in "the tortuous and distorted evolution of the next three centuries . . . a Third Revolution and a Fourth Revolution, and many Revolutions, all drowned in seas of blood, ere the world-movement of labor should come into its own."

Donnelly and London, unlike the other cataclysmists, dramatized rather than analyzed catastrophe. Donnelly, however, subordinated fiction to the cause. Gabriel Welstein is a mouthpiece for Populist doctrine and becomes the founder of an agrarian utopia. Ernest Everhard, on the other hand, is a pure projection of London's ego. He is the Nietzschean hero, an embodied will who dominates the movement. Everhard's social crusade is really London's fight to free himself from a frustrating environment. His death, and London's eventual suicide, are similar acts of defiance and resignation. Fiction and fact merge, and Ernest is martyred to Jack's own sense of victimization.

After focusing the conflict in the Philomath altercation, Everhard recedes into the background while London depicts the holocaust. In discussing the revolution, Jack's paranoia got the better of his ideology. At first, he seemed to be framing the uprising along orthodox Marxist lines. The petty *bourgeoisie* are wiped out by depression and repression after they refuse to join the workers. The middle-class success ideal is turned against itself, since the only virtuous capitalists are those who sacrifice themselves by resisting the moneyed cabal. The dialectic soon gives way to a conspiracy theory, however, and, instead of a social struggle between capitalists and workers, London portrays a paranoid conflict between the privileged and the persecuted. Labor's solidarity is broken when industrial unions bribed with high wages and better working conditions desert fellow workers. Betrayal defeats the general strike. The failure of this peaceful device clears the way for subsequent revolution and the plutocratic Iron Heel's victory. The picture of union treachery is a paranoid perversion of Marx. Instead of progressive working-class alienation culminating in an inevitable uprising, London drew a group of capitalists and workers uniting of their own free will to repeal the law of history. This doctrinal divergence occurred because Jack distrusted the masses and deprecated human nature. He did not believe that class-consciousness could overcome avarice. In his paranoid world, everybody was suspect, and even the dialectic did not make men brothers. Of all the cataclysmists, London was the most inconsistent ideologist because his own status was never involved with the cause he was defending.

After the plutocracy seizes power, London gives full reign to his suspicions. Socialists are driven underground, and a clandestine war, similar to that in *Caesar's Column,* begins. For both authors, these secret activities involve a flight from self as well as from reality. Identity is lost in the anonymity of disguise and duplicity. In London's book, revolutionaries organize "fighting groups," which the "Iron Heel" try to infiltrate. Cloak and dagger operations ensue, and Avis and Ernest become *agents provacateurs* masquerading as plutocrats. Conspiracy is everywhere; the paranoid's nightmare has become reality:

> The Iron Heel had triumphed in open warfare, but we held our own in the new warfare, strange and awful and subterranean, that we instituted. All was unseen, much was unguessed; the blind fought the blind; and through it all was order, purpose, control. We permeated the entire organization of the Iron Heel with our agents, while our own organization was permeated with the agents of the Iron Heel. It was warfare dark and devious, replete with intrigue and conspiracy, plot and counterplot. And behind all, ever menacing, was death, violent and terrible.[46]

As in Donnelly's case, conspiracy signified an aggressive withdrawal from the community. Secret organizations become sovereign

groups at war with the state. In standard cataclysmic fashion, secession was made a pretext for violent vengeance. Ostensibly formed
to fight dictatorial suppression, these fictional groups commit activities that they detest in the ruling élites. They too are violent and
conspiratorial; they too raise tension and behave dictatorially. If not
for the difference in allegiance, there would be little to distinguish
the élite from its opposition.

Above this underground skirmishing, the belligerents constantly
maneuver—the socialists to bring off the revolt and the Iron Heel to
crush it. An uprising is planned for 1918, but the oligarchy is able
to forestall it by precipitating a revolt in the Chicago slums. Plutocratic treachery is discovered in time, but socialist leaders are forced
to sacrifice the Chicago poor. Abortive insurgence enables London
to slake vicariously his neurotic taste for blood.

Jack's loathing for the masses complemented his adoration of the
superman. During his lecture tour, London expressed dislike for
downtrodden multitudes. "This is no spontaneous vague uprising of
a large mass of discontented and miserable people," he declared in
describing the coming revolution. "On the contrary, the propaganda
is intellectual; the movement is based upon economic necessity and
is in line with social evolution; while the miserable people have not
yet revolted." An aura of *bourgeois* respectability hung about the
"revolutionist," who was "no starved and diseased slave in the
shambles at the bottom of the social pit, but . . . a hearty, well-fed
workingman" who "sees the shambles waiting for him and his
children and recoils from the descent." [47] Those "miserable people"
not good enough to be revolutionaries were the Chicago slum-
dwellers. "People of the abyss," they lacked "education, . . . lived
like beasts in great squalid labor-ghettos, festering in misery and
degradation . . . were labor-slaves . . . housed in wretched barracks
where family life cannot exist, and where decency is displaced by
dull bestiality."

Gone was the pity London had shown in *The People Of The
Abyss*. Cast out with it was the Marxian doctrine of increasing
misery as precondition for revolution. In their stead was a
Nietzschean admiration for the master class, a sympathy with the
oligarchs' belief in their "high ethical righteousness." London discerned virtue in the Iron Heel because of its "belief that if ever they
weakened, the great beast would engulf them and everything of
beauty and wonder and joy and good in its cavernous and slimedrip-
ping maw." Donnelly feared the mob—anarchy reigned after the
"Brotherhood's" victory. London, on the other hand, had no Populist property consciousness to make him tremble at violent expro-

priation and too little respect for the masses to envision mob triumph. Sharing Donnelly's attraction to order and power, he too praised the enemy, but lacking the agrarian's apprehension of the masses, he depicted the plutocracy as crushing the unorganized rabble.

His revolutionary strategy reflected Jack's utopian dream. Everhard's plan entails the elimination of the two groups London most hated—the very rich because of his paranoia and the very poor because of his desire to dominate and destroy:

> Why we even depended much, in our plan, on the unorganized people of the abyss. They were to be located on the palaces and cities of the master. Never mind the destruction of life and property. Let the abysmal brute roar and the police and Mercenaries slay. The abysmal brute would roar anyway, and the police and Mercenaries would slay anyway. It would merely mean that various dangers to us were harmlessly destroying one another.

In describing the "Chicago Commune" battle, London revealed cruel enjoyment over the mutual destruction of his enemies. By keeping the action limited to Chicago and making the Iron Heel victorious, he escaped the communitarian implications of a successful revolt. Once the struggle begins, Jack gives his vivid imagination free reign and treats the reader to blood curdling scenes of gory devastation. Again paralleling Donnelly, he uses the mob as his most frightening image. In a passage notable for its similarity to *Caesar's Column* and its revelation of London's mentality, he portrays the slum people:

> . . . the people of the abyss, mad with drink and wrong, up at last and roaring for the blood of their masters. . . . a fascinating spectacle of dread. It surged past my vision in concrete waves of wrath, snarling and growling with lust for blood—men, women, and children, in rags and tatters, dim ferocious intelligences with all the god like blotted from their features and all the fiend like stamped in, apes and tigers, anaemic consumptives and great hairy beasts of burden, wan faces from which vampire society sucked the juice of life, bloated forms swollen with physical grossness and corruption, withered hags and death's heads bearded like patriarchs, festering youth and festering age, faces of fiends, crooked, twisted, misshapen monsters blasted with the ravages of disease and all the horrors of chronic innutriation— the refuse and the scum of life, a raging, screaming, screeching, demoniacal horde.

Thus the story reaches its climax. There is no more to tell after the terrible scene has been enacted. Hundreds of thousands of dead have sated all London's abnormal drives, and it remains only to extract that last bit of futility by showing the triumphant "Iron Heel, impassive and deliberate, . . . punishing without mercy and without malice, suffering in silence all retaliations that were made upon it, and filling the gaps in its fighting line as fast as they appeared." [48]

Jack London continued to dwell on catastrophe and power phantasies after finishing *The Iron Heel*. "The Enemy Of All The World," published in 1908, is about a man who revenges an unjust imprisonment by starting war between Germany and the United States. "The Dream of Debs," written the following year, depicts a successful general strike. The focus, however, is not on labor's victory but on the anarchy, robbery, and murder that occur when discipline lapses and the orderly processes of society are disturbed. "Goliah," which appeared in 1910, is a variation on *The Iron Heel* theme of a despotic oligarchy *versus* a Nietzschean savior. This narrative shows how much London had drifted from orthodox socialism. No longer is there even a proletarian movement to provide a backdrop for the hero. Goliah, disgusted with plutocratic rule, pre-empts global leadership. A benevolent sovereign, he imposes peace on the world, decreases labor hours, lowers the retirement age, and nationalizes industry.

In 1912, London brought out another novel, *The Scarlet Plague*, which foretold a dim future for America. A corrupt coterie has enslaved the workers in a caste system so rigid that they communicate with their rulers only through intermediaries. In 2012, "the year Morgan the fifth was appointed President of the United States by the Board of Magnates," a great plague destroys civilization. Despite London's atheism, this holocaust has an Old Testament tone of evil and retribution. Reminiscent of biblical vengeance, the plague is a visitation of justice upon a wicked land. After describing the carnage and brutality accompanying the old order's death throes, London paints an equally ugly picture of what emerges. Culture and discipline have been destroyed and the population decimated by plague. Survivors return to a natural state where the strongest and most savage dominate. Former underdogs now lord it over effete aristocratic remnants. Savagery so permeates the new age that speech is barely distinguishable from animal sounds. James Smith, former college professor, sums up the misery with a pessimistic peroration on humanity's fate in being doomed to an eternal cycle of dashed hopes:

Nothing can stop—it is the same old story over and over. Man will increase, and men will fight. The gunpowder will enable men to kill millions of men, and in this way only, by fire and blood, will a new civilization, in some remote day, be evolved. And of what profit will it be? Just as the old civilization passed, so will the new. It may take 50,000 years to build, but it will pass. All things pass. . . . Some will fight, some will rule, some will pray; and all the rest will toil and suffer sore while on their bleeding carcasses is reared again, and yet again, without end, the amazing beauty and surpassing wonder of the civilized state. It were just as well that I destroyed those cave-stored books— whether they remain or perish, all their old truths will be discovered, their old lies lived, and handed down. What is the profit? [49]

His portrayal of a destiny of unmitigated misery for society reveals the deep depression of London's last years. Even in an earlier work, "A Curious Fragment," in which he depicts a society with no hope of immediate deliverance, there is a promise of final salvation. The narrator of that tale comes to educate the workers with stories of sacrifices their brothers have made for freedom. His mission is to prepare the oppressed for their eventual emancipation. But there is no hope in *The Scarlet Plague*. At least order and culture are maintained by the rulers in *The Iron Heel* and "A Curious Fragment," but when the rabble triumphs in *The Scarlet Plague,* civilization is destroyed. London's old themes of life and vigor had been transmuted into despair and death. The return to nature once viewed as revivifying now is claimed to brutalize man. Socialist utopia, so much a part of orthodox Marxism and hovering at the end of London's earlier cataclysmic tales, had disappeared into the dead end of historical cycles. Perhaps Jack London no longer foresaw a final deliverance because of socialism's decline, but more likely the reason was something far deeper and more personal. He predicted doom after his expectations had been consistently disappointed. Wealth and prestige once won meant little to him and real power eluded him. Life seemed a vicious swindle and Jack dreamed of revenge. In retribution for his own frustrations he demanded society's destruction. Visions of catastrophe and the figures involved as agents served as vicarious grasps of power. Forecasting disaster, however, was as much a gesture of self-rejection as of self-assertion. Phantasy compensated for failure in the real world, and he dreamed of holocaust to make victory impossible. The aging adventurer, conscious of his own waning powers, was descending into the de-

spondency of his final years. He saw no hope for the world because
he could find no hope for himself.

Jack London means different things to different men. Some,
entranced with his generosity, sympathy for the unfortunate, and
socialist posturing, have seen him as a great fighter for the people.
He has been praised for remaining a socialist despite the facts that
his professional success had not involved the party and that his very
being depended upon the revolution's failure.

Others have maintained that London's individualism outweighed
his altruism. His *bourgeois* background and desire for wealth,
deification of the frontiersman, fascination with Darwin and Nietzsche, and superman self-image substantiate this view. Further evidence can be found in his childhood reading of Horatio Alger's
From Canal Boy To President, his desire for education in order to
avoid manual labor, his contempt for the masses, and his eventual
resignation from the Socialist Party. Particularly noteworthy in such
an analysis is its solution of the dualism between London's socialism
and individualism. According to one critic, Jack's socialism was the
refuge of a frustrated individualist. Ernest Everhard revolts against
an America that has become an Algeristic nightmare, the land of no
opportunity. Hence, the revolution must be defeated because victory
would end the superman's reign.[50]

Plausible as it is, there are some drawbacks to this approach.
Opportunity, even in the depression-ridden 1890's, had not
altogether disappeared, and few native-born Americans used the
dialectic as a battering ram to break down an insurmountable wall
of privilege. But even if others turned socialist to assuage their
desperate egos, why did London, who had achieved success under
the system, portray his protagonists as frustrated individuals with
no place to go? Of course, one explanation might be Jack's ambivalence toward worldly success. Here his socialism clashed with his
desire for literary fame, and, by criticizing the system while profiting
from it, he could have his cake and also eat it. Indeed, London's
writings show that he wanted both to play the game and to change
its rules after he won. This evidence indicates that he was not solely,
and perhaps not primarily, seeking status and wealth. It is worth
pointing out that, if his socialist heroes are killed off because they
are individualistic and their victory would mean social ruin, individualists like Wolf Larsen and Martin Eden are liquidated because
they try to be supermen. This point is especially striking in *Martin
Eden* because Eden is the personification of worldly achievement,
yet his success causes his suicide. As London wrote in his last liter-

ary note, "Martin Eden and Sea Wolf attacks on Nietzschean philosophy, which even the Socialists missed the point of." [51]

It is hardly fair, however, to set London's communitarian pronouncements against those who claim him to be individualistic and then to turn around and quote his superman themes at those who assert his altruism. Certainly London was an individualist and indubitably ambitious. The question is, Precisely how did these qualities manifest themselves?

He most certainly did not arrive via the conventional American success route. Horatio Alger's heroes have little more in common with Jack London than a desire for personal achievement. Modesty, prudence, regularity, hard work, and thrift are the attributes of the newsboys who become magnates. If these characteristics can be summed up in a word, it is "self-discipline." Scarcely any self-discipline, however, was present in the romantic egotist who burned himself out at forty after twenty-five years of riotous extravagance. London's adulthood began with drinking and brawling on the San Francisco waterfront, was punctuated with promiscuity, was haunted by a search for romantic love, and was highlighted by escapes to faraway places like Tahiti or danger spots like Manchuria. It ended amid the wreckage of that financial white elephant, Beauty Ranch, where he poured money into stud stallions and distributed lordly largesse to a following of friends, artists, bohemians, and ne'er-do-wells. Such an existence can hardly be labeled Algeristic.

Jack London may have hungered for status, but he chose the adventurer-artist, rather than the sober-minded businessman, as his model. Thomas Bailey Aldrich, William Dean Howells, and Mark Twain were living examples of writers who had won their places in the sun. Perhaps London had kept them in mind, because he was ruthlessly opportunistic about his work. Here is a strong argument for belief in Jack's desire for wealth, but only if we forget that, to romantic heroes, wealth and even art are merely the means to life. Martin Eden, it must be remembered, kills himself because his recognition has come for his success rather than his self.[52]

Another indication of London's attitude can be seen in the heroes of his stories. His protagonists are rarely businessmen; they are usually sea captains, professors, trappers, or writers. Elam Harnish in *Burning Daylight,* one of the few characters who is a tycoon, renounces business as decadent and regains his virtue by going back to the soil. In Jack's most autobiographical novel, *Martin Eden,* the very pursuit of worldly success is couched in romantic terms. Martin discovers "that he loved beauty more than fame, and that what desire he had for fame was largely for Ruth's sake. . . .

He wanted to be great in the world's eyes; 'to make good,' as he expressed it, in order that the woman he loved should be proud of him and deem him worthy." [53] After Ruth rejects him, renown and fortune come his way, but Eden spurns them because they are not genuine. They are plaudits from the herd, from people who cannot appreciate him for what he is. In other words success is anti-life. It is false and vulgar, creating a public idol by destroying the inner man. Martin is simply another successful writer, a world-famous anonymity. Elam Harnish and Martin Eden, London's examples of the dream of success come true, flee the world to save their souls. Harnish, the tycoon, goes to a farm to regain vitality, and Eden commits suicide in despair at the emptiness of achievement. In both novels, romantic love and ego-fulfillment triumph over the desire for wealth and status. Harnish is saved by Dede Mason, who will not marry him unless he gives up business. Martin Eden is destroyed because, without Ruth Morse, success is unbearable.

Fabulous adventure rather than mundane achievement appealed to London's nature. He was the great swashbuckler, "Prince of the Oyster Pirates," the greatest drinker, fighter, and lover on the water-front; or, in another guise, "tramp royal," master of the road and rail—rootless wanderer. Jack's romantic view of himself and of his fictional heroes was a combination of reality, half-conscious myth-making, and image-projection. Above all, it was food for a ravenous ego.

Romantic egotism led Jack to create all his works in his own image. Self-involvement could be carried to the point of narcissism, as when he described "my gorgeous constitution, . . . my strong head, my broad shoulders and deep chest." [54] Fictional characters were extensions of himself, reliving his actual or desired experiences. These Adonis-like adventurers are everlastingly engaged in deeds of strength, danger, and conflict. They are eternally Byronic youths who fight life and defy maturity. Intervals between action are occupied with reflections upon rootlessness and isolation. These figures ape their creator, who also sought to escape loneliness and self-doubt through excitement. Incessant restlessness took Jack London to the world's frontiers, where he hunted danger in leper colonies, among South Sea headhunters, in the Alaskan Gold Rush, in the Far East during the Russo-Japanese War, and in revolutionary Mexico. Always the boy adventurer, he sought the primitive and the thrilling. In his books and in his life, the frontier was the matrix of existence. There the simple and the savage prevailed, civilization was torn away, and manly courage determined success and survival.

In the contest with nature, virility was regained or proven anew. The great tragedy of London's life was his inability to remain close to the wilds. Part adventurer and part intellectual, he quested after two worlds—and one spoiled him for the other. Jack always came back from the frontier to books, only to flee again when he heard the call of the wild.

A similar dichotomy ran through his love affairs. Again the dualism between civilization and savagery, between responsibility and adventure tore him apart. On returning from Alaska, he slipped into the classical Alger pattern of striving to marry above his station, but the attempt failed when he refused to surrender his goal of artistic fame for a more conventional road to success. A few years later, he rushed into marriage with Bessie Maddern. Once more responsibility had won out. Jack saw in Bessie "a mate, not in the lust of my eyes, but in the desire of my fatherhood." [55] She was the "Mother-Woman" who appealed to civilized man, to the Jack London who might rise from canal boy to President. But the siren of romance again proved stronger. The "Mate-Woman," Charmian Kittridge, "wonderful, unmoral and filled with life to the brim," captured him in 1903.[56] London thought she would satisfy his need for empathy and companionship. He who had hunted the "great man-comrade" in vain, found in her both "comradeship and . . . the great woman-love as well." Charmian would go any place and do anything. "God! and you have grit! I love you for it," said Jack. "You are my comrade for it, too. I think of you swimming, and jumping and diving, and my arms go out to the dear, sensitive, gritty body of yours, as my arms go out to the gritty soul of you within that body." [57]

Even the all-embracing "Mate-Woman" could not satisfy Jack. His life continued to be a mad search for escape, driving him to the Far East, Hawaii, the South Seas, Mexico, and finally to Glen Ellen, California. Here, at the Beauty Ranch, he lived in seigneurial fashion, surrounded by retainers who came to box, wrestle, talk, and drink. It was, as Kenneth Lynn says, a great "barony" where London held court for those like himself who tried to keep their youths by fleeing a world that had become intolerably lonely and interminably dull.

The other ranchers were living memories, and so was their lord. The boy pirate, now a paunchy forty, became painfully aware that his god-like body was mortal after all. "Never again would" he "have the thumbs of my youth" and his "lean runner's stomach has passed into the limbo of memory." [58]

Physical disintegration was accompanied by moral breakdown.

Heretofore inspiring causes now evoked feeble confessions of fatigue and futility. "It is a good many years since I jumped into the battle to right political affairs," replied the mellowing property-owner to a plea to join one more crusade. "Really, I feel a sort of veteran when I think over the long years of the fight. I am not exactly a beaten veteran, but unlike the raw recruit, I do not expect to storm and capture the enemy's position by the next sunrise." Visions of early victory had vanished. Indeed, he did not even hope "to see the end of the campaign." [59] In 1916, with the socialist utopia no longer in prospect, the aging squire of Glen Ellen resigned from the party.

London's personal life was also deteriorating. "Wolf House" burned down the day it was finished, and a part of his soul was consumed in that fire. Accidents on the farm put him into debt and enslaved him to magazine contracts. Charmian, soul-mate of yore, and Jack, "God's own mad lover," became unfaithful to each other. When Jack turned to his daughter for comfort, he was rebuffed. Disappointed in his most intimate relationships, London drew away from the ranch companions whom he had once found so congenial. Close friends like Cloudesley Johns remarked on "his periods of mental depression when his splendid will to live almost left him." [60]

As the years passed, Jack grew increasingly despondent. Personal failures bred feelings of resentment and persecution. His readers misunderstood him, and people whom he had befriended turned against him. When his sister Eliza, the person who knew him best, remarked, "Jack, you are the loneliest man in the world. The things your heart wanted, you've never had," he replied, "How the devil did you know?" [61]

Suicide offered the only relief from irreversible degeneracy and unresolvable contradiction. Disaffected since childhood, Jack never sank deep roots and was always ready to trade life for a thrill. Ending his existence, therefore, seemed the perfect solution. It was the only adventure left for a man who had experienced everything and whose existence was meaningless without new thrills. Suicide meant escape from himself and this escape became more imperative and more impossible through any other means as age cut down mobility and loneliness forced him back on his own thoughts. The act also supported his illusion of mastery and strength by allowing him to end the debilitation of age. Finally, it was a dramatic gesture characteristic of the Byronic figure. London, who had martyred his heroes to society's betrayal, now sacrificed himself. Self-destruction was the microcosm of global holocaust. Both were variations of desperation that combined aggressive defiance with impotence and submission. Suicide, like cataclysm, was the summation rather than the solution of a tormented life.

Self-destruction occurred more than once to Jack. In *John Barleycorn,* he described an attempt he had made to drown himself while still a punk-hero on the waterfront. "Thoughts of suicide . . . entered my head. . . . I thought of a fine, a splendid culmination, a perfect rounding off of my short but exciting career. . . . I decided that this was all, that I had seen all, lived all, been all, that was worthwhile, and that now was the time to cease." [62] Excitement was his credo: Live to the hilt, compress everything into a few glorious years, and then depart before being surfeited by dullness or having to live on memories. Life was an adventure, and, when there were no more thrills, there should no longer be life:

> I would rather be ashes than dust! I would rather that my spark should burn out in a brilliant blaze than it should be stifled by dry rot. I would rather be a superb meteor, every atom of me in magnificent glow, than a sleepy and permanent planet. The proper function of man is to live, not to exist, I shall not waste my days in trying to prolong them. I shall use my time.[63]

Jack next considered suicide during his struggle for literary success. Rebuffed by the magazines, rejected by Mabel, and pressured by family poverty, London penned farewell letters. His troubled state was apparent from a letter he wrote to Mark DeWolfe Howe after Howe, a complete stranger, had rejected one of his stories. "I have been quite sick but am better now. . . . I was on the verge of breaking down, so I suppose my letter had a strong tinge of hysteria. I had no friend to go to and had to break out on somebody. This working out one's soul is not a pleasant task." [64]

A few years later, amid the wreck of his first marriage, the death wish returned again. Once again the vital life spirit seemed to have vanished. "I don't seem to care for anything," he wrote Charmian. "I am sick, my dear. It's Nietzsche's 'Long Sickness' that is mine, I fear." [65] In *John Barleycorn,* he attributed this malaise to drink, the terrible "white logic" through which he penetrated life's raw core. Crushed by what he beheld, he "meditated suicide coolly, as a Greek philosopher might." Just as he was about to fall into the abyss, however, "one remaining illusion—the PEOPLE" saved him.[66]

At the ranch, he again contemplated taking his life. This time, Jack no longer had the resiliency of youth or the belief in socialism to pull him through. He was in the same position as Martin Eden. The struggle, the adventure, the romance and excitement of daring and winning were over. Once one had arrived, there was no place to go. The only end was death, for life had lost all meaning. Accordingly, on November 21, 1916, Jack London took the ultimate step of the romantic hero by committing suicide. He asked to have his body cremated and his ashes placed under a high red stone on the hill of his Beauty Ranch. Even in death, London remained the Byronic figure at war with the world, for he had ordered his tomb inscribed, "The stone the builders rejected." [67]

A Postscript from the Past

THE CATACLYSMISTS provide a warning to the present as well as a comment on the past. Their inability to come to terms with themselves or their time is not a calamity confined to a group or even an age. It is a result of the human situation—of disappointed desires, of man's yearning to be greater than he is or can be. At its noblest, it is tragedy. In the case of the cataclysmists, however, estrangement restricted horizons and stifled humanity. Thwarted ambition accomplished nothing except to make them dare even less than they could do.

Today we are in another period of cataclysmic thinking. The elements that pervaded thoughts of catastrophe in previous eras are appearing once more. A state of mind has re-emerged that sees human relations solely in terms of power struggles. Again words like "conspiracy," "betrayal," "swindle," and "confrontation with force" are heard. Terms like "peace," "democracy," "equality," and "brotherhood" are still used to rationalize the ruthless quest for power—while such slogans as "better red than dead," "massive retaliation," or "pre-emptive war" recall the old polarizations of withdrawal and surrender or aggrandizement and aggression.

Doubts about America have reappeared as part of the cataclysmic psychology. Many contemporary critics have come to agree with Donnelly and London that this nation is no longer a youthful land of promise. Other observers echo the Adamses in claiming that the United States is administratively ill-adapted to modern times or that the country is losing vital energy. Some even share the pessimistic conclusions of those anxious aristocrats, foreseeing national defeat or a global holocaust.

The return of haunting fears and suspicions has been accompanied by the fulfillment of old prophecies. World wars, betrayed revolutions, class strife, exploitation of the downtrodden, and racial conflict have plagued our time. Even the major participants in global crises were accurately designated by the cataclysmists. The turbulence of the twentieth century has resulted from struggles involving Britain and America against Russia, Japan, and Germany. As the Cassandras predicted, man has made the conditions of his own destruction by suppressing just demands and meeting the threat of force with counterforce.

Despite similarities in outlook, there is one great difference between present forebodings and former fears. Not even the frequent accuracy of previous predictions can obscure the discrepancy between possibility and phantasy. But the prospect of real holocaust has not greatly changed the nature of cataclysmic forces. In the earlier era, man was confused by the denial of tradition, dwarfed when small communities gave way to metropolises, and enfeebled by economic and political forces beyond his comprehension and control. Those days marked the emergence of the cities, the great bureaucracies, and the world conflicts that dominate modern times. Now, man has lost his way and his self in the megalopolis, the huge corporation, and the super-nation. These forces have become bigger than life, and their continued growth threatens to end it.

Notes

Notes to Chapter 2

1 Henry George, *Progress And Poverty* (Doubleday, Page and Co.: Garden City, 1916), pp. 486, 540, 530, 534, 482, 555.
2 Edward Bellamy, *Equality* (D. Appleton and Co.: New York, 1897), pp. 319, 337; cf. *Looking Backward* (Little, Brown and Co.: Boston, 1941), p. 9.
3 Bellamy, *Looking Backward*, p. 276; cf. *Equality*, p. 346.
4 William Dean Howells, *A Traveller From Altruria* (Harper and Bros.: New York, 1894), pp. 221, 281-282, 293.
5 Samuel Clemens, *The Mysterious Stranger* (Harper and Bros.: New York, 1929), p. 131.
6 Theodore Dreiser, "The American Financier," *Hey Rub-A-Dub-Dub: A Book Of The Mystery And Wonder And Terror Of Life* (Boni and Liveright: New York, 1920), p. 74.
7 Washington Gladden, *Applied Christianity* (Houghton Mifflin Co.: Boston, 1894), p. 312.
8 Lyman Abbott, *The Rights of Man* (Houghton Mifflin Co.: Boston, 1901), p. 312.
9 Walter J. Rauschenbusch, *Christianity and the Social Crisis* (The Macmillan Co.: New York, 1908), p. 285.
10 Josiah Strong, *Our Country: Its Possible Future and Its Present Crisis* (Baker and Taylor Co.: New York, 1885), p. 40.
11 Abbott, *The Industrial Problem* (G. W. Jacobs and Co: Philadelphia, 1905), pp. 16-17.
12 Strong, *The Next Great Awakening* (Baker and Taylor Co.: New York, 1902), p. 17; cf. Rauschenbusch, *op. cit.*, p. 59.
13 Strong, *Studies In The Gospel Of The Kingdom* (The American Institute Of Social Service: New York, 1910), p. 65.

14   Abbott, *Christianity And Social Problems* (Houghton Mifflin Co.:
     Boston, 1896), p. iii; Strong, *The Twentieth Century City*
     (Baker and Taylor Co.: New York, 1898), p. 140; Gladden,
     Social Salvation (G. P. Putnam's Sons: New York, 1902),
     p. 27.
15   Richard T. Ely, *The Labor Movement in America* (T. Y. Crowell
     Co.: New York, 1890), pp. v-vi.
16   Ely, *Studies in the Evolution of Industrial Society* (The Macmillan
     Co.: New York, 1912), pp. 144-145, 164.
17   Ely, *Social Aspects of Christianity* (T. Y. Crowell Co.: New York,
     1889), p. 53.
18   Ely, *The Social Law of Service* (T. Y. Crowell Co.: New York,
     1896), p. 21.

Notes to Chapter 3

1   Morrell Heald, "Business Attitudes Toward European Immigration,
     1880-1900," *Journal Of Economic History*, XIII (Summer,
     1953), 294; John Higham, *Strangers in the Land* (Rutgers
     University Press: New Brunswick, 1955), pp. 16-17, 22-23.
2   "The Late Riots," *The Nation*, XXV (August 2, 1877), 68.
3   Robert V. Bruce, *1877: Year of Violence* (Bobbs-Merrill and Co.:
     Indianapolis, 1959), pp. 135-136, 225-226, 242-243, 276.
4   "Editor's Easy Chair," *Harper's New Monthly Magazine*, CV
     (October, 1877), 782-783. Cf. Thomas Scott, "The Recent
     Strikes," *North American Review*, CXXV (September, 1877),
     351-362.
5   "The Great Strike," *Scribner's Monthly Magazine*, XIV (October,
     1877), 852-853. Cf. Charles Francis Adams, "Prevention of
     Railroad Strikes, *The Nation*, XXV (August 30, 1877),
     133-134; Bruce, *op. cit.*, pp. 161, 164, 171, 313-314, 316.
6   "The Silver Crisis," *Nation*, XXXVIII (February 28, 1884), 182.
     Frederic Albert Shannon points out that the greatest lag be-
     tween farm prices and other commodities came between 1861
     and 1865 and that the gap was much smaller in the Eighties
     when the farm protest began on a large scale. The farmers,
     however, were not aware of this gap and measured their
     prosperity in terms of high crop prices. For Shannon's
     argument, *America's Economic Crisis* (The Macmillan Co.:
     New York, 1940), p. 24.
7   Selig Perlman, "Upheaval and Reorganization," in John R. Com-
     mons *et al.*, *History of Labor in the United States* (The Mac-
     millan Co.: New York, 1918), II, 277, 300.
8   Eugene Hilgard, "Progress in Agriculture, Education and Govern-
     ment," *The Atlantic Monthly*, XLIX (April, 1882), 531.

9   New York *Sun,* quoted in Commons, *op. cit.,* p. 371.
10 "The New Monists—The Labor Agitators, II, *The Chautauquan,* VI (June, 1886), 641. Cf. George Frederic Parsons, "The Labor Question," *Atlantic,* LVIII (July, 1886), 98-99.
11 Washington Gladden, "Is It Peace Or War," *The Century Illustrated Magazine,* XXXII (August, 1886), 567, 571, 575.
12 Lyman Abbott, "Danger Ahead," *Century,* XXXI (November, 1885), 53, 54.
13 "Pittsburgh Manifesto," quoted in Commons, *op. cit.,* pp. 283-295.
14 "The Alarm," quoted in Henry David, *The History of the Haymarket Affair* (Farrar and Rinehart, Inc.: New York, 1936), pp. 120-121.
15 "Die Arbeiter Zeitung," quoted in Louis Adamic, *Dynamite* (Viking Press: New York, 1931), p. 48.
16 Carter Harrison, quoted in David, *op. cit.,* p. 112.
17 *New York Times,* January 16, 1886, p. 4. Cf. *New York Tribune* January 16, 1886, p. 4.
18 *Chicago Inter Ocean,* May 5, 1886, quoted in David, *op. cit.,* p. 112.
19 *Chicago Tribune,* May 6, 1886, quoted in *Public Opinion,* I (May 15, 1886), 81. Cf. *Chicago Herald,* quoted in David, *op. cit.,* 209.
20 *New York Tribune,* May 7, 1886, p. 7; *New York Times,* May 7, 1886, p. 4; *Cleveland Plain Dealer,* quoted in *Public Opinion,* I, 85. Cf. *Philadelphia Telegraph,* quoted in *Ibid.;* Arthur Edwards, "Chicago's Experience With Anarchy," *Chautauquan,* VII (March 1887), 168.
21 "Organizing Against Lawlessness," *Chautauquan,* VII (March, 1887), 179.
22 By the end of 1892, The Amalgamated Association of Iron and Steel Workers had only 5,000 workers. The union was made up of skilled workers, and its constitution urged members to protect "the business of all employers" signing agreements with the union. It had an annual wage conference with employers and observed its contracts with few work stoppages. David, "Upheaval At Homestead," in Daniel Aaron, ed., *America in Crisis* (Oxford University Press: New York, 1952), pp. 136, 139-140, 170.
23 *The Standard,* July 13, 1892, quoted in *Public Opinion,* XIII (July 24, 1892), 370.
24 John Brisben Walker, "The Homestead Strike: Object Lesson," *Cosmopolitan,* XIII (September, 1892), 572, 574. Cf. Thomas B. Preston, "Are We Socialists," *The Arena Magazine,* VII (December, 1892), 90-99.
25 *Cleveland Plain Dealer,* July 25, 1892, quoted in *Public Opinion,* XIII (July 31, 1892), 394.
26 Preston, *op. cit.,* pp. 98-99.

27 Harold U. Faulkner, *Politics, Reform and Expansion, 1890-1900* (Harper and Bros.: New York, 1959), pp. 142-143, 169.
28 Thomas Byrnes, "The Menace of 'Coxeyism,' " *North American Review,* CLVIII (May, 1894), 700.
29 "The New Lawlessness," *Nation,* LVIII (May 10, 1894), 340. Cf. *New York Tribune,* May 27, 1894, p. 6; "Social Unrest and Disorder," *Chautauquan,* XIX (May, 1894), 233-234.
30 Henry Frank, "The Crusade of the Unemployed," *Arena,* X (July, 1894), 242. Cf. "General" Fry quoted in Byrnes, "Coxeyism," *op. cit.,* p. 690.
31 Nelson A. Miles, "The Lesson of the Recent Strikes," *North American Review,* CLIX (August, 1894), 184.
32 *New York Herald,* July 3, 1894, quoted in Almont Lindsey, *The Pullman Strike* (University of Chicago Press: Chicago, 1942), p. 311. Cf. Rev. Dr. Herrick Johnson, quoted in *Ibid.,* pp. 319-320; *St. Paul Globe* and *Philadelphia Times,* quoted in *Public Opinion,* XVII (July 21, 1894), 630-631; H. P. Robinson, quoted in "The Lesson of the Recent Strikes," *op. cit.,* p. 199.
33 William H. Carwardine, *The Pullman Strike* (Charles H. Kerr and Co.: Chicago, 1894), p. 121. Cf. James C. Clark, "The Coming Industrial Order," *Arena,* XI (January, 1895), 238-239.
34 *New York Tribune,* May 7, 1886, p. 4. Cf. "A Word To Social Philosophers," *Nation* XXXV (November 17, 1887), 388.
35 "The Harm Of Immigration," *Nation,* LVI (January 19, 1893), 43.
36 T. T. Munger, "Immigration By Passport," *Century,* XXXV (March, 1888), 794; John H. Denison, "The Survival of the American Type," *Atlantic,* LXXV (January, 1895), 16. Cf. Josiah Strong, "City Evangelization," *Chautauquan,* IX (November, 1888), 99.
37 W. Scott Morgan, *History of the Wheel and Alliance and the Impending Revolution* (C. B. Woodward Co.: St. Louis, 1891), p. 83. Cf. Georgia Farmer's Alliance, quoted in C. Vann Woodward, *Tom Watson: Agrarian Rebel* (Rinehart and Co.: New York, 1955), p. 137. James B. Weaver, quoted in Fred Emory Haynes, *James Baird Weaver* (Iowa State Historical Society: Iowa City, 1919), p. 255.
38 Strong, *The New Era* (Baker and Taylor Co.: New York, 1893), pp. 187-188.
39 The National Board of Trade, quoted in Higham, *op. cit.,* p. 52; Heald, *op. cit.,* p. 296.
40 *New York Times,* August 2, 1886, p. 4. Cf. *New York Tribune,* August 2, 1886, p. 4; Parsons, *op. cit.,* p. 99.
41 Higham, *op. cit.,* pp. 56-58.

42 Munger, *op. cit.*, p. 791. Cf. Peri Ander, "Our Foreign Immigration," *Arena*, II (August, 1890), 277; *New York Times*, November 11, 1887, p. 4.
43 "The New Immigration," *Nation*, LIII (September 17, 1891), 209-21. Cf. E. A. Hempstead, "Shall Immigration Be Restricted," *Chautauquan*, VIII (July, 1888), 610.
44 Munger, *op. cit.*, p. 797.
45 "The Harm of Immigration," *Nation*, LVI (January 19, 1893), 43.
46 Munger, *op. cit.*, pp. 793-794.
47 A. Cleveland Coxe, "Government By Aliens," *The Forum*, VII (July, 1889), 600.
48 Munger, *op. cit.*, p. 793.
49 "City Immigrant Population," *Chautauquan*, XII (January, 1891), 522.
50 Hempstead, *op. cit.*, p. 612.
51 Ander, *op. cit.*, p. 277.
52 Coxe, *op. cit.*, p. 606. Cf. Hjalmar H. Boysen, "Dangers of Unrestricted Immigration," *Forum*, III (July, 1887), 533.
53 Hempstead, *op. cit.*, p. 612.
54 Henry Cabot Lodge, quoted in Barbara Miller Solomon, *Ancestors And Immigrants* (Harvard University Press: Cambridge, 1956)), p. 68.
55 Lodge, "The Census and Immigration," *Century*, XLVI (September, 1893), 737.
56 Francis Amasa Walker, quoted in Solomon, *op. cit.*, pp. 71-72.
57 F. A. Walker, "Restriction Of Immigration," *Atlantic*, LXXVII (June, 1896), 827-828. For evidence of restrictionism among other Brahmins, see Charles Eliot Norton, "Some Aspects of Civilization," *Forum*, XX (February, 1896), 641-652; Thomas Bailey Aldrich to G. D. Woodberry, May 14, 1892, in Ferris Greenslet, *The Life of Thomas Bailey Aldrich* (Houghton Mifflin Co.: Boston, 1908), pp. 168-169; Solomon, *op. cit.*, p. 87.
58 Noble Canby, "Immigration," *Chautauquan*, XVI (November, 1892), 199. Cf. Lodge, *loc. cit.*, F. A. Walker, *op. cit.*, pp. 827-829; Samuel Lane Loomis, "Foreigners and American Churches," *Chautauquan*, XVII (May, 1893), 180-184.
59 For this quotation and that on p. 82, see F. A. Walker, *op. cit.*, pp. 827-828, 823. Cf. N. S. Shaler, "European Peasants as Immigrants," *Atlantic*, LXXI (May, 1893), 649, 651-652; Lodge, *loc. cit.*
60 Loomis, *op. cit.*, p. 183; Canby, *op. cit.*, p. 201; Denison, *op. cit.*, p. 17; Shaler, *op. cit.*, pp. 47-48.
61 James B. Weaver, *A Call to Action* (Iowa Printing Co.: Des Moines, 1892), p. 5.

62 Thomas A. Watson, *The People's Campaign Book 1892: Not A Revolt Its A Rebellion!* (National Watchman's Publishing Co.: Washington, D. C., 1892), pp. 219-220.

63 H. R. Chamberlain, "Farmer's Alliance and Other Political Parties," *Chautauquan*, XIII (June, 1891), 339. Cf. John R. Dodge, "The Discontent of the Farmer," *Century*, XXI (January, 1892), 447.

64 Rodney Welch, "The Farmers' Changed Condition," *Forum*, X (November, 1890), 700.

65 "Crazes," *Nation*, LIII (November 26, 1891), 403. Cf. "The Farm Change In Politics," *Nation*, LII (June 14, 1891), 453.

66 "The Kansas Situation," *Nation*, LVI, (January 19, 1893), 44.

67 "Western Socialism," *Nation*, LVI (May 4, 1893), 324.

68 Henry Litchfield West, "Two Republics or One?" *North American Review*, CLXII (April, 1896), 510.

69 "A Real Business Campaign," *Nation*, LXIII (July 30, 1896), 80; "The Triumph of Sectionalism and Communism," *Harper's Weekly*, XL (July 18, 1896), 698. For other frantic reactions, see *New York Tribune*, September 17, 1896, p. 4; "The Platform Of Revolution," *Nation*, LXIII (July 23, 1896), 62; *New York Mail and Express, Brooklyn Standard Union, Philadelphia Press, Boston Journal*, all quoted in *Public Opinion*, XXI (July 16, 1896), 76.

70 *Chicago Staats-Zeitung*, quoted in *Public Opinion*, XXI (July 16, 1896), 75.

71 *New York Tribune*, July 6, 1896, p. 6; *Philadelphia Press and New York Mail and Express*, quoted in *Public Opinion*, XXII (July 16, 1896), 75-76.

72 *Boston Journal*, quoted in *Ibid.*, p. 136.

73 *New York Times*, August 6, 1896, p. 5. Cf. "Business Campaign," *op. cit.*, p. 80; "Triumph of Sectionalism," *op. cit.*, p. 698; Ingersoll Lockwood, *1900 or the Last President* (American News Co.: New York, 1896); *New York Mail and Express* and *Brooklyn Standard Union*, both quoted in *Public Opinion*, XXI (July 16, 1896), 75-76.

74 Andrew D. White, quoted in *Public Opinion*, XXI (July 30, 1896), 136. Cf. White, "Encouragements in the Present Crisis," *Forum*, XXII (September, 1896), 16-30.

75 Theodore Roosevelt, quoted in Henry Pringle, *Theodore Roosevelt: A Biography* (Harcourt, Brace and Co.: New York, 1931), p. 164.

76 *Philadelphia Press*, quoted in *Public Opinion*, XXI (July 16, 1896), 76.

77 *New York Tribune*, November 4, 1896, p. 6. Cf. *Worcester Spy*, quoted in *Public Opinion*, XXI (November 12, 1896), 613; *New York Herald, New York Commercial Advertiser*.

78 *New York World*, quoted in *Ibid.*, p. 583.

79 *Brooklyn Times,* quoted in *Ibid.,* p. 614. Cf. *Philadelphia North American, Hartford Post, Philadelphia Inquirer* and *Toledo Blade,* all quoted in *Ibid.*

Notes to Chapter 4

1 Charles M. Harger, "The New Era in the Middle West," *Harper's New Monthly Magazine,* XCVII (July, 1898), 282.
2 Thomas A. Watson, "Why I Am Still a Populist," *Review of Reviews,* XXXVIII (September, 1908), 304.
3 *Boston Traveller,* quoted in *Public Opinion,* XXI (November 12, 1896), 614; *Boston Traveller,* quoted in *Ibid.,* XXIX (July 12, 1900), 37. Cf. *Ibid.,* XXVIII (July 5, 1900), 387-388, and XXIX (July 12, 1900), 37-41; "Mr. Bryan," *The Atlantic Monthly,* XC (September, 1902), 290.
4 Harger, "The Kansas of Today," *The Atlantic Monthly,* XC (September, 1902), 363.
5 Watson, *Political and Economic Handbook* (Jeffersonian Publishing Co.: Thomason, Ga., 1916), p. 457.
6 *Public Opinion,* a good index to the contemporary press, did not carry articles on labor troubles in the Cripple Creek and Telluride mining districts until December 17, 1903. None of the papers quoted associated the strikes with anarchists or thought the conflicts were threats. *Public Opinion,* XXXVI (December 17, 1903), 805. Other *cause célèbres* were treated in the same way. When Steunenberg, who had been governor of Idaho during the Coeur D'Alene Strike, was murdered, it was reported without comment in the magazines and newspapers. See, for example, *New York Herald,* December 31, 1905, p. 2; *New York Tribune,* December 31, 1905, p. 1. Even the indictment of Moyer, Pettibone, and Haywood drew no editorial comment from the *New York Tribune.* Summaries of the press, *Public Opinion,* and *Review of Reviews,* carried no stories about Steunenberg's assassination or the indictment of the Western Federation of Miners' leaders. The dynamiting of the *Los Angeles Times* building was also reported without comment. See, for example, *New York Tribune,* October 2, 1910, pp. 1-2, October 3, 1910, pp. 1, 3; *Philadelphia Press,* October 2, 1910, pp. 1-2. Even the indictment of union officers did not bring forth enraged press comment. The *New York Herald* and *Christian Science Monitor* reported it without editorial comment. See *New York Herald,* April 23, 1911, p. 1, April 24, 1911, pp. 1, 2, April 25, 1911, pp. 1, 8; *Christian Science Monitor.* April 24, 1911, p. 4. Many magazines car-

ried no editorials or stories on the affair: *Atlantic Monthly, The Forum, Cosmopolitan,* and *The Review of Reviews.* Magazines and dailies that ventured opinions did not associate labor with anarchism or cataclysm, nor did they attempt to smear unionism in general. They called instead for a fair trial. See, for example, *New York Times,* October 4, 1910, p. 10, April 24, 1911, p. 2; *New York Tribune,* April 24, 1911, p. 6, April 25, 1911, p. 6; *Philadelphia Press,* April 25, 1911, p. 6; *The Outlook,* C (May 6, 1911), 1-2; Theodore Roosevelt, *Ibid.,* p. 12-13; Harvey J. O'Higgins, "The Dynamiters," *McClure's Magazine,* XXXVII (August, 1911), 347-364. The last article stressed the role of William J. Burns and the detective aspects of the case and had nothing on its social implications. The I.W.W. strike in Paterson, New Jersey, received the same treatment. Commentators mostly emphasized the need for fairness and the plight of the workers. See, for example, John A. Fitch, "The I.W.W. an Outlaw Organization," *The Survey,* XXX (June 7, 1913), 355-362; Gregory Mason, "Industrial War In Paterson," *Outlook,* CIV (June 7, 1913), 283-287. Some papers commented on the futility of the strike: *New York Times,* February 27, 1913, p. 12. Others reported it with no comment; *Review of Reviews,* XLVIII (September, 1913), 277-278.

7   W. Jett Lauck, "The Lesson From Lawrence," *North American Review,* CXCV (May, 1912), 665-672. Cf. Harry Emerson Fosdick, "After the Strike in Lawrence," *Outlook,* CI (June 15, 1912), 340-346.

8   R. F. Hoxie, "The Truth About the I.W.W.," *The Journal of Political Economy,* XXI (November, 1913), 787.

9   *New York Evening Post,* Saturday Supplement, November 2, 1912, p. 2. Other articles that discussed the I.W.W. dispassionately and discounted its dangers: Arno Dosch, "What the I.W.W. Is," *The World's Work,* XXVI (August, 1913), 406-420; Lorin F. Deland, "The Lawrence Strike: A Study," *Atlantic,* CIX (May, 1912), 694-705. The newspapers did not consider the strike nor the union too important or dangerous. The story went off the front page of the *New York Tribune* on January 15, 1912. The paper ran no editorial on the strike until January 23, and the next editorial was February 3. These editorials were not even vaguely cataclysmic, and the I.W.W. was not mentioned. The strike was discussed as an issue of employee-liability and work-hour legislation. *New York Tribune,* January 13 and February 3, 1913, p. 6. The *New York Times* and the *New York Sun* had no editorials on the strike from January 16 to February 16.

10 Dosch, *op. cit.,* p. 417.

11 Deland, *op. cit.,* p. 705.

12 National Civic League Charter quoted in Selig Perlman, "Labor Movements," in Commons, *et al., History of Labor in the United States*: *1896-1932,* IV (The Macmillan Co.: New York, 1935), 48.

13 Dosch, *op. cit.,* p. 407. Cf. Lauck, *op. cit.,* p. 672.

14 From 1897 to 1907, there was a tremendous spurt of economic growth, which rejuvenated the middle class and kept the spotty economic performance of the next few years from having more than a slight negative influence. For the economic cycles see H. U. Faulkner, *The Decline of Laissez-Faire: 1897-1917* (Rinehart: New York, 1951), pp. 29-31; Fred Albert Shannon, *America's Economic Growth* (The Macmillan Co.: New York, 1940), pp. 636, 660; Warren R. Persons, "An Index Of General Business Conditions 1875-1913," *Review Of Economic Statistics,* IX (1927), 20-29.

15 *Boston Traveller,* quoted in *Public Opinion,* XXXIII (July 3, 1902), 6. Cf. *Cleveland Leader,* quoted in *Ibid.; Philadelphia Times,* quoted in *Ibid.,* XXXII (May 22, 1902), 647.

16 Ambrose P. Winston, "A Quarter-Century Of Strikes," *Atlantic,* XC (November, 1902), 665.

17 Frank Luther Mott, *Golden Multitudes* (The Macmillan Co.: New York, 1947), p. 158.

18 Theodore Roosevelt, "Address to Congress," 1902, quoted in Richard Hofstadter, *The American Political Tradition* (6th ed; Alfred A. Knopf: New York, 1959), pp. 222-223.

19 Theodore Roosevelt, quoted in *Ibid.,* p. 215. Cf. Roosevelt, *Outlook,* C, 12-13.

20 Ray Stannard Baker, "A New Industrial Conspiracy," *McClure's* XXI (September, 1903), 463. The idea of a balance between labor and capital is discussed in Hofstadter, *op. cit.,* pp. 203-234.

21 Roosevelt, quoted in Hofstadter, *op. cit.,* p. 223.

22 Robert M. LaFollette, *The Political Philosophy Of Robert M. LaFollette* (Robert M. LaFollette Co.: Madison, 1920), p. 104; William E. Borah, *Bedrock* (National Home Library: Washington, D.C., 1936), p. 13. Cf. Albert Baird Cummins, quoted in John D. Hicks and Theodore Salutos, *Agricultural Discontent in the Middle West* (University of Wisconsin Press: Madison, 1951), p. 45.

23 Cummins, *The Political Issues* (Des Moines, 1906), pp. 3, 14; Borah, *op. cit.,* p. 10.

24 Cummins, *op. cit.,* p. 12.

25 Borah, *op. cit.,* p. 11. Significantly, he was speaking to the Union League.

26 *San Francisco Call,* quoted in *Public Opinion,* XXXI (July 19, 1901), 360.

27 *Cleveland Plain Dealer,* quoted in *Ibid.,* I (May 15, 1886), 85;

Cleveland Plain Dealer, quoted in *Ibid.,* XXXI (July 19, 1901), 360. For a similar switch in opinion, compare *New York Tribune,* May 5, 1886, p. 4, with *Ibid.,* September 15, 1901, p. 9; "A Word To Social Philosophers," *Nation,* XLV (November 17, 1886), 398, with "The Bill Against Anarchists," *Ibid.,* LXXIV (February 20, 1902), 85. For other statements about the insignificance of the anarchists, see *American Review of Reviews,* XXIX (October, 1901), 388; "The Death of the President," *Atlantic,* LXXXVIII (October, 1901), 432; "The Anarchists and the President," *North American Review,* CLXXIII (October, 1901), 441; *Birmingham News, Baltimore World, Boston Journal,* all quoted in *Public Opinion,* XXXI (July 19, 1901), 360.

28 *New York Evening Post,* quoted in *Public Opinion,* XXXVI (May 26, 1904), 645. Cf. *Philadelphia Record,* quoted in *Ibid.,* p. 645; Francis Lamont Pierce, "The Agitator: His Function in Social Evolution," *Arena,* XXXVIII (September, 1907), 306-310.

29 A. M. Simons, "The United States and World Politics," *The International Socialist Review,* I (February, 1901), 463. Cf. "A Year Of Disintegration," *Ibid.,* VII (January, 1907), 434; Robert Hunter, "The Socialist Party in the Present Campaign," *Review of Reviews,* XXXVII (September, 1908), 299.

30 *Review of Reviews,* XXXVII (May, 1908), 538.

31 Seymour Stedman, "Immediate Demands," *International Socialist Review,* III (January, 1902), 25. Cf. Francis Marshall Elliot, "The National Strike," *Ibid.,* VII (February, 1907), 465; Simons, "Better than Barricades," *Ibid.,* XII (February, 1912), 930; Ed Moore, "When the Workers Fold Their Arms," *Ibid.,* XI (June, 1911), 729-730; James Connolley, "Ballots, Bullets, Or—," *Ibid.,* X (October, 1919), 354-358.

32 Victor Berger, quoted in Ira Kipnis, *The American Socialist Movement: 1897-1912* (Columbia University Press: New York, 1952), p. 154. Cf. Morris Hillquit, quoted in *Ibid.,* p. 202; John Spargo, quoted in *Ibid.,* 203; Eugene V. Debs, quoted in *Ibid.,* p. 22. For the resolution condemning violence, *Ibid.,* pp. 408, 417.

33 John Graham Brooks, "Recent Socialist Literature," *Atlantic,* XCIX (February, 1907), 278.

34 J. N. Larned, "Prepare for Socialism," *Ibid.,* CVII (May, 1911), 579.

35 Frederic C. Howe, *The Modern City and Its Problems* (Charles Scribner's Sons: New York, 1915), p. 7.

36 John J. Hamilton, *The Dethronement of the City Boss* (Funk and Wagnalls: New York, 1910), p. 17.

37 Raymond L. Bridgeman, "Civic Righteousness Via Percentages," *Atlantic,* CII (May, 1911), 579.

38 Hamilton, *op. cit.*, pp. 24-25. Cf. Howe, *op. cit.*, pp. 375-376;
    Howe, *The City: The Hope of Democracy* (Charles Scribner's
    Sons: New York, 1905), pp. 2, 7, 15-16, 305-306; George C.
    Sykes, "The Tenement House Problem," *Atlantic*, XCIII
    (March, 1904), 414-416; Burton J. Hendrick, "A Great
    Municipal Reform," *Ibid.*, XCII (October, 1903), 408-415;
    Hamilton, *op. cit.*, pp. 15-17.
39 Hamilton, *op. cit.*, p. 25. Cf. Bridgeman, *op. cit.*, pp. 797-802;
    Charles Mumford Robinson, "Improvement in City Life,"
    Atlantic, LXXXIII (April, 1899), 524-537; Everett P.
    Wheeler, "The Unofficial Government of Cities," *Ibid.*, LXXV
    (November, 1900), 370-376; Hutchins Hapgood, "The Mu-
    nicipal Voters' League of Chicago," *Ibid.*, pp. 834-843; Charles
    Zueblin, "A Decade of Civic Improvement," *Chautauquan*,
    XXXVI (November, 1902), 174-177; Note 38.
40 Howe, *Modern City*, p. 7; Howe, *Hope of Democracy*, p. 301.
41 Deland, *op. cit.*, p. 705. Cf. Lauck, *op. cit.*, pp. 671-672.
42 John Higham, *Strangers in the Land* (Rutgers University Press:
    New Brunswick, 1955), pp. 118, 120-122, 128-129, 167-174.
    For Progressives and reformers who were also restrictionists,
    see Edward Alsworth Ross, "The Old World in the New and
    Immigrant Blood," *Century* LXXXVII (November, 1913),
    28-35; Agnes Reppelier, "The Modest Immigrant," *Atlantic*,
    CXVI (September, 1915), 303-312; William Hemstreet,
    "Agrarian Revival," *Arena*, XXIX (February, 1903), 142-
    151; "Americanization," *New Republic*, V (January 29, 1916),
    322-323. John R. Commons and David Starr Jordan were
    members of the Immigration Restriction League. Barbara
    Miller Solomon, *Ancestors And Immigrants* (Harvard Uni-
    versity Press: Cambridge, 1957), p. 123. For the connection
    between restrictionists and municipal reformers see Higham,
    op. cit., p. 102.
43 W. A. Northcott, "The Rights Of Men," *Arena*, XXVI (De-
    cember, 1901), 569.
44 "National Deterioration," *Nation*, LXXXVII (August 16, 1906),
    135.
45 Benjamin Orange Flower, "The Gathering Together and Onward
    March of the Forces of Free Government," *Arena*, XXXV
    (April, 1907), 414.
46 Benjamin Parke De Witt, *The Progressive Movement* (The Mac-
    millan Co.: New York, 1915), p. 4.
47 Frederic C. Howe, quoted in C. C. Regier, *The Era of the Muck-
    rakers* (University of North Carolina Press: Chapel Hill,
    1932), pp. 200-201.

Notes to Chapter 5

1 George S. Boutwell, speech endorsing Bryan at the Anti-Imperialist Convention, August 15, 1900, quoted in *Public Opinion*, XXIX (August 23, 1900), 227-228.

2 Moorfield Storey to George F. Hoar, February 28, 1900, quoted in Mark DeWolfe Howe, *Portrait of an Independent: Moorfield Storey* (Houghton Mifflin Co.: Boston, 1931), p. 227. Cf. "Democratic Fatalism," *The Nation*, LXVII (December 1, 1898), 404.

3 John Clark Ridpath, "The Republic and the Empire," *The Arena*, XX (September, 1898), 344. Cf. Samuel C. Parks, "Imperialism," *Arena*, XXV (June, 1901), 586.

4 "Militarism in a Republic," *Nation*, LXIII (March 5, 1896), 190. Cf. "Suppression," *Nation*, LXVIII (May 25, 1899), 388; "The White Peril," *Nation*, LXXI (August 2, 1900), 81; Parks, *op. cit.*, pp. 579, 586; E. V. Long, "The Anti-thesis of True Expansion," *Arena*, XXIV (October, 1900), 344-345.

5 Storey, *Our New Departure* (George H. Ellis, Printer: Boston, 1900), p. 53.

6 Solomon Solix-Cohen, "The Spectre of Imperialism," *Arena*, XX (October, 1898), 452. Cf. Ridpath, *Ibid.*, pp. 344-345; H. D. Money, "Conquest and the Constitution," *Arena*, XXIII (April, 1900), 338; "The Cause of Peace," *Nation*, LXVIII (April 20, 1896), 290.

7 Benjamin Orange Flower, "The Proposed Federation of the Anglo-Saxon Nations," *Arena*, XX (August, 1898), 232.

8 Alexander Hume Ford, "The Warfare of Railroads in Asia," *Century*, LIX (March, 1900), 794. Cf. Frederic Austin Ogg, "Saxon and Slav: The Lion and the Bear in the Far East," *Chautauquan*, XXXVII (March, 1903), 14-15; Charles A. Conant, "The United States as a World Power," *The Forum*, XXIX (July, 1900), 816; Franklin Henry Giddings, *Democracy and Empire*, (The Macmillan Co.: New York, 1900), p. 289.

9 Richmond P. Hobson, "The Defense of Our Outlying Possessions," *The World Today*, XX (July, 1908), 741-742.

10 Eleanor Tupper and George E. McReynolds, *Japan in American Public Opinion* (The Macmillan Co.: New York, 1937), pp. 42-54, 101, 108; Foster Rhea Dulles, *Forty Years of American-Japanese Relations* (Appleton-Century Co.: New York, 1937), pp. 80-81, 107-108.

11 "The Deeper Preparedness," *The New Republic*, III (July 24, 1915), 299-300.

12 Sigmund Henschen, "What Is Behind the Japanese Peril?"
    Forum, LVI (July, 1916), 63-78. Cf. Thomas Millard, "The
    Japanese Menace," *Century,* XCI (March, 1916), 673-682;
    "Being Candid With Japan," *New Republic,* V (December
    11, 1915), 136-137; Sydney L. Gulick, *Anti-Japanese War
    Scare Stories* (Fleming H. Revell Co.: New York, 1917), pp.
    19-64.

13 Homer Lea, quoted by Clare Booth, ed., in Homer Lea, *The Valor
    of Ignorance* (Harper and Bros.: New York, 1942), p. 12.

14 Adna R. Chaffee, "Introduction," *Ibid.* (1909), pp. 23-24.

15 For quotations in the foregoing pages, see *Ibid.,* pp. 27-31, 52, 57,
    49, 206, 19, 87, 93, 178, 220.

16 Lea, *The Day of the Saxon* (Harper and Bros.: New York, 1912),
    pp. 5, 239-240.

17 W. Morgan Shuster, "The Breakdown of Civilization," *Century,*
    LXXXIX (November, 1914), 52, 59. Cf. Edwin Davies
    Schoonmaker, "Has the Church Collapsed," *Century,* XCIX
    (February, 1915), 481-489; P. Gavan Duffy, "The Bondage
    of Modern Religion," *Century* (March, 1915), 867-895; "If
    We Enter the War," *New Republic,* VI (April 22, 1916),
    305-306; Herbert W. Horwill, "The Cost to Humanity,"
    Atlantic, CXV (March, 1915), 417-426; William Austin
    Smith, "Some False Consolations of War," *Atlantic,* CXVI
    (December, 1915), 843-847. The group most consistently de-
    nouncing the war was the socialists. See, for example, the
    following articles in *International Socialist Review,* XV:
    Phillip S. Russell, "Europe in the Clutch of War" (September,
    1914), 133-135; Henry L. Slobodin, "After the War—What?"
    (April, 1915), 587-588; William E. Bohn, "The War, the
    World, and the Future" (April, 1915), 581-585; "When
    We Go To War" (June, 1915), 753-754.

18 Eric Fisher Wood, *The Writing on the Wall: The Nation on
    Trial* (The Century Co.: New York, 1916), p. 147. Cf. Julius
    W. Muller, *The Invasion Of America* (George H. Doran:
    New York, 1915); Hudson Maxim, *Defenseless America*
    (Hearst's International Publishing Co.: New York, 1915);
    Cleveland Moffett, *The Conquest Of America* (George H.
    Doran: New York, 1916).

19 Some prominent examples of those who became enthusiastic after
    we entered the war are Woodrow Wilson; "America Tested
    By War," *The New Republic,* XV (June 22, 1918), 220-221;
    and The American Peace Society, which, after we declared war,
    said that "we must help in the bayonetting of a normally
    decent German soldier in order to free him from a tyranny
    which he at present accepts." "Advocate of Peace," quoted in
    Merle Curti, *Peace Or War* (W. W. Norton and Co.: New
    York, 1936), p. 254.

20 George W. Alger, "Preparedness and Democratic Discipline," *Atlantic,* CXVII (April, 1916), 480. Cf. R. K. Hack "Drift," *Atlantic,* CXVIII (September, 1916), 358; Frank Buffington Vrooman, "Our Next Step," *Century,* XCII (June, 1916), 192.

21 "Patriotism in War and Peace," *Nation,* XCIX (October 8, 1914), 423.

22 Alger, *op. cit.,* p. 480. Cf. John Jay Chapman, "The Crisis," *Atlantic,* CXIV (November, 1914), 714-715; H. M. Chittenden, "Questions For Pacifists," *Atlantic,* CXVI (August, 1915), 168; R. M. Johnson, "Arms and the Race," *Century,* LXXXIX (March, 1915), 649; Edwin Davies Schoonmaker, "The Fall or Rise of Socialism," *Century,* LXXXIX (April, 1915), 871; Eric Fisher Wood, "Army Reform," *Century,* XCI (December, 1915), 249.

23 Robert W. Herrick, "Recantation of a Pacifist," *New Republic,* IV (October 30, 1915), 329.

24 John Jay Chapman, "Ode on the Sailing of Our Troops," *North American Review,* CCVI (November, 1917), 682. For other aristocrats who shared these views, see Henry F. May, *The End of American Innocence: A Study of the First Years of Our Own Time: 1912-1917* (Alfred A. Knopf: New York, 1959), pp. 365-366, 377; Henry James to Prime Minister Asquith, 1915, quoted in Leon Edel, ed., *The Selected Letters of Henry James* (Straus and Cudahy: New York, 1955), pp. 227-228; Barrett Wendell to Edward Bowditch, December 8, 1914, quoted in M. A. DeWolfe Howe, *Barrett Wendell and His Letters* (Atlantic Monthly Press: Boston, 1924), p. 264.

25 David A. Shannon, *The Socialist Party of America* (The Macmillan Co.: New York, 1955), p. 98; Daniel Bell, "The Background and Development of Marxian Socialism in the United States," Donald Egbert and Stow Persons, eds., *Socialism and American Life* (Princeton University Press: Princeton University, 1952), p. 311. For evidence of the unifying effect that the war had on American communities, see W. Lloyd Warner, *Democracy in Jonesville* (Harper and Bros.: New York, 1949), pp. 287-288; Elin L. Anderson, *We Americans: A Study of Cleavage in an American City* (Harvard University Press: Cambridge, 1937), pp. 183-185; Lee J. Levinger, *A Jewish Chaplain in France* (The Macmillan Co.: New York, 1922), p. 214.

26 Ernest Hunter Wright, "What Shall We Win with the War?" *Century,* LXXIV (July, 1918), 341-342.

27 "The Unity Of America," *Nation,* CVI (March 21, 1918), 311. Cf. "America Tested by War," *New Republic,* XV (June 20, 1918), 220.

28 William E. Borah, quoted in Robert Endicott Osgood, *Ideals and Self-Interest in America's Foreign Relations: The Great Trans-*

formation of the Twentieth Century (University of Chicago Press: Chicago, 1953), p. 259. Cf. Theodore Roosevelt, quoted in *Ibid.,* p. 269.

29 James to Asquith, quoted in Edel, *op. cit.,* pp. 227-228. Cf. Chapman, "Ode," *North American Review,* pp. 682-687; Wendell to Bowditch, quoted in Howe, *op. cit.,* p. 264; May, *op. cit.,* pp. 365-366, 377.

30 Woodrow Wilson, quoted in Joseph Tumulty, *Woodrow Wilson as I Know Him* (Doubleday, Page and Co.: New York, 1921), pp. 80-81.

31 Wilson, quoted in E. M. House, *The Intimate Papers of Colonel House,* II (Little, Brown and Co.: Boston, 1926), 412.

32 Wilson's conversation with Frank I. Cobb, quoted in John L. Heaton, *Cobb of the World* (E. P. Dutton: New York, 1924), pp. 268-270.

33 Wilson, quoted in Tumulty, *op. cit.,* pp. 258-259.

34 Wilson, "Memorial Day Address," May 30, 1917, quoted in Wilson, *In Our First Year of War* (Harper and Bros.: New York, 1918), pp. 56, 58.

Notes to Chapter 6

1 Theodore L. Nydahl, ed., "The Diary of Ignatius Donnelly," (Ph.D. dissertation: 1859-1884, University of Minnesota, 1941), p. 8.

2 Donnelly, *Minnesota* (Folger and Turner: New York, 1857), p. 5. Cf. Donnelly, "The Mourner's Vision," (Privately printed, Philadelphia, 1850), pp. 34-35, 63, 71, 79. For Donnelly's part in Minnesota real-estate ventures, see Ralph L. Harmon, "Ignatius Donnelly and His Faded Metropolis," *Minnesota History,* XXVII (September, 1936), 262-276.

3 Donnelly, *Minnesota,* p. 13.

4 For Donnelly's nationalism, see *Congressional Globe,* 38th Congress, 1st Session, Part 3 (May 2, 1864), 2038-2039; 39th Congress, 1st Session, Part 3 (June 5, 1866), 2968; 40th Congress, 2nd Session, Part 4 (July 1, 1868), 3660; Nydahl, "*Diary,*" July 25, 1869 (Microfilm, Harvard University), 347.

5 Donnelly, *Globe,* 38th Congress, 1st Session, Part 1 (February 27, 1864), 857.

6 Donnelly, "Speech on Reconstruction," *Globe,* 38th Congress, 1st Session, Part 3 (May 2, 1864), 2037. Donnelly aggressively sought federal aid. For his bills to obtain land grants for railroads, see *Ibid.* (May 16, 1864), p. 2293; 38th Congress, 2nd Session, Part 1 (January 11, 1865), 202, (January 17, 1865), 295, (February 6, 1865), 616. For a bill to have the

government endorse and guarantee Northern Pacific stock, see 39th Congress, 1st Session, Part 3 (April 26, 1866), 2208-2211. For some of Donnelly's internal improvement measures, see 39th Congress, 1st Session, Part 1 (February 1, 1866), 579, 585 (February 13, 1866), 811; Part 2 (April 4, 1866), 1751-1752; 40th Congress, 2nd Session, Part 3 (June 4, 1868), 2830. For a bill increasing the wool tariff, see 39th Congress, 1st Session, Part 3 (April 12, 1866), 1925.

7   Donnelly to Jay Cooke, quoted in John D. Hicks, "The Political Career of Ignatius Donnelly," *Mississippi Valley Historical Review,* VIII (September, 1928), 84.

8   Donnelly, *Globe,* 40th Congress, 2nd Session, Part 2 (May 7, 1868), 2385.

9   Donnelly, *Globe,* 40th Congress, 3rd Session, Part 3 (March 3, 1869), 1881. For the bill to sell Indian lands cheaply to settlers, see 40th Congress, 2nd Session, Part 2 (March 6, 1868), 1704-1705. For extension of payment time to homesteaders, see 40th Congress, 2nd Session, Part 1 (January 15, 1868), 538-540. For the bills taxing government bondholders, see 38th Congress, 2nd Session, Part 3 (February 6, 1865), 804, and 40th Congress, 2nd Session, Part 4 (July 6, 1868), 3758.

10 For examples of his tender familial attitude, see Nydahl, "Diary," (September 10, 1881), pp. 890-891, 888; Kate Donnelly to Ignatius Donnelly, January 23, 1891, "Donnelly Papers," (microfilm at Columbia University); Donnelly, *In Memoriam,* (Privately printed, 1895).

11 Nydahl, "Diary," December 8-15, 1873, pp. 596-597, November 17, 1881, p. 904; 1867, p. 291, March 24, 1868, p. 317, 1866, p. 242.

12 For Donnelly's arguments on education, see *Globe,* 39th Congress, 1st Session, Part 1 (December 14, 1865), 60, (February 1, 1866), 585; 39th Congress, 1st Session, Part 3 (May 1, 1866), 2571; 40th Congress, 1st Session, Part 1 (March 25, 1867), 338 (July 13, 1867), 633; 40th Congress, 2nd Session, Part 1 (January 20, 1868), 637; 40th Congress, 2nd Session, Part 2 (May 27, 1868), 2620.

13 Donnelly, "Reconstruction," *Globe,* 2037.

14 Donnelly, *Globe,* 40th Congress, 1st Session, Part 1 (March 13, 1867), 91.

15 Nydahl, "Diary," July 21, 1869, p. 343, July 25, p. 347. Cf. Donnelly, *A Tribute to Abraham Lincoln* (Washington, D.C., 1942); "Memoranda 1866," p. 309.

16 Donnelly, *Globe* (May 2, 1864), 2038.

17 Nydahl, "Diary," March, 1870, p. 373, April 21, 1870, p. 381; "Memoranda 1870," pp. 400-401.

18 Donnelly to Jay Cooke, July 29, 1871, quoted in Martin Ridge, "Ignatius Donnelly: The Making of a Tribune" (Unpublished Ph.D. dissertation, Northwestern University, 1951), pp. 541-542.

19 Donnelly, "Red Wing Speech," July 4, 1871, quoted in Ridge, *op. cit.,* p. 538.

20 Donnelly, quoted in Hicks, "Donnelly," p. 92.

21 Donnelly, quoted in Ridge, "Ignatius Donnelly and the Granger Movement in Minnesota," *Mississippi Valley Historical Review,* XLII (March, 1956), 707-708.

22 Donnelly, quoted in Hicks, "Donnelly," pp. 95-96.

23 Nydahl, "Diary," March 14, 1880, p. 798, May 16, 1880, p. 814, October 27, 1880, p. 850, April 21, 1880, pp. 809-810.

24 *Ibid.,* December 31, 1881, pp. 910-911.

25 Donnelly, *Ragnarok: The Age of Fire and Gravel* (D. Appleton and Co.: New York, 1883), pp. 43, 107, 108, 110, 438-439, 406, 407, 439, 441.

26 Donnelly, *The Great Cryptogram: Francis Bacon's Cipher in the So-Called Shakespeare Plays* (R. S. Peale and Co.: London, 1888), pp. 57-58.

27 For adverse criticism of *The Great Cryptogram,* see Nydahl, "Diary," pp. 78-79. For Donnelly's reaction, see Donnelly "Diary: 1888-1889," (July 16, 1888), microfilmed from type-written copies made by Theodore Nydahl, Mankato State Teachers College, Mankato, Minnesota. Microfilm at Harvard University, Cambridge, Massachusetts. The pages are not numbered.

28 Donnelly, "Diary," May 17, 1889.

29 *Ibid.*

30 One student lists forty-nine utopian novels published between 1884-1900. Allyn B. Forbes, "The Literary Quest For Utopia," *Social Forces,* VI (December, 1927), 188-189. For biblio-graphical information on *Caesar's Column,* see Glenn Negley and J. Max Patrick, *The Quest for Utopia* (Harper and Bros.: New York, 1952), pp. 6-7; Walter J. Rideout, ed., *Caesar's Column* (John Harvard Press: Cambridge, 1960), p. xix; Nydahl, "Diary," pp. 81-82; Frank J. Schulte to Donnelly, September 15, 1890, Donnelly Papers.

31 Jansen McClury and Co., refused to publish *Caesar's Column,* according to Nydahl, *Diary,* December 31, 1890. Schulte refers to another reluctant publisher in a letter to Donnelly, January 20, 1890, Donnelly Papers. For approving comments by Cardinal Gibbons, Frances Willard, and others, see Everett W. Fish, *Biography of Ignatius Donnelly* (F. J. Schulte and Co.: Chicago, 1895), p. 121. For the nationalists and socialists, see Schulte to Donnelly, April 8, 1890, April 9, 1890, Donnelly

Papers. For the *Arena,* see Schulte to Donnelly, April 21, 1890, Donnelly Papers.

32   Milton George, quoted in Schulte to Donnelly, April 12, 1890, Donnelly Papers. H. L. Loucks, President of the Farmers' Alliance, said that "it should be read by every farmer in the land." Loucks, quoted in Fish, *Biography,* p. 121. Other examples of agrarian support can be found in letters to Donnelly among the Donnelly Papers for 1890.

33   Donnelly, *Caesar's Column* (1st ed. reprinted by John Harvard Press: Cambridge, 1960), pp. 34-35, 185, 184, 18, 38, 39, 40-41, 96-97, 113-114, 122, 100, 190.

34   Similar uses of Rome as a symbol of decadence and disaster are found in Thomas A. Watson, *The People's Campaign Book 1892: Not a Revolt Its a Rebellion!* (National Watchman Publishing Co.: Washington, D.C., 1892), pp. 207-208; W. Scott Morgan, *History of the Wheel and Alliance and The Impending Revolution* (C. B. Woodward: St. Louis, 1891), pp. 664-665; James B. Weaver, *A Call to Action* (Iowa Printing Co.: Des Moines, 1892), pp. 211-286, 295. The association between Rome and the United States is doubly significant in view of the fact that, in the nation's early days, emulation of Rome was ardently encouraged, and Rome was the symbol of a virtuous republic.

35   Donnelly wrote to Schulte that " 'Gabriel' has some reference to the Angel Gabriel: and 'Weltstein' means 'the stone of the world': Gabriel Weltstein may be supposed to imply a mystical meaning: Gabriel blows a trumpet to revive the sleeping nations; and his doctrines are the foundation stone of the world! Some such thought was in my head." Donnelly to Schulte, January 13, 1890, quoted in Rideout, ed., *Caesar's,* 19n.

36   Donnelly, *Caesar's,* pp. 135, 163, 170.

37   Donnelly, "Memoranda 1888."

38   Donnelly, *Caesar's,* pp. 175, 174-175, 250, 254-255, 256, 282, 280, 291, 45.

39   James B. Weaver quoted in Fred Emory Haynes, *James Baird Weaver* (Iowa Printing Co.: Iowa City, 1919), p. 322. Cf. William Allen White, *The Autobiography of William Allen White* (The Macmillan Co.: New York, 1946), p. 218.

40   Mary Elizabeth Lease, quoted in Dale Kramer, *The Wild Jackasses: The American Farmer in Revolt* (Hastings House: New York, 1956), p. 94.

41   Mrs. Lease, quoted in Frank Zornow, *A History of the Jayhawk State* (University of Oklahoma Press: Norman, 1957), p. 206.

42   Mrs. Lease, quoted in Meridel LeSueur, *North Star Country* (Sloan and Pearce: New York, 1945), p. 221.

43   Mrs. Lease, quoted in Kramer, *op. cit.,* p. 94.

44 *New York Times,* August 11, 1896, p. 3.
45 Mrs. Lease, quoted in Elizabeth N. Barr, "The Populist Uprising,"
    William E. Connelley, ed., *A Standard History of Kansas and
    Kansans,* II (Lewis Publishing Co.: Chicago, 1918), 1151.
46 *New York Times,* August 11, 1896, p. 3.
47 Mrs. Lease, quoted in Barr, *op. cit.,* p. 1151.
48 Mrs. Lease, *The Problem Of Civilization Solved* (Laird and Lee:
    Chicago, 1895), Introduction; pp. 21, 103-104, 99, 104, 23,
    28-29, 32-33, 322-323, 353-354.

Notes to Chapter 7

1 Ignatius Donnelly, *Caesar's Column* (1st ed. reprinted by John
   Harvard Press: Cambridge, 1960), pp. 31-32, 127, 149-150.
2 I have drawn this evidence from two studies of anti-Semitism in
   Populism. From Richard Hofstadter, *The Age of Reform*
   (Alfred A. Knopf: New York, 1956), the following references are taken: the statement of the New Jersey Grange, p. 78;
   the Associated Press account of the St. Louis Convention, p.
   80; remarks by Gordon Clark and Coin Harvey, pp. 78, 78n,
   79, 79n. From Edward Flower, "Anti-Semitism in the Free
   Silver and Populist Movements and the Election of 1896"
   (Unpublished Master's Thesis, Columbia University, 1952), a
   work also cited by Hofstadter, come the following references:
   eastern newspaper accounts of the Populist Convention, pp. 27-
   28; Jewish magazines considering Populists and their campaign
   anti-Semitic, pp. 46-57; alleged connections between Dr. Ahl-
   wardt, a German anti-Semite and Bryan, p. 31; for remarks by
   Populist speakers, pp. 33, 35, 30; for the vogue of *Puck* and
   The Police Gazette, p. 28; for Mrs. Lease's remarks in New
   York, p. 30. For these New York remarks and other anti-
   Semitic utterances by Mrs. Lease and Donnelly, see Hofstadter,
   op. cit., pp. 60, 74, 79.
3 Flower, *op. cit.,* p. 29.
4 In my own research, I have found only two isolated anti-Semitic
   references, aside from further statements by Donnelly and Mrs.
   Lease. One is in Thomas K. Norwood, *Plutocracy or American
   White Slavery* (Metropolitan Publishing Co.: New York,
   1888), p. 110. George Otis, the agrarian hero, is killed by
   Jacob Jacobsen and Thomas Schwarz, agents of the millionaire aristocracy. Norwood was a senator and congressman from
   Georgia and had Populist sympathies, although he was not
   actually a Populist. The other case occurs in W. Scott Morgan,
   History of the Wheel and Alliance and the Impending Revolu-

tion (C. B. Woodward Co.: St. Louis, 1891), p. 146. Here
Morgan refers to "the final struggle" between the money
power and the farmers as "the great issue between the people
and Shylock." These references, it should be noted, are
isolated statements and not the themes of the books.

5 *New York Times,* August 11, 1896, p. 3.

6 Flower, *op. cit.,* p. 44.

7 *Jewish Chronicle,* November 30, 1896, quoted in Flower, *op. cit.,*
p. 40.

8 Donnelly, *The American Peoples' Money* (Laird and Lee: Chicago,
1895), p. 136. Cf. Thomas A. Watson, *The Peoples' Campaign Book: 1892. Not A Revolt Its A Rebellion!* (National
Watchman's Publishing Co.: Washington, D.C., 1892), p.
221; Leonard Brown, *Popular Perils* (Des Moines Journal Co.:
Des Moines, 1892), p. 162.

9 "Populist Manifesto," quoted in Frank K. L. McVey, *The Popu-
list Movement* (The Macmillan Co.: New York, 1896), pp.
201-202. Cf. "Populist Platform of 1896," quoted in John W.
Ballman, *The Presidential Campaign of 1896* (Walter J. Berg:
Cincinnati, 1896), p. 90; Thomas A. Watson, *Political and
Economic Handbook* (Jeffersonian Publishing Co.: Thomson,
Georgia, 1892), p. 168; C. C. Post, *Congressman Swanson*
(Charles H. Sergel: Chicago, 1892), p. 258; S. M. Brice and
C. Vincent, *A Financial Catechism* (Vincent Publishing Co.:
Indianapolis, 1896), p. 5; Thomas N. Norwood, *Plutocracy
or American White Slavery* (Metropolitan Publishing Co.:
New York, 1888), p. 110; Sarah V. Emery, *Seven Financial
Conspiracies Which Have Enslaved the American People* (L.
Thompson: Lansing, 1896), p. 10; J. M. Thompson, "The
Farmers' Alliance In Nebraska," *Proceedings and Collections
of the Nebraska State Historical Society,* V (1902), p. 204;
Joseph Columbus Manning, *Fadeout of Populism* (T. A. Heb-
bons: New York, 1928), pp. 101-108; James B. Weaver, *A
Call to Action* (Iowa Publishing Co.: Des Moines, 1892),
pp. 5-6; W. Scott Morgan, *History of the Wheel and Alliance
and the Impending Revolution* (C. B. Woodward Co.: St.
Louis, 1891), pp. 426-427; Leonard Brown, *The Pending Conflict* (Des Moines Journal Co.: Des Moines, 1890), p. 14.

10 Brown, *Popular Perils,* p. 181. Cf. note 9.

11 Leonidas Polk, quoted in N.A. Dunning, *The Farmers' Alliance
History and Agricultural Digest* (Alliance Publishing Co.:
Washington, D.C., 1891), p. 19.

12 Morgan, *op. cit.,* pp. 559-560. Cf. Winfield, *Non-Comformist*
(May 1, 1890), quoted in "The Coming Cataclysm," *The
Arena,* II (August, 1890), 293n; Resolutions of a mass meeting in Ottawa, Kansas, April, 1890, quoted in *Ibid.,* pp. 294-
295n; Brown, *Perils,* p. 26; Brown, *Pending,* p. 14; Brice and

Vincent, *op. cit.*, pp. 5-6; Emery, *op. cit.*, p. 67; Dunning, *op. cit.*, p. 158; E. A. Allen, *The Lives of Weaver and Field and Achievements of the Peoples Party* (Peoples Party Publishing Co.: 1892), p. 19; Norwood, *op. cit.*, pp. 126-128.

13 For example, see Hofstadter, *op. cit.*, pp. 70-81. One sound Populist idea that came out of the conspiracy theory was criticism of an inadequate money supply caused by adhering to the gold standard. This policy led agrarians to suggest proposals to increase the volume and velocity of money in circulation, which were adopted with some success in the New Deal. Two Populist works in which these suggestions may be found are Ignatius Donnelly, *The Golden Bottle or the Story of Ephraim Benezet of Kansas* (D. D. Merrill Co.: New York, 1892), pp. 122, 128, 136-138, and Donnelly, *American People's Money* pp. 33-34, 84-85.

14 Donnelly, *Caesar's*, pp. 130, 32. His sympathy for the Jews is brought out very strongly in *The Golden Bottle*, a novel of Populist utopia. When the world is divided up, the Jews are given Palestine. They are entitled to it because from "this great race . . . we had derived our religion and so much of our literature, . . ." They are to have "some share in the awakening of the world . . . . and to revive the ancient glories of their people." After awhile "the Jews, too shall have a nation and a flag; illustrious and honored in the world; . . . And their delegates shall hold high seats, too, in the Congress of 'The Universal Republic,' respected as representatives of the race which preserved the worship of the true God in the midst of the darkness and foulness of ages of barbarism." Donnelly, *The Golden Bottle*, p. 280.

Notes to Chapter 8

1 Barbara Miller Solomon, *Ancestors and Immigrants* (Harvard University Press: Cambridge, 1956), p. 20. Cf. Charles Eliot Norton, "The Lack of Old Homes in America," *Scribner's Magazine*, V (May, 1889), 638.

2 Norton, "Some Aspects of Civilization," *The Forum*, XX (February 18, 1896), 650, 664.

3 Norton to Samuel G. Ward, April 26, 1896, quoted in Sara Norton and Mark DeWolfe Howe, eds., *The Letters of Charles Eliot Norton*, II (Houghton Mifflin Co.: Boston, 1913), 243-244.

4 Norton to W. L. Mackenzie King, January 26, 1903, quoted in Norton and Howe, *op. cit.*, p. 333.

5   Norton, "William Eustis Russell," *Harvard Graduates Magazine,*
    V (December, 1896), 191.
6   Norton to Leslie Stephen, June 24, 1898, quoted in Howe and
    Norton, *op. cit.,* pp. 270-271. Cf. Norton to Edward Lee-
    Childe, June 26, 1898, quoted in *Ibid.,* pp. 272-273; Norton
    to Ward, October 10, 1898, quoted in *Ibid.,* p. 275; Norton to
    Ely Godkin, July 7, 1900, quoted in *Ibid.,* pp. 293-294.
7   Norton, "Memorials of Two Friends" (New York, 1902), pp.
    101-102.
8   Norton, "Reminiscences of Old Cambridge," *Proceedings: Cam-
    bridge Historical Society,* I (1905), 13.
9   Moorfield Storey, *Politics as a Duty and as a Career* (G. P. Put-
    nam's Sons: New York, 1889), p. 4.
10 Storey, "The American Legislature," Annual Address before the
    American Bar Association, August 22, 1894, *Transactions of
    the American Bar Association,* pp. 16-17. Cf. Storey, "A Years
    Legislation," Presidential Address, American Bar Association,
    August 19, 1896 (Dando Printing and Publishing Co.: Phila-
    delphia, 1896), p. 2.
11 Storey to George F. Hoar, February 28, 1900, quoted in M. A.
    DeWolfe Howe, *Portrait of an Independent: Moorfield Storey*
    (Houghton Mifflin Co.: Boston, 1932), p. 227.
12 Storey, *Our New Departure,* October 26, 1900 (George H. Ellis,
    Printer: Boston, 1901), p. 15. Cf. pp. 43, 53.
13 Storey, "The Democratic Party and Philippine Independence"
    (George H. Ellis, Printer: Boston, 1913), p. 7.
14 Storey, "New Departure," p. 43.
15 Storey, "Philippine Independence," p. 60.
16 Storey to Charles Francis Adams, Jr., September 12, 1912, quoted
    in Howe, *Portrait,* p. 303.
17 Storey to T. S. Perry, September 6, 1914, quoted in *Ibid.,* p. 309.
18 Barrett Wendell, *The Privileged Classes* (Charles Scribner's Sons:
    New York, 1908), pp. 114, 112, 118-119.
19 Wendell, "Conflict Of Idolatries," Phi Beta Kappa Address,
    Harvard Graduates Magazine, XXVII (September, 918), 4,
    15-16.
20 Thomas Bailey Aldrich to G. E. Woodbury, May 14, 1892, quoted
    in Ferris Greenslet, *The Life of Thomas Bailey Aldrich*
    (Houghton Mifflin Co.: Boston, 1908), pp. 168-169.
21 *Ibid.,* May 16, 1894, p. 178.
22 *Ibid.,* May 12, 1899, pp. 205-206.
23 For John Adams's attitude, see Adrienne Koch and William Peden,
    Selected Writings of John and John Quincy Adams (Alfred A.
    Knopf: New York, 1946), January 3, 1759, p. 8; July 21,
    1756, p. 7; January 30, 1768, p. 27; February 16, 1775, pp.
    4-5; Adams to James Madison, June 17, 1817, p. 203; Adams

to Benjamin Rush, December 30, 1800, p. 145; Adams to Skelton Jones, March 11, 1809, p. 150; Adams to Rush, August 28, 1811, p. 160; Adams to James Lloyd, March 31, 1815, pp. 189-191.

24 John Quincy Adams, February 28, 1829, quoted in *Ibid.*, p. 70.

25 J. Q. Adams to Charles W. Upham, February 2, 1837, *Ibid.*, p. 389. Cf. J. Q. Adams, *Ibid.*, July 30, 1834, pp. 382-383.

26 Henry Adams, *The Education of Henry Adams* (Houghton Mifflin Co.: Boston, 1918), p. 260.

27 Brooks Adams to H. Adams, March 6, 1809, Houghton Library. Cf. B. Adams to H. Adams, January 28, 1910, Houghton; B. Adams, "Unpublished Biography of John Quincy Adams" in the Massachusetts Historical Society.

28 H. Adams to Charles Milnes Gaskell, August 7, 1908, quoted in Worthington Chauncy Ford, ed., *The Letters of Henry Adams* II (Houghton Mifflin Co.: Boston, 1938), 504n. All Henry Adams's letters, unless otherwise noted come from one of the two volumes in this study.

29 B. Adams to H. Adams, June 24, 1915, Houghton. Cf. B. Adams to H. Adams, October 1, 1913, Houghton.

30 H. Adams to Gaskell, November 25, 1877, p. 302. Cf. Adams to Gaskell, January 1, 1881, p. 328; Adams to Gaskell, February 3, 1884, p. 342; Adams to Isaac Wayne MacVeagh, July 9, 1881, quoted in Harold Dean Cater, ed., *Henry Adams and His Friends* (Houghton, Mifflin Co.: Boston, 1947), p. 108.

31 Adams to Gaskell, September 25, 1868, p. 145; cf. Adams to Gaskell, November 11, 1868, p. 147; to Gaskell, June 20, 1869, p. 149; Adams to Gaskell, January 13, 1870, p. 177; Adams to Gaskell, April 27, 1872, p. 224; Adams to Henry Cabot Lodge, July 9, 1880, p. 325.

32 Adams to Gaskell, November 25, 1877, p. 302.

33 Adams to Charles Francis Adams, Jr., November 21, 1862, quoted in Ford, *A Cycle of Adams Letters*, I (Houghton, Mifflin Co.: Boston, 1920), 195-196.

34 Adams to C. F. Adams, Jr., April 11, 1862, quoted in *Ibid.*, p. 135.

35 Adams to Gaskell, September 25, 1868, p. 156. Cf. Adams to Gaskell, November 4, 1875, p. 273.

36 Adams to C. F. Adams, Jr. November 11, 1858, p. 5. For evidence that he rejected the family career, see Adams to C. F. Adams, November 16, 1867, p. 136; Adams to C. F. Adams, Jr., May 21, 1869, p. 160; Adams to Gaskell, June 20, 1869, p. 161; Adams's biography in his Harvard Class Book, quoted in Robert A. Hume, *Runaway Star: An Appreciation of Henry Adams* (Cornell University Press: Ithaca, 1951), p. 36; Adams to C. F. Adams, Jr., November 30, 1863, *Cycle*, II, 96-97.

37 Adams to Gaskell, March 8, 1888, p. 387. Cf. Adams to Gaskell, April 21, 1889, p. 404; Adams to Lodge, May 11, 1915, quoted in Cater, *op. cit.,* p. 772.

38 Adams to Gaskell, February 19, 1914, p. 620. Cf. Adams to John Hay, May 11, 1892, Cater, *op. cit.,* p. 264; Adams, *Education,* p. 28.

39 Adams to Lodge, May 11, 1915; *Education,* p. 254.

40 Adams to Edward H. Davis, February 3, 1911, quoted in *Yale Review,* XI (October, 1921), 220; cf. Adams to Davis, January 12, 1912, quoted in *Ibid.,* p. 220; Adams to Margaret Chanler, April 11, 1909, p. 517; Adams to Gaskell, December 17, 1908, quoted in Cater, *op. cit.,* p. 514.

41 Adams to Elizabeth Cameron, June 10, 1888, p. 388.

42 Adams to Gaskell, November 26, 1893, p. 34.

43 Adams to Gaskell, January 23, 1894, p. 35.

44 Adams to Mrs. Cameron, September 15, 1893, p. 33.

45 H. Adams, *Education,* pp. 343-344, 496. Cf. Adams to B. Adams, August 10, 1902, p. 391. For the nadir of his scientific pessimism, in which he speculates on the Second Law of Thermodynamics, showing that the universe is in a permanent state of deterioration because it is losing irreplaceable energy, see Adams, *The Degradation of the Democratic Dogma* (The Macmillan Co.: New York, 1919).

46 Adams to B. Adams, September, 1895, pp. 82-83.

47 Adams to Mrs. Cameron, August 4, 1896, p. 114, 115.

48 Adams to B. Adams, June 11, 1898, p. 184n.

49 Adams to B. Adams, June 11, 1897, pp. 129-130; Adams to Mrs. Cameron, February 7, 1904, p. 424.

50 Adams to Mrs. Cameron, July 22, 1911, p. 570.

51 Adams to B. Adams, September 20, 1910, p. 549.

52 Adams to B. Adams, September, 1895, pp. 82-83.

53 Adams to Mrs. Cameron, January 25, 1903, p. 393.

54 Adams to Mrs. Cameron, August 20, 1905, p. 460; cf. Adams to B. Adams, November 1, 1910, p. 551.

55 Adams to Mrs. Cameron, March 1, 1914, p. 622.

56 Adams to Mrs. Cameron, September 5, 1917, p. 645.

57 Adams to B. Adams, January 30, 1910, p. 532.

58 Adams to B. Adams, September 20, 1910, p. 529.

59 Adams to Mrs. Cameron, February 7, 1904, pp. 423-424. Cf. Adams to Margaret Chanler, August 11, 1905; p. 457; Adams to Mrs. Cameron, January 13, 1910, p. 529; Adams to Gaskell, January 4, 1897, p. 120; Adams to Mrs. Cameron, February 7, 1904, p. 423.

60 Adams to C. F. Adams, Jr., November 10, 1911, p. 576.

61 Adams, *Education,* pp. 260, 434-435. Cf. Adams, *Mont-St. Michel and Chartres* (Houghton Mifflin Co.: Boston, 1905), p. 45.

62 Adams to Alan Stanburrough Cook, August 6, 1910, pp. 546-547;

Adams to Hay, September 7, 1895, p. 347; Adams to Hay, November 7, 1900, p. 301; Adams to B. Adams, May 6, 1899, quoted in Cater, *op. cit.,* p. 463; *Education,* pp. 384-385, 388; *Chartres,* p. 45.

63 Adams to Henry Osborn Taylor, May 7, 1901, quoted in Cater, *op. cit.,* p. 510.

64 Adams, *Chartres,* pp. 145, 265-266, 128, 260, 196.

65 Adams, "Prayer to the Virgin of Chartres," quoted in Mabel La Farge, ed., *Henry Adams: Letter to a Niece* (Houghton Mifflin Co.: Boston, 1920), p. 131.

66 Adams, *Education,* p. 459.

67 Adams, *Chartres,* p. 276.

68 Adams to Frederick Bliss Luquiens, March 21, 1912, quoted in *Yale Review,* X (October, 1920), 122-123. This remark may be an unconscious explanation for his turning from history to personal studies like *The Education* or to aesthetic-impressionistic works like *Mont-St. Michel and Chartres.* American history was painful after 1885, while these areas could give him solace, since through them he formulated the aristocratic sensibility. At the same time, however, he realized that the Church and the Middle Ages had limited relevance for him in contemporary America. Cf. Adams to Taylor, January 22, 1905, p. 630; Adams to Taylor, February 5, 1915, quoted in Cater, *op. cit.,* p. 769.

Notes to Chapter 9

1 Charles Francis Adams, Sr., "Diary," June 24, 1861, microfilmed Adams Papers, Widener Library (Cambridge). Cf. December 19, 1871.

2 Brooks Adams, "The Seizure of the Laird Rams," *Proceeedings: Massachusetts Historical Society,* XLV (December, 1911), 243-244, 247.

3 Adams to C. F. Adams, January 26, 1868, Adams Papers.

4 Adams to C. F. Adams, March 24, 1868, Adams Papers.

5 Adams to C. F. Adams, February 24, 1868, Adams Papers.

6 Adams, "The Platform of the New Party," *North American Review,* CXIX (July, 1874), 47, 60, 60-61.

7 Adams, "Review Of James Fitzjames Stephen's *Liberty, Equality, Fraternity,*" *North American Review,* CXVIII (April, 1874), 445, 447.

8 Adams to Henry Cabot Lodge, August 20, 1879. All letters to Lodge cited here are in the Lodge Papers, Massachusetts Historical Society.

9   Adams, "The Last Stage of English Whiggery," *Atlantic Monthly,*
    XLVII (April, 1881), 569.

10 C. F. Adams, "Diary," July 21, 1877.

11 Mrs. Duncan Cryden, quoted in Arthur F. Beringause, *Brooks
    Adams* (Alfred A. Knopf: New York, 1955), pp. 71-72.

12 Adams to Lodge, September 4, 1881.

13 Adams to H. Adams, March 7, 1887. Unless otherwise noted,
    Adams's letters are from Houghton Library (Cambridge).

14 Adams, *The Emancipation of Massachusetts* (Houghton Mifflin
    Co.: Boston, 1887), pp. 42, 363-364, 40.

15 Adams to H. Adams, March 11, 1887.

16 Adams, *The Plutocratic Revolution* (New England Tariff Reform
    League: Boston, 1892), pp. 1-2, 4.

17 Adams to Lodge, November 23, 1892.

18 Adams to H. Adams, January 4, 1893.

19 Adams, *The Law of Civilization and Decay,* (2nd ed., Alfred A.
    Knopf: New York, 1943), pp. 58-59, 60, 184, 303, 304-305;
    326, 328-329, 336-339.

20 Adams, *The Gold Standard: An Historical Study* (New England
    News Co.: Boston, 1894), p. 34.

21 Adams to Lodge, May 6, 1894.

22 Adams to H. Adams, June 24, 1895, Adams Papers, Massachusetts
    Historical Society. Cf. Adams to H. Adams, October 28, 1896,
    Adams Papers.

23 H. Adams to Elizabeth Cameron, September 5, 1917, quoted in
    Worthington Chauncy Ford, ed., *The Letters of Henry Adams:
    1892-1918,* II (Houghton Mifflin Co.: Boston, 1938), 645.

24 Adams to H. Adams, April 22, 1896.

25 Adams to H. Adams, July 12, 1896.

26 Adams to H. Adams, October 31, 1896.

27 Adams, *Law,* pp. 58-59.

28 Adams to Cecil Spring Rice, June, 1888, quoted in Stephen
    Gwynn, ed., *The Letters and Friendships of Cecil Spring Rice,*
    I (Constable and Co.: London, 1929), 97.

29 Adams to H. Adams, February 2, 1895.

30 Adams to H. Adams, May 14, 1895.

31 Adams to H. Adams, June 24, 1895, Massachusetts Historical
    Society. Cf. Adams to H. Adams, September 21, 1895; Adams
    to H. Adams, October 13, 1895; Adams to H. Adams, August
    17, 1896; Adams to H. Adams, November 15, 1896.

32 Adams to H. Adams, September 9, 1896.

33 Adams to H. Adams, August 17, 1896. Cf. Adams to H. Adams,
    August 25, 1896; October 15, 1896.

34 Adams to H. Adams, October 15, 1896; Adams to H. Adams,
    March 25, 1896.

35 Adams to H. Adams, July 26, 1896.

36 Adams to H. Adams, September 21, 1895.

37 Adams to H. Adams, December 23, 1895.

38 Adams to H. Adams, March 7, 1896.

39 Adams to H. Adams, February 27, 1898; Adams to H. Adams, April 29, 1898.

40 Adams to H. Adams, May 22, 1898; Adams to Abigail Homans, April 26, 1898.

41 Adams to Abigail Homans, May 25, 1898.

42 Adams to H. Adams, May 22, 1899. Cf. Adams to A. Homans, May 25, 1898.

43 Adams, *Springfield Republican,* September 20, 1898, quoted in Daniel Aaron, *Men of Good Hope* (Oxford University Press: New York, 1951), p. 267.

44 Adams to H. Adams, October 13, 1901. Cf. Adams to H. Adams, April 30, 1901.

45 Adams to Mrs. Cameron, February 3, 1901, quoted in Ford, *op. cit.,* II, 313.

46 Adams to Theodore Roosevelt, September 12, 1901, quoted in Beringause, *op. cit.,* p. 203.

47 Adams, to H. Adams, October 13, 1901.

48 Adams to Lodge, March 27, 1901.

49 Adams, "Address at the Memorial Service to Lieutenant Edward Bumpus," *Boston Evening Transcript,* October 16, 1901, p. 9. Cf. Adams to Holmes, April 13, 1902; Adams, "Address at the Reform Club Dinner," *The American Architect,* LXXIV December 28, 1901), 99-100.

50 Adams, "The New Industrial Revolution," *Atlantic,* LXXVII, (February, 1901), 165. Cf. "War and Economic Competition," *Scribner's Magazine,* XXXI (March, 1902), 352; Adams to H. Adams, July 5, 1901; July 27, 1901; September 12, 1902.

51 Adams, "Reciprocity or the Alternative," *Atlantic,* LXXVIII (August, 1901), 153-155; "War as the Ultimate Form of Economic Competition," *Proceedings: American Naval Institute* (December, 1903), 829-881; "Economic Conditions for Future Defense," *Atlantic,* XCII (November, 1903), 632-649.

52 Adams to H. Adams, September 26, 1902; Adams to H. Adams, December 11, 1902.

53 Adams, *Railways as Public Agents: A Study in Sovereignty* (Plimpton Press: Boston, 1910), pp. 53-54, 136-138, 143, 144. Cf. Adams to Henry Teller, December 19, 1907.

54 Adams to H. Adams, April 10, 1906.

55 Adams to H. Adams, April 28, 1902.

56 Adams to H. Adams, February 3, 1903.

57 Adams to H. Adams, October 6, 1904.

58 Adams to H. Adams, July 2, 1905.

59 Adams to H. Adams, January 9, 1906; Adams to H. Adams, April 15, 1908.

60 Adams to H. Adams, January 1, 1908. Cf. Adams to H. Adams, January 9, 1906; May 21, 1905.

61 Adams, "John Quincy Adams" (1909), Unpublished ms. in the

Massachusetts Historical Society, pp. 165, 396, 564-565, 299, 256, 80, 406.

62 Adams to H. Adams, March 6, 1909. Cf. Adams to H. Adams, January 28, 1910.

63 Adams to H. Adams, January 28, 1910.

64 Adams to H. Adams, November 12, 1910. Cf. Adams to H. Adams, April 9, 1911.

65 Adams to Holmes, June 29, 1911, private collection of Mark DeWolfe Howe, Harvard Law School.

66 Adams to H. Adams, March 1, 1910.

67 Adams to H. Adams, March 2, 1910.

68 Adams to H. Adams, March 10, 1910; Adams to H. Adams, April 5, 1910.

69 Adams to H. Adams, October 22, 1910; Adams to H. Adams, November 12, 1912.

70 Adams to H. Adams, April 9, 1911.

71 Adams to B. Adams, January 30, 1910, quoted in Ford, *op. cit.*, II, 532. Cf. Theodore Roosevelt to John Hay, May 3, 1897, quoted in Elting Morison, ed., *The Letters of Theodore Roosevelt*, I (Harvard University Press: Cambridge, 1951), 609; Oliver Wendell Holmes to Sir Frederick Pollack, August 9, 1897, quoted in Mark DeWolfe Howe, ed., *Holmes-Pollack Letters*, II (Harvard University Press: Cambridge, 1941), 76.

72 Adams to Holmes, March 9, 1913, private collection of Mark DeWolfe Howe.

73 Adams, *The Theory of Social Revolutions* (The Macmillan Co.: New York, 1913), pp. 3-4, 17-19, 27-30, 6-7. Cf. Adams, "The Collapse of Capitalistic Government," *Atlantic,* CXI (April, 1913), 433-444.

74 Adams, "Can War Be Done Away With," *Publications: American Sociological Society,* X (December, 1915), 104, 104-105, 104, 105-106.

75 Adams, "The American Democratic Ideal," *Yale Review,* V (January, 1916), 233.

76 Adams, quoted in Mark DeWolfe Howe, *Who Lived Here* (Little, Brown and Co.: Boston, 1952), p. 12.

77 Adams, "Can War Be Done Away With," pp. 106, 115, 106.

78 Adams, "Democratic Ideal," p. 225.

79 Adams to H. Adams, March 20, 1915.

80 Adams to Holmes, April 18, 1918, private collection of Mark DeWolfe Howe.

81 Adams, *The Emancipation of Massachusetts* (Houghton Mifflin Co.: Boston, 1919), pp. 152, 166-167. Cf. Adams, "Collective Thinking in America," *Yale Review,* VIII (April, 1919), 623-640.

82 Adams, "Introductory Note," in H. Adams, *The Degradation of*

the Democratic Dogma (The Macmillan Co.: New York, 1919), pp. v-vi, vii, viii.

83 Adams, "The Heritage of Henry Adams," *Ibid.,* p. 121.
84 Holmes to Pollack, May 25, 1906, quoted in Howe, ed., *Holmes-Pollack Letters,* II, 123.
85 Adams to H. Adams, July 5, 1901. Cf. Adams to H. Adams,
86 Adams to Mark DeWolfe Howe, June 22, 1921.
    December 21, 1899.

Notes to Chapter 10

1   Charmian Kittredge London, *The Book of Jack London,* I (The Century Co.: New York, 1921), 213, 33-34.
2   Flora Wellman London, quoted in Irving Stone, *Sailor On Horseback* (Houghton Mifflin Co., Boston, 1938), p. 14.
3   Fred Lewis Pattee, *Sidelights on American Literature* (The Century Co.: New York, 1922), pp. 102, 103.
4   Jack London, quoted in George Wharton James, "A Study of Jack London In His Prime," *Overland Monthly,* LXIX (May, 1917), 365-366.
5   London, quoted in C. London, *Book,* II, 15.
6   London, quoted in *Ibid.,* I, 68, 266, 264, 75, 265.
7   London, quoted in James, *op. cit.,* p. 367.
8   London, *John Barleycorn* (The Century Co.: New York, 1908), p. 83.
9   London, quoted in Pattee, *Sidelights,* p. 104.
10 London, *Barleycorn,* p. 107.
11 *Jack London: A Sketch Of His Life And Work* (The Macmillan Co.: New York, 1905), p. 7.
12 London to Mabel Applegarth, quoted in C. London, *Book,* I, 269.
13 London, *Barleycorn,* pp. 187-188, 204.
14 London, quoted in C. London, *Book,* I, 13.
15 London, *Barleycorn,* p. 22.
16 London to Cloudesley Johns, February 10, 1899, quoted in C. London, *Book,* I, 277. Protagonists Humphrey Van Weyden in *The Sea Wolf,* Ernest Everhard in *The Iron Heel,* and Darrell Standing in *The Star Rover,* are all given old American pedigrees.
17 London to Johns, April 17, 1899, quoted in C. London, *Book,* I, 285-286.
18 London, "The God of His Fathers," *The God of His Fathers,* (Doubleday, Page and Co.: New York, 1901), p. 1.
19 London, quoted in Joan London, *Jack London and His Times* (Doubleday, Doran and Co.: New York, 1939), pp. 212-213.

For his socialist appeal to all races, see Jack London, "Explanation of the Great Socialist Vote of 1904," in Philip S. Foner, ed., *Jack London: American Rebel* (The Citadel Press: New York, 1947), p. 404.

20 London, "The Question of the Maximum," *The War of the Classes* (The Regent Press: New York, 1905), pp. 151, 155-156, 185, 189-190, 191. For a similar discussion of these matters, see Jack London, "The Shrinkage of the Planet," *Revolution and Other Essays* (The Macmillan Co.: New York, 1910), pp. 147-149.

21 London to Johns, November 11, 1899, quoted in C. London, *Book*, I, 313.

22 London, May 22, 1904, quoted in C. London, *Book*, I, 420. Cf. London, March 5, 1904, quoted in Irving Shepard, ed., *Jack London's Tales of Adventure* (Hanover House, New York, 1956), pp. 415-416.

23 London, "The Yellow Peril," *Revolution*, p. 289. Cf. London, "If Japan Awakens China," *Sunset Magazine*, XXIII (December, 1909), 601.

24 London, "The Unparalleled Invasion," *The Strength of the Strong* (Grosset and Dunlap: New York, 1914), p. 99.

25 London, quoted in C. London, *Book*, II, 6. Cf. London, "What Life Means to Me," *Revolution*, pp. 300-303.

26 London, quoted in Henry Bland Meade, "Jack London: Traveller, Novelist and Social Reformer," *The Craftsman*, IX (February, 1906), 619; London, quoted in C. London, *Book*, II, 162-163.

27 London to Anna Strunsky, December 26, 1900, quoted in C. London, *Book*, I, 347.

28 London, quoted in Ninetta Eames, "Jack London," *Overland Monthly*, XXXV (May, 1900), 420-421.

29 London, "How I Became a Socialist," *War of the Classes*, p. 302. Cf. pp. 267-271.

30 London to Anna Strunsky, August 25, 1902, quoted in Foner, *op. cit.*, p. 49.

31 London, "Introduction" to Upton Sinclair, ed., *The Cry for Justice*, quoted in Foner, *op. cit.*, pp. 525-526. Cf. "What Communities Lose by the Competitive System," quoted in *Ibid.*, pp. 419-431.

32 London, quoted in Foner, *op. cit.*, p. 74.

33 C. London, *Book*, II, 293. Cf. London, quoted in Foner, *op. cit.*, p. 72.

34 John Spargo, "Review Of The Iron Heel," *The International Review*, VIII (April, 1908), 629.

35 London, "Letter of Resignation to the Sonoma County Socialists," March 7, 1916, quoted in C. London, *Book*, II, 336. By accusing the "Ghetto Socialists" of New York City of

pacifism (see London, quoted in Foner, *op. cit.*, p. 124), London revealed mild anti-Semitism. Meyer London and Morris Hillquit were Jews, and the eastern wing of the party was dominated by Jews. In London's later years, anti-Semitism was introduced into his novels. Elam Harnish is swindled by the Guggenheims in *Burning Daylight* (The Macmillan Co.: New York, 1910), pp. 142-143. Simon Nishikanta, an Armenian Jew, is portrayed as "a bulking colossal bodied, greasy seeming grossness of flesh—the Armenian Jew and San Francisco Pawnbroker," *Michael, Brother Of Jerry* (The Macmillan Co.: New York, 1919), p. 63. Anti-Jewishness, however, was never a major theme in his writings.

36 London, quoted in C. London, *Book*, II, 266, 337.

37 London, "Revolution," *Revolutions*, p. 8.

38 London, quoted in C. London, *Jack London and Hawaii* (Mill and Boon Ltd.: London, 1918), p. 23.

39 London, quoted in Joan London, *op. cit.*, pp. 334, 336.

40 London, quoted is C. London, *Book*, II, 41. Cf. pp. 34, 162.

41 London, quoted in Stone, *op. cit.*, p. 227.

42 For this opinion, see *Outlook*, LXXXIX (June 20, 1908), 388; *The Nation*, LXXVI (March 19, 1908), 264; *Dial*, XLIV (April 16, 1908), 247; *The Independent*, LXIV (April 16, 1908), 865.

43 *The Arena*, XXXIX (April, 1908), 506.

44 For Bukharin's statement, see Martin Russak, "Jack London," *The New Masses*, IV (January, 1929), 13; Trotsky is quoted in Joan London, *op. cit.*, p. 313; Lenin is quoted in Kenneth Lynn, *The Dream Of Success* (Little, Brown and Co.: Boston, 1955), p. 75.

45 Trotsky, quoted in Joan London, *op. cit.*, p. 313. Cf. Anatole France, "Introduction," *The Iron Heel*, (Harper and Bros.: New York, 1934), pp. xiii-xvii; Max Lerner, "Introduction," *The Iron Heel* (Harper and Bros.: New York, 1958), pp. ix-xii; R. H. S. Grossman, "The Prophecies Of Jack London," *The New Statesman And Nation*, XIX (June 8, 1940), 723-724.

46 London, *The Iron Heel* (The Regent Press: New York, 1913), pp. 6, 19, 72, 73, 83, 97, xiv, 248-249.

47 London, "Revolution," *Revolution*, pp. 12-13.

48 London, *Iron Heel*, pp. 302-303, 300-301, 326-327, 353.

49 London, *The Scarlet Plague* (The Macmillan Co.: New York, 1923), pp. 19, 178-179.

50 By far the best among these studies is Kenneth Lynn, *The Dream Of Success*, pp. 75-118, which treats London as motivated by Algerism. It is from this study that much of the evidence for this view has been taken. Lynn's thesis is also valuable because it tries to reconcile London's individualism with his socialism.

51 London, quoted in C. London, *Book,* II, 381.
52 The following remarks are examples of London's less-than-inspirational attitude toward his writings: "A strong will can accomplish anything— . . . There is no such thing as inspiration, and very little of genius. Dig, blooming under opportunity, results in what appears to be the former, and certainly makes possible the development of what original modicum of the latter one may possess." London, to Johns, May 30, 1899, quoted in C. London, *Book* I, 284. His materialism came out in this letter to Johns: "Why certes, if they wish to buy me, body and soul, they are welcome,—if they pay the price. I am writing for money; if I can procure fame, that means more money. More money means more life to me. I shall always hate the task of getting money; everytime I sit down to write it is with great disgust." (Note that his pragmatic attitude is not Algeristic, because he makes money to spend it, to live.) London to Johns, March 1, 1900, quoted in C. London, *Book,* I, 331. Cf. London to Johns, September 20, 1899, quoted in *Ibid.,* pp. 307-308; London to Johns, May 2, 1900, quoted in *Ibid.,* p. 341. For Martin Eden's predicament, *Martin Eden* (The Macmillan Co.: New York, 1919), pp. 374, 377, 386.
53 London, *Martin Eden,* p. 192.
54 London, *Barleycorn,* p. 132.
55 For London's romance with Mabel Applegarth, see Stone, *op. cit.,* pp. 130-132. For his marriage to Bessie Maddern, see Joan London, *op. cit.,* pp. 223-224.
56 London, quoted in Joan London, *op. cit.,* p. 224.
57 London, quoted in C. London, *Book,* II, 83, 77.
58 London, *Barleycorn,* p. 314.
59 London, quoted in C. London, *Book,* II, 340.
60 Johns, quoted in Stone, *op. cit.,* pp. 313, 323-324.
61 For the Eliza-Jack conversation, see *Ibid.,* p. 427. Cf. pp. 323-324; Jack London, quoted in C. London, *Book,* II, 375-376.
62 London, *Barleycorn,* p. 115.
63 London, quoted in Joan London, *op. cit.,* p. 372.
64 London to M. A. DeWolfe Howe, July 7, 1899, Houghton Library, Harvard University.
65 London to C. London, February 2, 1905, quoted in C. London, *Book,* II, 29.
66 London, *Barleycorn,* pp. 254-255.
67 Stone, *op. cit.,* pp. 330-332.

Bibliography

THE FOLLOWING TITLES *are a selection of the most important sources cited or consulted. A more complete bibliography is in Widener Library, Harvard University.*

Aaron, Daniel. *Men of Good Hope.* Oxford University Press: New York, 1951.

Abbott, Lyman. *Christianity and Social Problems.* Houghton Mifflin Co.: Boston, 1896.

———. *The Industrial Problem.* G. W. Jacobs and Co.: Philadelphia, 1905.

———. *The Rights of Man.* Houghton Mifflin Co.: Boston, 1901.

Adamic, Louis. *Dynamite.* Viking Press: New York, 1931.

Adams, Brooks. "Address at the Memorial Service of Lieutenant Edward Bumpus," *Boston Evening Transcript,* November 16, 1901, p. 16.

———. "The American Democratic Ideal," *Yale Review,* V (January, 1916), 225-233.

———. *America's Economic Supremacy.* The Macmillan Co.: New York, 1900.

———. "Can War Be Done Away With?" *Publications; American Sociological Society,* X (December, 1915), 103-124.

———. *The Emancipation of Massachusetts.* Houghton Mifflin Co.: Cambridge, 1887.

———. *The Emancipation of Massachusetts.* Houghton Mifflin Co.: Cambridge, 1919.

———. *The Gold Standard: An Historical Study.* New England News Co.: Boston, 1895.

———. "The Heritage of Henry Adams," Introduction to Henry Adams, *The Degradation of the Democratic Dogma.* The Macmillan Co.: New York, 1919.

————. "John Quincy Adams," Unpublished biography in the Adams Papers, Massachusetts Historical Society.

————. "The Last Stage of English Whiggery," *Atlantic Monthly* XLVII (April, 1881), 567-572.

————. *The Law of Civilization and Decay,* 2nd ed., 1896. Reprinted by Alfred A. Knopf: New York, 1943.

————. *The New Empire.* The Macmillan Co.: New York, 1902.

————. *The Plutocratic Revolution.* New England Tariff Reform League: Boston, 1892.

————. *Railways as Public Agents: A Study in Sovereignty.* Plimpton Press: Boston, 1910.

————. "Reciprocity or the Alternative," *Atlantic Monthly,* LXXXVIII (August, 1901), 145-155.

————. "Review of James Fitzjames Stephen's *Liberty, Equality, Fraternity,*" *North American Review,* CXVIII (April, 1874), 444-447.

————. "The Seizure of the Laird Rams," *Proceedings: Massachusetts Historical Society,* XLV (December, 1911), 243-333.

————. *Theory of Social Revolutions.* The Macmillan Co.: New York, 1913.

Adams, Charles Francis, Jr. "Prevention of Railroad Strikes," *The Nation,* XXV (August 30, 1877), 133-134.

Adams, George Burton. "A Century of Anglo-Saxon Expansion," *Atlantic Monthly,* LXXIX, (April, 1897), 528-538.

Adams, Henry. *The Degradation of the Democratic Dogma.* The Macmillan Co.: New York, 1919.

————. *The Education of Henry Adams.* Houghton Mifflin Co.: Boston, 1918.

————. *Mont-Saint Michel and Chartres.* Houghton Mifflin Co.: Boston, 1905.

Alger, G. W. "Preparedness and Democratic Discipline," *Atlantic Monthly,* CXVII (April, 1916), 476-486.

Anderson, Thornton. *Brooks Adams: Constructive Conservative.* Cornell University Press: Ithaca, 1951.

The Arena Magazine, 1889-1909.

The Atlantic Monthly, 1885-1918.

Bailey, T. A. *America Faces Russia.* Cornell University Press: Ithaca, 1950.

————. "The Election of 1900: A Mandate on Imperialism," *Mississippi Valley Historical Review,* XXIV (June, 1937), 43-52.

Baker, Ray Stannard. "The Trust's New Tool—The Labor Boss," *McClure's Magazine,* XXII (November, 1903), 30-43.

————. "What the United States Steel Corporation Really Is," *McClure's Magazine,* XVIII (November, 1901), 3-13.

Baskett, Sam S. "Jack London on the Oakland Waterfront," *American Literature,* XXVII (November, 1955), 363-372.

Bellamy, Edward. *Equality.* D. Appleton and Co.: New York, 1897.

————. *Looking Backward.* Little, Brown, and Co.: Boston, 1941.

Beringause, Arthur F. *Brooks Adams*. Alfred A. Knopf: New York, 1955.

Borah, William E. *Bedrock*. National Home Library: Washington, D.C., 1936.

Bridgeman, Raymond L. "Civic Righteousness Via Percentages," *Atlantic Monthly*, CII (December, 1908), 797-802.

Brissenden, Paul F. *The I.W.W.* Russell and Russell Inc.: New York, 1956.

Brooks, John Graham. "Recent Socialist Literature," *Atlantic Monthly*, XCIX (February, 1907), 278-283.

Brown, Leonard. *The Pending Conflict*. Des Moines Journal Co.: Des Moines, 1890.

————. *Popular Perils*. Des Moines Journal Co.: Des Moines, 1892.

Bruce, Robert V. *1877: Year of Violence*. Bobbs-Merrill and Co.: Indianapolis, 1959.

Canby, Henry Seidel. "Immigration," *Chautauquan*, XVI (November, 1892), 197-201.

Carwardine, William H. *The Pullman Strike*. Charles H. Kerr and Co.: Chicago, 1894.

Cater, Harold Dean, ed. *Henry Adams and His Friends*. Houghton Mifflin Co.: Boston, 1947.

The Century Illustrated Magazine, 1885-1918.

Chamberlain, H. R. "Farmers' Alliance and Other Political Parties," *Chautauquan*, XIII (June, 1891), 338-342.

Chapman, John Jay. "The Bright Side of the War," *Atlantic Monthly*, CXXI (January, 1918), 138-140.

————. "Ode on the Sailing of Our Troops," *North American Review*, CCVI (November, 1917), 682-683.

The Chautauquan, 1885-1914.

Clark, Gordon. *Shylock as Banker, Bondholder, Corruptionist, Conspirator*. American Bimetallic League: Washington, D.C., 1894.

Clemens, Samuel. *The Mysterious Stranger*. Harper and Bros.: New York, 1924.

Cline, H. F. "Benjamin Orange Flower and The Arena: 1889-1909," *Journalism Quarterly*, XVII (June, 1940), 139-150.

Commons, John R. *et al. History of Labor in the United States*, II-IV. The Macmillan Co.: New York, 1935.

Congressional Globe, 39th, 40th, 41st Congresses, 1864-1869.

Connelley, William E. *A Standard History of Kansas and Kansans*, II. Lewis Publishing Co.: Chicago, 1918.

Coxe, A. Cleveland. "Government By Aliens," *The Forum*, VII (July, 1889), 597-608.

Cummins, Albert Baird. *The Political Issues*. Des Moines, 1906.

David, Henry. *The History of the Haymarket Affair*. Farrar and Rinehart, Inc.: New York, 1936.

————. "Upheaval at Homestead," in Daniel Aaron, ed., *America in Crisis*. Alfred A. Knopf: New York, 1952.

Deland, Lorin F. "The Lawrence Strike: A Study," *Atlantic Monthly*, CIX (May, 1912), 694-705.

Denison, John H. "The Survival of the American Type," *Atlantic Monthly*, LXXV (January, 1895), 16-28.

De Witt, Benjamin Parke. *The Progressive Movement*. The Macmillan Co.: New York, 1915.

Dodge, John R. "The Discontent of the Farmer," *Century*, XXI (January, 1892), 447-456.

Donnelly, Ignatius. *The American People's Money*. Laird and Lee: Chicago, 1895.

———. *Atlantis: The Antideluvian World*. Harper and Bros.: New York, 1882.

———. *Caesar's Column*, 1890. Reprinted by John Harvard Press: Cambridge, 1960.

———. (Edmund Boisgilbert, pseud.). *Doctor Huguet*. Laird and Lee: Chicago, 1891.

———. (Edmund Boisgilbert, pseud.). *The Golden Bottle or the Story of Ephraim Benezet of Kansas*. D. D. Merrill Co.: New York, 1892.

———. *The Great Cryptogram*. R. S. Peale and Co.: London, 1888.

———. *In Memoriam*, privately printed, New York Public Library.

———. *Minnesota*. Folger and Turner: New York, 1857.

———. "The Mourner's Vision," privately printed, Philadelphia, 1850.

———. *Ragnarok: The Age of Fire and Gravel*. D. Appleton and Co.: New York, 1883.

———. *A Tribute to Abraham Lincoln*, 1865. Reprinted, Washington, D.C., 1942.

Dosch, Arno. "What the I.W.W. Is," *The World's Work*, XXVI (August, 1913), 406-420.

Dreiser, Theodore. *Hey Rub-A-Dub-Dub: A Book of the Mystery and Wonder and Terror of Life*. Boni and Liveright: New York, 1920.

Dulles, Foster Rhea. *Forty Years of American-Japanese Relations*. Appleton-Century Co.: New York, 1937.

———. *The Imperial Years*. T. Y. Crowell Co.: New York, 1956.

Dunning, N. A. *The Farmers' Alliance History and Agricultural Digest*. The Alliance Publishing Co.: Washington, D.C., 1891.

Edel, Leon. *Henry James: Selected Letters*. Farrar, Straus: New York, 1955.

Ely, Richard T. *The Labor Movement in America*. T. Y. Crowell Co.: New York, 1890.

———. *Social Aspects of Christianity*. T. Y. Crowell Co.: New York, 1889.

———. *The Social Law of Service*. T. Y. Crowell Co.: New York, 1896.

———. *Studies in the Evolution of Industrial Society*. The Macmillan Co.: New York, 1912.

Faulkner, Harold U. *Politics, Reform and Expansion, 1890-1900*. Harper and Bros.: New York, 1959.

Fish, Everett. *Biography of Ignatius Donnelly.* F. J. Schulte and Co., Publishers: Chicago, 1892.

Flower, Benjamin Orange. "The Gathering Together and Onward March of the Forces of Free Government," *Arena,* XXXV (April, 1907), 414-415.

———. "The Proposed Federation of the Anglo-Saxon Nations," *Arena,* XX (August, 1898), 223-238.

Flower, Edward. "Anti-Semitism in the Free Silver and Populist Movements and the Election of 1896." Unpublished Master's thesis, Department of History, Columbia University, 1952.

Foner, Philip. *Jack London: American Rebel.* The Citadel Press: New York, 1947.

Ford, Alexander Hume. "The Warfare of Railroads in Asia," *Century,* LIX (March, 1900), 794-800.

Ford, Worthington Chauncey, ed., *The Letters of Henry Adams: 1858-1918.* 2 vols. Houghton Mifflin Co.: Boston, 1930, 1938.

———. *A Cycle of Adams Letters.* 2 vols. Houghton Mifflin Co.: Boston, 1920.

Fosdick, Harry Emerson. "After the Strike in Lawrence," *The Outlook,* CI (June 15, 1912), 340-346.

Frank, Henry. "The Crusade of the Unemployed," *Arena,* X (July, 1894), 239-244.

George, Henry. *Progress and Poverty.* Doubleday, Page and Co.: Garden City, 1911.

Gladden, Washington. *Applied Christianity.* Houghton Mifflin Co.: Boston, 1894.

———. *Social Facts and Forces.* G. P. Putnam's Sons: New York, 1897

"The Great Strike," *Scribner's Monthly Magazine,* XIV October, 1877), 852-853.

Greenslet, Ferris. *The Life of Thomas Bailey Aldrich.* Houghton Mifflin Co.: Boston, 1908.

Gwynn, Stephen. *The Letters and Friendships of Cecil Spring Rice,* I. Constable and Co.: London, 1929.

Hamilton, John J. *The Dethronement of the City Boss.* Funk and Wagnalls: New York, 1910.

Handlin, Oscar. "American Views of the Jew at the Opening of the Twentieth Century," *Publications of the American Jewish Historical Society,* XL (June, 1951), 326-336.

Harger, Charles M. "The New Era in the Middle West," *Harper's New Monthly Magazine,* XCVII (July, 1898), 276-282.

Harmon, Ralph L. "Ignatius Donnelly and His Faded Metropolis," *Minnesota History,* XVII (September, 1936), 262-276.

Harper's New Monthly Magazine, CV (October, 1877), 782-783.

Harrington, Fred H. "The Anti-Imperialist Movement in the United States," *Mississippi Valley Historical Review,* XXII (September, 1935), 211-230.

Haynes, Fred Emory. *James Baird Weaver*. Iowa State Historical Society: Iowa City, 1919.

Heald, Morrell. "Business Attitudes Toward European Immigration, 1880-1900," *Journal of Economic History*, XIII (Summer, 1953), 291-305.

Heaton, John L. *Cobb of the World*. E. P. Dutton: New York, 1924.

Hempstead, E. A. "Shall Immigration Be Restricted," *Chautauquan*, VIII (July, 1888), 610-612.

Henschen, Sigmund. "What Is Behind the Japanese Peril?" *Forum*, LVI (July, 1916), 63-78.

Herrick, Robert. "Recantation of a Pacifist," *New Republic*, IV (October 30, 1915), 328-330.

Hicks, Granville. *The Great Tradition*. The Macmillan Co.: New York, 1935.

Hicks, John D. "The Birth of the Populist Party," *Minnesota History*, IX (September, 1928), 219-247.

———. "The Political Career of Ignatius Donnelly," *Mississippi Valley Historical Review*, VIII (June, 1921), 80-132.

Higham, John. *Strangers in the Land*. Rutgers University Press: New Brunswick, 1955.

Hobson, Richmond Pearson. "The Defense of Our Outlying Possessions," *The World Today*, XV (July, 1908), 741-744.

Hofstadter, Richard. *The Age of Reform*. Alfred A. Knopf: New York, 1956.

———. *The American Political Tradition*. Alfred A. Knopf: New York, 1959.

Holbrook, Stewart H. *Lost Men of American History*. The Macmillan Co.: New York, 1946.

Howe, Frederic C. *The City: The Hope of Democracy*. Charles Scribner's Sons: New York, 1905.

———. *The Modern City and Its Problems*. Charles Scribner's Sons: New York, 1915.

Howe, M. A. DeWolfe. *Barrett Wendell and His Letters*. Atlantic Monthly Press: Boston, 1924.

———. *Portrait of an Independent: Moorfield Storey*. Houghton Mifflin Co.: Boston, 1932.

———. *Who Lived Here*. Little, Brown and Co.: Boston, 1952.

Howe, M. A. DeWolfe, Jr. *Holmes-Pollack Letters*, 2 vols. Harvard University Press: Cambridge, 1941.

Howells, William Dean. *A Traveller from Altruria*. Harper and Bros.: New York, 1894.

Hoxie, R. F. "The Truth about the I.W.W.," *The Journal of Political Economy*, XXI (November, 1913), 785-797.

Hume, Robert A. *Runaway Star: An Appreciation of Henry Adams*. Cornell University Press: Ithaca, 1951.

Hunter, Robert. "The Socialist Party in the Present Campaign," *Review of Reviews*, XXXVIII (September, 1908), 293-299.

The International Socialist Review, 1900-1917.
James, George Wharton, "A Study of Jack London in His Prime,"
Overland Monthly, LXIX (May, 1917), 361-400.
Keim, Jeanette. *Forty Years of German-American Relations.* William J.
Doran: New York, 1919.
Kipnis, Ira. *The American Socialist Movement: 1897-1912.* Columbia
University Press: New York, 1952.
Knapp, Adeline. "San Francisco and the Civic Awakening," *Arena,* XII
(April, 1895), 241-249.
Koch, Adrienne, and William Peden. *Selected Writings of John and
John Quincy Adams.* Alfred A. Knopf: New York, 1946.
Kramer, Dale. *The Wild Jackasses: The American Farmer in Revolt.*
Hastings House: New York, 1956.
La Farge, Mabel, ed. *Henry Adams: Letters to a Niece.* Houghton
Mifflin Co.: Boston, 1920.
LaFollette, Robert M. *The Political Philosophy of Robert M. LaFollette.*
Robert M. LaFollette Co.: Madison, 1920.
Larned, J. N. "Prepare for Socialism," *Atlantic Monthly,* CVII (May,
1911), 577-588.
Lauck, W. Jett. "The Lesson from Lawrence," *North American Review,*
CXCV (May, 1912), 665-672.
Lea, Homer. *The Day of the Saxon.* Harper and Bros.: New York, 1912.
———. *The Valor of Ignorance,* 1909. Reprinted, Harper and Bros.:
New York, 1942.
Lease, Mary Elizabeth. *The Problem of Civilization Solved.* Laird and
Lee: Chicago, 1895.
LeSueur, Meridel. *North Star Country.* Sloan and Pearce: New York,
1945.
Lindsey, Almont. *The Pullman Strike.* University of Chicago Press:
Chicago, 1942.
Lodge, Henry Cabot. "The Census and Immigration," *Century,* XLVI
(September, 1893), 737-739.
———. "A Million Immigrants a Year," *Century,* LXVII (January,
1904), 466-473.
London, Charmian Kittredge. *The Book of Jack London.* 2 vols. The
Century Co.: New York, 1921.
———. *Jack London and Hawaii.* Mill and Boon Ltd.: London, 1918.
Jack London: A Sketch of His Life and Work. The Macmillan Co.:
New York, 1905.
London, Jack. *Burning Daylight.* The Macmillan Co.: New York, 1913.
———. *Call of the Wild.* The Macmillan Co.: New York, 1923.
———. "Explanation of the Great Socialist Vote," *San Francisco
Examiner,* November 10, 1904, Foner, *American Rebel.*
———. "If Japan Wakens China," *Sunset Magazine,* XXIII (December,
1909), 597-602.
———. "Introduction" to Upton Sinclair, ed., *Cry For Justice.* The John
C. Winston Co.: New York, 1906.

———. *The Iron Heel.* The Regent Press: New York, 1913.
———. *John Barleycorn.* The Century Co.: New York, 1913.
———. *Martin Eden.* The Macmillan Co.: New York, 1919.
———. *The People of the Abyss.* The Macmillan Co.: New York, 1907.
———. *Revolution and Other Essays.* The Macmillan Co.: New York, 1910.
———. *The Scarlet Plague.* The Macmillan Co.: New York, 1923.
———. *The Sea Wolf.* The Macmillan Co.: New York, 1904.
———. *The Son of the Wolf.* Houghton Mifflin Co.: Boston, 1900.
———. *The Strength of the Strong.* Grosset and Dunlap: New York, 1914.
———. *Tales of Adventure,* Irving Shepard, ed. Hanover House: Garden City, 1956.
———. *The War of the Classes.* The Regent Press: New York, 1905.
———. *When God Laughs.* The Macmillan Co.: New York, 1911.
London, Joan. *Jack London and His Times.* Doubleday, Doran and Co.: New York, 1939.
Loomis, Samuel Lane. "Foreigners and American Churches," *Chautauquan,* XVII (May, 1893), 180-184.
Luce, Claire Booth, "Introduction," in H. Lea, *The Valor of Ignorance,* Harper and Bros.: New York, 1942.
Lynn, Kenneth S. *The Dream of Success: A Study of Modern American Literature.* Little, Brown and Co.: Boston, 1955.
McVey, Frank L. *The Populist Movement.* The Macmillan Co.: New York, 1896.
May, Henry F. *The End of American Innocence: A Study of the First Years of Our Own Time: 1912-1917.* Alfred A. Knopf: New York, 1959.
"The Menace of Coxeyism," *North American Review,* CLVIII (May, 1894), 687-705.
Miles, Nelson A. "The Lesson of the Recent Strikes," *North American Review,* CLIX (August, 1894), 180-188.
Morgan, W. Scott. *History of the Wheel and Alliance and the Impending Revolution.* C. B. Woodward Co.: St. Louis, 1891.
Morison, Elting, ed. *The Letters of Theodore Roosevelt,* I. Harvard University Press: Cambridge, 1951.
Munger, T. T. "Immigration by Passport," *Century,* XXXV (March, 1888), 791-799.
The Nation, 1885-1918.
The New Republic, 1914-1918.
New York Times, 1885-1918.
New York Tribune, 1885-1918.
Norton, Charles Eliot. *Memorials of Two Friends.* New York, 1902.
———. "Reminiscences of Old Cambridge," *Cambridge Historical Society,* I (1905), 11-23.
———. "Some Aspects of Civilization," *Forum,* XX (February, 1896), 641-652.

————. *Tercentenary Festivals of Emmanuel College.* Cambridge, England, 1884.
————. "William Eustis Russell," *Harvard Graduates Magazine,* V (December, 1896), 177-194.
Norton, Sara, and M. A. DeWolfe Howe. *The Letters of Charles Eliot Norton.* Houghton Mifflin Co.: Boston, 1913.
Norwood, Thomas K. *Plutocracy or American White Slavery.* Metropolitan Publishing Co.: New York, 1888.
Nydahl, Theodore, ed. "The Diary of Ignatius Donnelly: 1859-1884." Unpublished Ph.D. dissertation, Department of History, University of Minnesota, 1941.
Osgood, Robert Endicott: *Ideals and Self-Interest in America's Foreign Relations: The Great Transformation of the Twentieth Century.* University of Chicago Press: Chicago, 1953.
Phillips, David Graham. "The Menace of Plutocracy," *Arena,* XXXV (March, 1906), 258-264.
Pierce, Francis Lamont. "The Agitator: His Function in Social Evolution," *Arena,* XXXVIII (September, 1907), 306-310.
Pringle, Henry. *Theodore Roosevelt: A Biography.* Harcourt, Brace and Co.: New York, 1931.
Public Opinion, 1886-1906.
Quint, Howard. *The Forging of American Socialism.* University of South Carolina Press: Columbia, 1953.
Rauschenbusch, Walter J., *Christianity and the Social Crisis.* The Macmillan Co.: New York, 1908.
Regier, C. C. *The Era of the Muckrakers.* University of North Carolina Press: Chapel Hill, 1932.
The Review of Reviews, 1889-1918.
Rideout, Walter B. "Introduction," in Ignatius Donnelly, *Caesar's Column.* John Harvard Press: Cambridge, 1960.
Ridge, Martin. "Ignatius Donnelly: The Making of a Tribune." Unpublished Ph.D. dissertation, Department of History, Northwestern University, 1951.
Ridpath, John Clark. "City Immigrant Population," *Chautauquan,* XII (January, 1891), 522-523.
————. "The Invisible Empire," *Arena,* XIX (June, 1898), 828-840.
————. "The Mixed Populations of Chicago," *Chautauquan,* XII (January, 1891), 483-493.
————. "Plutocracy and War," *Arena,* XIX (January, 1898), 97-103.
————. "The Republic and the Empire," *Arena,* XX (September, 1898), 344-363.
Robinson, H. P. "The Lesson of the Recent Strikes," *North American Review,* CLIX (August, 1894), 195-201.
Russak, Martin. "Jack London," *The New Masses,* IV (January, 1929), 13.
Saloutous, Theodore, and John D. Hicks. *Agricultural Discontent in The West: 1900-1939.* University of Wisconsin Press: Madison, 1951.

Schieber, Clara Eve. *The Transformation of American Sentiment Toward Germany: 1870-1914.* Corn Hill Publishing Co.: Boston, 1923.

Scott, Thomas. "The Recent Strikes," *North American Review*, CXXV (September, 1877), 351-362.

Seymour, Charles, ed. *Intimate Papers of Colonel House*, II. Houghton Mifflin Co.: Boston, 1926.

Shaler, N. S. "European Peasants as Immigrants," *Atlantic Monthly*, LXXI (May, 1893), 646-655.

Shannon, David A. *The Socialist Party of America.* The Macmillan Co.: New York, 1955.

Shippee, Lester B. "Germany and the Spanish American War," *American Historical Review*, XXX (July, 1925), 754-775.

Shuster, W. Morgan. "The Breakdown of Civilization," *Century*, LXXXIX (November, 1914), 51-59.

Solix-Cohen, Solomon. "The Spectre of Imperialism," *Arena*, XX (October, 1898), 445-452.

Solomon, Barbara Miller. *Ancestors and Immigrants.* Harvard University Press: Cambridge, 1956.

Stone, Irving. *Sailor On Horseback: The Biography of Jack London.* Houghton Mifflin Co.: Boston, 1938.

Storey, Moorfield. "The American Legislature," *Transactions of the American Bar Association*, August 22, 1894.

———. "The Democratic Party and Philippine Independence," May, 1913. George H. Ellis, Printer: Boston, 1913.

———. *Our New Departure.* George H. Ellis, Printer: Boston, 1900.

———. *Politics as a Duty and as a Career.* C. P. Putnam's Sons: New York, 1889.

———. "A Years Legislation," Presidential Address, American Bar Association, August 19, 1896. Dando Printing and Publishing Co.: Philadelphia, 1896.

Strong, Josiah. "City Evangelization," *Chautauquan*, IX (November, 1888), 96-103.

———. *The New Era.* Baker and Taylor Co.: New York, 1893.

———. *The Next Great Awakening.* Baker and Taylor Co.: New York, 1902.

———. *Our Country: Its Possible Future and Its Present Crisis.* Baker and Taylor Co.: New York, 1885.

———. *Studies in the Gospel of the Kingdom.* The American Institute of Social Service: New York, 1910.

———. *The Twentieth Century City.* Baker and Taylor Co.: New York, 1898.

"The Triumph of Sections and Communism," *Harper's Weekly*, XI (July 18, 1896), 698.

Tumulty, Joseph. *Woodrow Wilson as I Know Him.* Doubleday, Page and Co.: New York, 1921.

Tupper, Eleanor, and George R. McReynolds. *Japan in American Public Opinion.* The Macmillan Co.: New York, 1937.

Walker, Francis A. "Restriction of Immigration," *Atlantic Monthly,* LXXVII (June, 1896), 823-828.

Walker, John Brisben. "The Homestead Strike: Object Lesson," *Cosmopolitan,* XIII (September, 1892), 572-575.

Watson, Thomas A. *The People's Campaign Book: 1892. Not A Revolt Its a Rebellion!* National Watchman's Publishing Co.: Washington, D.C., 1892.

―――. *Political and Economic Handbook.* Jeffersonian Publishing Co.: Thomson, Georgia, 1916.

―――. "Why I Am Still a Populist," *Review of Reviews,* XXXVIII (September, 1908), 303-306.

Weaver, James B. *A Call to Action.* Iowa Printing Co.: Des Moines, 1892.

Welch, Rodney. "The Farmers' Changed Condition," *Forum,* X (November, 1890), 689-700.

Wendell, Barrett. "Conflict of Idolatries," *Harvard Graduates Magazine,* XXVII (September, 1918), 1-16.

―――. *The Privileged Classes.* Charles Scribner's Sons: New York, 1908.

West, Henry Litchfield. "Two Republics or One?" *North American Review,* CLXII (April, 1896), 509-511.

White, Andrew D. "Some Practical Lessons of the Recent Campaign," *Forum,* XXII (December, 1896), 414-422.

White, William Allen. *The Autobiography of William Allen White.* The Macmillan Co.: New York, 1946.

Wilson, Woodrow. *In Our First Year of War.* Harper and Bros.: New York, 1918.

Wood, Eric Fisher. *The Writing on the Wall: The Nation on Trial.* The Century Co.: New York, 1916.

Woodward, C. Vann. *Tom Watson: Agrarian Rebel.* Rinehart and Co.: New York, 1955.

Zornow, Frank. *A History of the Jayhawk State.* University of Oklahoma Press: Norman, 1957.

MANUSCRIPTS AND MICROFILMS

Adams Papers, Massachusetts Historical Society.
Adams Papers, Microfilm, Harvard University.
Brooks Adams Letters, Houghton Library, Harvard University.
Ignatius Donnelly, "Diary," 1888-1889, Microfilm, Harvard University.
Ignatius Donnelly, Papers, 1889-1890, Microfilm, Columbia University.
Henry Cabot Lodge Papers, Massachusetts Historical Society.
Jack London Letters, Houghton Library, Harvard University.

INDEX

Index